CW00762886

Journey Through Wine

An Atlas

56 countries, 100 maps,
8000 years of history

*Adrien
Grant Smith Bianchi*

hardie grant books

*Jules
Gaubert-Turpin*

Contents

The countries are organised primarily by order of appearance of wine-growing, from the earliest to the most recent.

Save the earth; it's the only
planet with wine.

Introduction

Unique and exciting, uniting the richness of the soil and human passion, wine is surely the best gastronomic ambassador for our planet. And so this atlas tells of the earth and the people to whom we owe this fabulous nectar.

What better way to understand the world's wine-growing regions than with a map? If the borders of our world are well defined, those of the grape never stop expanding. Whether lining the banks of the Danube or gripping the foothills of the Andes, the grapevine draws inspiration from the climate, the soil and its environment to offer a singular taste.

Writing this book resembled a quest, one that demanded we gather the clues scattered here and there – by dissecting a botanical thesis on Madagascan viticulture here, or spending an evening on a translation site to decipher Hungarian there.

What's fascinating is that as we went along, everything became clear, and everything was connected. Whether fortifying the warriors of the ancient world or providing true social glue in the exclusive areas of San Francisco, wine has always followed the route of civilisation, and this book summarises its travel itinerary.

To recount the history of the world's wine-growing regions, we are embarking on a tour of those parts of the world where vineyards have taken shape and come to life. We begin where wine first saw the light of day and then, page by page, follow its astonishing and epic journey.

Thanks to the Cité du Vin in Bordeaux for its inspiring works,
to La Ligne Rouge for its rare pearls,
to Hélène d'Argentré, Raphaële Wauquiez
and Emmanuel Le Vallois for their confidence,
and to Marcel Turpin for his meticulous read-through.

How to use this book

At a glance

Here we attempt to evoke in a few words what is specific to the character of the wine-growing area in question.

Surface area and production

These two numbers tell you the size of the region and its annual production, two essential landmarks for understanding a wine-growing region and its global importance.

Hungary

With its world-famous tokaj (or tokay), Hungary was the first country to devise a meticulously detailed classification of its wine areas.

Tokaj
The Danube
LOUIS XV
The drink of the Tsars
Bor

Global ranking
(by production)
18

Hectares planted
68,000

Annual production
(in millions of litres)
190

Proportion
of red/white grapes
30%   70%

Harvest period
September
October

Period when wine-
growing appeared
400
AD

Influences
Celts

Slovakia

Upper
Hungary   MISKOLC   To

Northern
Transdanubia   EGER   Bükk   NYÍREG

Mátra   Eger

Lake
Neusiedl   Austria

SOPRON   GYŐR   Neszmély   BUDAPEST   Lake Tisza   DEBREC

Sopron   Pannonhalma   TATABÁNYA

SZOMBATHELY   Nagy-Somló   SZÉKESFEHÉRVÁR   Etyek-Buda   SZOLNOK

VESZPRÉM

Balaton   Balaton-Felvidék   Balatonfüred-Csopak   DUNAÚJVÁROS   Danube   KECSKEMÉT

Zala   Badacsony

ZALAEGERSZEG   Pannon   Kunság

Zala   Tolna   Csongrád   HÓDMEZŐVÁSÁRHELY

NAGYKANIZSA   Balatonboglár

Slovenia   Balatonboglár   KAPOSVÁR   Szekszárd   Hajós-Baja   SZEGED

Croatia   PÉCS   Pécs

Villány   Serbia

Proportion of red/white grapes

This pie chart tells you the proportion of red and white grapes planted in the region.

Don't forget that rosé and certain sparkling whites are made using red grapes!

5 appellations
to start with

Tokaj
Kunság
Hajós-Baja
Eger
Szekszárd

0   20   40   60 km

Main varieties

● Blaufränkisch,* Kadarka,
Cabernet Sauvignon

● Furmint, Hárslevelű,
Welschriesling

* *locally called Kékfrankos*

Endemic variety

Then

The best publicity ever given to to tokaj was by the French King Louis XV, who said to his mistress Madame de Pompadour, 'Here, Madame, is the wine of kings and the king of wines.'

Tokaj (pronounced *tockay*) is a legendary syrupy wine. History tells that soldiers who returned home later than expected discovered a strange type of rot on their grapes. There is

Here, Madame, is the wine of kings and the king of wines.'

Certification

Some countries use certification systems to verify the origin of certain wines; these are included when applicable.

Appellations

Appellation refers to a wine's provenance and terroir, a geographic indication of its origins. Our shortlist of appellations highlights some of the most distinctive, notable and celebrated wines from this part of the world.

Key

Médoc	Name of major wine-growing region		Lake
Saint-Julien	Name of winemaking sub-region/appellation		River
	Outline of winemaking region		Neighbouring country
□	Capital city		Country/region/ area in question
○	Other city		Coastline of area in question
MILAN	Name of city		Border
ADRIATIC SEA	Name of ocean or sea	*Albania*	Name of neighbouring country
Lake Skadar	Name of lake/river/ island		

Bearings

The indispensable kit for the reader-traveller: a compass indicates a country's position and orientation so you never lose north.

NORTH

The story

The information is often divided into two parts: then and now. A tour of the past is the key to a thorough understanding of the challenges of tomorrow.

when they e with this ng the grapes pe gives le aromatic s to evolve of the wine ope. On the narchs of s of the east, ly improved ne the ry, so much ed in the or us on the ou ripened pe fields of weet nectar.'

, Hungarian where the doesn't come m.

region ver the rvest: Hungary?

Whichever it was, tokaj is the oldest appellation in the world, given it dates back to 1730, making it 125 years earlier than the first classification of the Bordeaux Grands Crus. As is the case with several Eastern European nations, the fall of Soviet Communism renewed investment, and today Hungary exports a quarter of its wine throughout the world.

Kunság (in the Danube region) is the largest wine-growing area in the country, accounting for 30 per cent of national production. When you choose a Hungarian wine, look for the words *minőségi bor* or *különleges minőségű bor*. These measures of quality indicate that the wine belongs to one of the country's 22 appellations. Another point of national pride: while the whole world snaps up American or French oak for making its barrels, the Hungarians make the most of their own oaks, which lend themselves perfectly to the maturation of wine.

115

Main varieties

This section lists the main grape varieties used to make wine in this area. The underlined varieties originated in the country concerned.

Who made wine in 3000 BC?

Researchers are constantly moving back further in time to determine the origin of wine-growing, but one thing is certain: humans invented wine before the wheel. You could say they had their priorities right.

• Georgia

• *First traces of wine in history*

Arctic Circle

45° North

Tropic of Cancer

Equator

Tropic of Capricorn

35° South

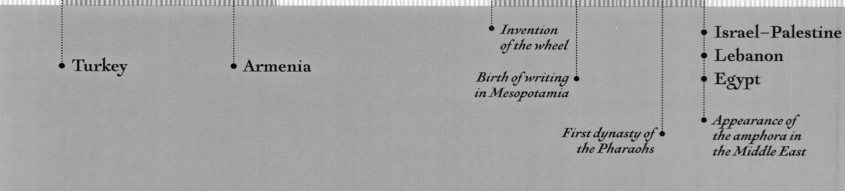

4500 BC	4000 BC	3500 BC	3000 BC

- Invention
of the wheel

- Turkey

- Armenia

Birth of writing
in Mesopotamia

- Israel–Palestine

- Lebanon

- Egypt

First dynasty of
the Pharaohs

Appearance of
the amphora in
the Middle East

9

1 Moldavia Ukraine

Romania

2 Serbia *BLACK SEA*

Bulgaria # Turkey

Macedonia

Albania **ISTANBUL** ○ **ADAPAZARI**
Sea of Marmara
GEBZE
3 Greece ○ **BURSA**
ESKISEHIR **ANKARA** □

Aegean Sea *Lake Tuz* **KAYSE**

○ **IZMIR** *Lake Egirdir*
KONYA ○ **ADAN**
DENIZLI ○
MERSIN ○

ANTALYA ○
Gulf of Antalya

4 *MEDITERRANEAN SEA* Cyprus

5

Black Sea

GEORGIA, TURKEY & ARMENIA

Although some might find it hard to believe, red wine was actually born on the shores of the Black Sea. But it should not be so surprising that wine was born in the region that has been called the 'Fertile Crescent' of Mesopotamia. It's here that we commence our journey.

Main varieties

- ● Saperavi, Pinot Noir Cabernet Sauvignon
- ● Rkatsiteli, Mtsvane, Chardonnay

Endemic variety

Georgia

With one foot in Europe and the other in Asia, this small country in the Caucasus is considered the cradle of global wine-growing. From grape varieties to winemaking techniques, the Georgians were the first to speak the language of wine.

Then

The *qvevri* is the emblem of Georgian wine. This large earthenware jar, which could hold anywhere between 300 and 3500 litres of wine, is the ancestor of the French *barrique*. Once filled with grape juice, *qvevri* were buried underground for several weeks in order to guarantee fermentation at a stable temperature. Thanks to its 6000-year history, this winemaking process was inscribed on UNESCO's Representative List of the Intangible Cultural Heritage of Humanity in 2013.

> The *qvevri* is the emblem of Georgian wine.

With Ethiopia and Armenia, Georgia was one of the first nations to adopt Christianity as its official religion, which reinforced the place of wine in sacred rituals and celebrating religious holidays. Having lived under the yoke of the Persians, Romans, Byzantines, Arabs, Mongols and Ottoman Turks, Georgia was annexed by Imperial Russia in 1800. In 2006, Russia decided to boycott Georgian wines on its territory. This embargo drove the winemakers to become organised. They quickly decided to turn towards the West while refining the quality of their products.

Now

Georgia has less than a hundred wine producers, but numerous families make their own wines. For the country's 18 appellations, 525 endemic varieties are cultivated, a world record. The Kakheti region is responsible for close to 70 per cent of national production. The eastern regions produce dry wines, while those of the west excel in sweet wines, both white and red.

> For the country's 18 appellations, 525 endemic varieties are cultivated, a world record.

The country is also the origin of a rare but exciting drop: orange wine. This is a white wine made like a red, where fermentation takes place with the skins and sometimes even the stalks. This method still inspires Slovenian, Italian, French and even Australian winemakers.

The determined Georgian government is now working with NASA to prove scientifically, and once and for all, that it really was the first wine-growing country in history.

Kindzmarauli
Mukuzani
Kardenakhi

Azerbaijan

Global ranking
(by production)
20

Hectares planted
48,000

Annual production
(in millions of litres)
170

Proportion of red/white grapes
40% — 60%

Harvest period
September October

Period when wine-growing appeared
6000
BC

5 appellations to start with
Tsinandali
Mukuzani
Napareuli
Kardenakhi
Kindzmarauli

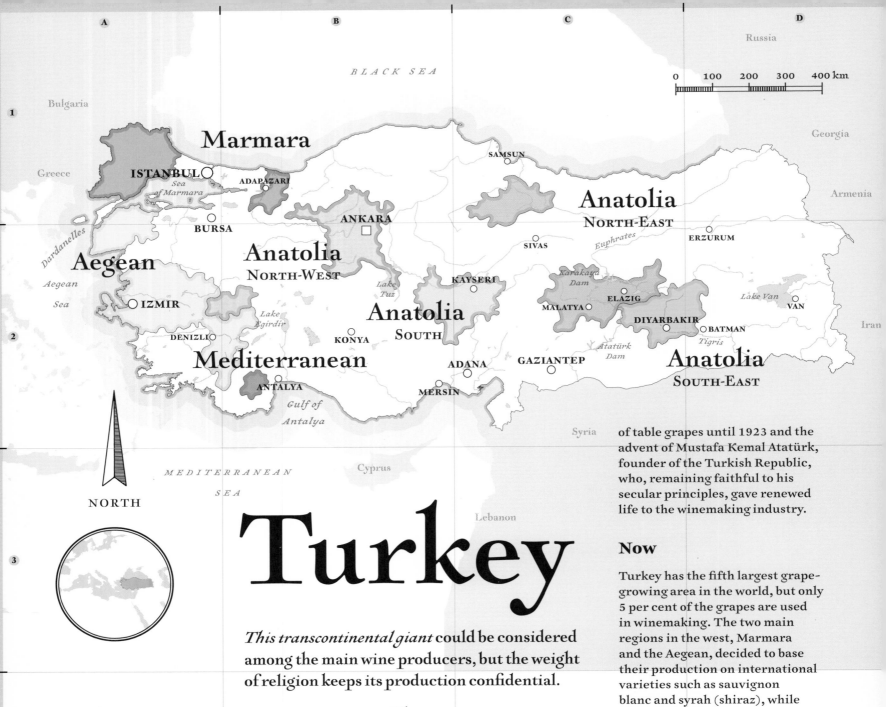

Turkey

This transcontinental giant could be considered among the main wine producers, but the weight of religion keeps its production confidential.

of table grapes until 1923 and the advent of Mustafa Kemal Atatürk, founder of the Turkish Republic, who, remaining faithful to his secular principles, gave renewed life to the winemaking industry.

Now

Turkey has the fifth largest grape-growing area in the world, but only 5 per cent of the grapes are used in winemaking. The two main regions in the west, Marmara and the Aegean, decided to base their production on international varieties such as sauvignon blanc and syrah (shiraz), while those in central Turkey are more interested in endemic varieties.

> Turkey has the fifth largest grape-growing area in the world, but only 5 per cent of the grapes are used in winemaking.

Wine-growing is still in the throes of reorganisation but remains a virtual monopoly: 90 per cent of production comes from a handful of large producers.

Then

Anatolia (modern Turkey) was surely one of the most civilised regions of prehistory. It was also here that bronze and the beginnings of metallurgy appeared. Enjoying an ideal geographic position for trade with Europe, Asia and Africa, Turkey was coveted by all the great emperors of history. We can distinguish two great epoques in the history of Turkish wine-growing. The first was that of the Roman and Byzantine (Holy Roman) Empire, when the wine flowed freely and travelled as far as the north of Europe. The second began with the fall of Constantinople in 1453 and the arrival of the Ottomans. In the name of Islam, wine was banished for five centuries. Grape-growing was restricted to the production

Global ranking
(by production)
32

Hectares planted
480,000

Annual production
(in millions of litres)
54.6

Proportion of red/white grapes
40%
60%

Harvest period
September

Period when wine-growing appeared
4500
BC

Main varieties

- Öküzgözü, Syrah, Boğazkere
- Sultaniye, Emir, Narince

Endemic variety

Global ranking (by production)

47

Hectares planted

17,000

Annual production (in millions of litres)

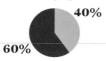

6

Proportion of red/ white grapes

40%

60%

Harvest period

September October

Period when wine-growing appeared

4100 BC

Armenia

Georgia's challenger on the question of 'Who made wine first?'

Then

Armenia is one of the rare wine-growing countries lacking a coastline. In this landlocked country, the wine-growing regions are situated at an altitude of 800–1900 metres. This didn't stop it being one of the first lands to cultivate grapes and discover wine. In Genesis, the first book of the Bible, Noah appears as the first wine-grower in history: after the flood, he plants three vines in the foothills of Mount Ararat.

To this day, it remains the oldest winemaking site ever discovered.

Wine-growing continued in this extremely Christian country; however, under Soviet rule, Moscow forced producers to concentrate on making brandy. The brandy-making tradition survived, and the Armenians still devote half their harvest to making this *eau de vie*, known locally as 'cognac'.

Now

Modern Armenian winemaking occurs at two speeds: agricultural and industrial. Faced with low rainfall, the majority of modern producers have turned to irrigation. If you happen to visit, you will notice that the humblest winemakers sell their wines in plastic bottles.

Between 2007 and 2010, a team of Irish, American and Armenian archaeologists discovered prehistoric traces of grape seeds, vine stems and a wine press in the bottom of a cave near Areni (in Vayots Dzor province). To this day, it remains the oldest winemaking site ever discovered. It's enough to make them gnash their teeth in Georgia, which also considers itself to be the birthplace of wine.

Georgia

GYUMRI

VANADZOR

Dzoraget

Debed

Azerbaijan

Hrazdan

HRAZDAN

Aragatsotn

GAVAR

ABOVYAN

Lake Sevan

VAGHARSHAPAT

YEREVAN

ARMAVIR

Aras

ARTASHAT

Armavir

Ararat

Vayots Dzor

Turkey

GORIS

Vorotan

Azerbaijan

KAPAN

Main varieties

● Areni Noir, Khndogni

● Tchilar, Voskehat, Rkatsiteli, Mskhali

Endemic variety

NORTH

0   50   100 km

1

NORTH

2

3

Libya

Middle East

LEBANON, EGYPT & ISRAEL–PALESTINE

*The Phoenicians – the original inhabitants of the region
corresponding to modern Lebanon – were the first to make
wine a commercial commodity. Thanks to their powerful
shipping fleet, they went on to export their amphorae
and knowledge throughout the Mediterranean region.*

4

5

Turkey

Lebanon

Cyprus

MEDITERRANEAN

TRIPOLI

SEA

BEIRUT

Syria

HAIFA

Egypt

TEL AVIV
JERUSALEM

Israel–
Palestine

ALEXANDRIA

PORT SAID

*Dead
Sea*

MANSOURA

Jordan

TANTA

*Suez
Canal*

BANHA

ISMAILIA

GIZA   CAIRO

SUEZ

Qarun Lake

FAIYUM

BENI SUEF

Saudi
Arabia

MINYA

MALLAWI

Gulf of Suez

Gulf of Aqaba

ASYUT

Nile

SOHAG

Red

QENA

Sea

LUXOR

ASWAN

*Lake
Nasser*

Sudan

0   100   200   300 km

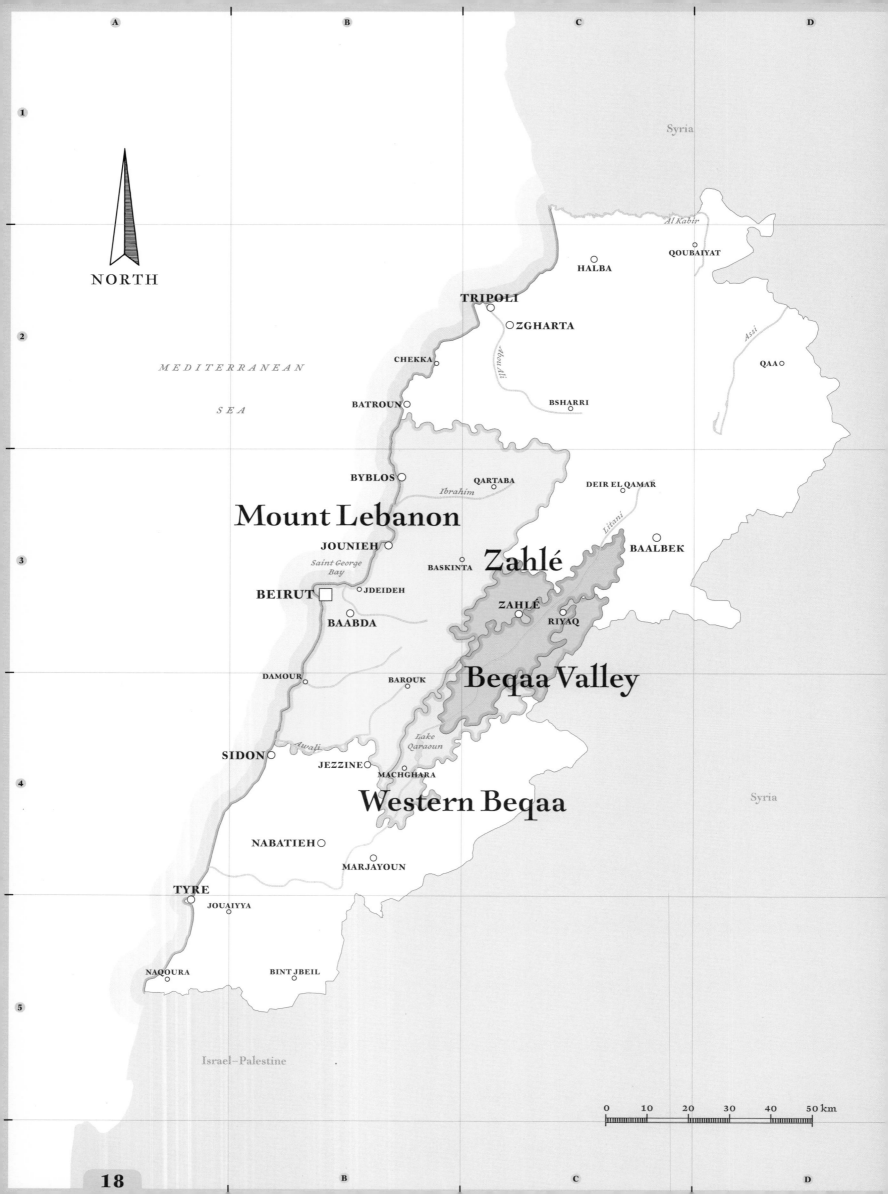

Lebanon

The history of Lebanese wine dates back to ancient times, but an organised wine industry is very recent in this country, which in 1900 had only three wine producers.

Then

Present-day Lebanon was known as Phoenicia in ancient times. The Phoenicians quickly realised that grapevines grew happily on their sun-bathed hills, and they went on to spread wine-growing across the Mediterranean. In the Middle Ages, Venetian merchants sold Lebanese wines throughout Europe. In the 16th century, the Ottoman Empire took control of the region. Winemaking was forbidden outside of religious practices. It was therefore the monks, on the slopes of Mount

In the Middle Ages, Venetian merchants sold Lebanese wines throughout Europe.

Lebanon, who maintained the traditions and terroirs for winemaking. The country was under French administration between 1920 and 1943, which explains the domination of Bordeaux and Rhône grape varieties.

Now

Lebanon is now primarily a producer of table grapes. Of the 27,000 hectares of grapevines,

Lebanon is the most promising of the Middle Eastern countries.

barely 20 per cent are grown for the production of wine. At the heart of the wine industry are the vines of the Beqaa Valley, growing at more than 1000 metres above sea level. With 300 days of sunshine per year and close to seven months without rain, the influences of the Mediterranean are indispensable for successful grape-growing in Lebanon. It is the most promising of the Middle Eastern wine-growing countries.

Main varieties

●	Cabernet Sauvignon, Merlot, Carignan, Cinsault
●	Chardonnay, Clairette, Merwah, Obeidi

<u>Endemic variety</u>

Global ranking
(by production)

50

Hectares planted

27,000

Annual production
(in millions of litres)

5.25

Proportion
of red/white grapes

25%

75%

Harvest period

September

Period when wine-growing appeared

3000
BC

Egypt

It's the biggest grape-grower of the region, but only 1 per cent of Egypt's grapes are used for wine. We're far from the time when its wine ran like its rivers.

Global ranking (by production)
51

Proportion of red/white grapes

25%
75%

Hectares planted
70,000

Annual production (in millions of litres)
4

Harvest period
June to August

Period when wine-growing appeared
3000
BC

Influences
Phoenicians

Then

Wild grapevines don't grow in Egypt, and they owe their introduction to the Canaanites. In ancient times, wine was mainly produced in the Alexandria region, and the Pharaohs pushed for its development along the length of the Nile. Long limited to the elites, wine only became accessible to all during the reign of Ramses II (1200 BC). Despite this, it was beer that won the status of drink of the people. Hieroglyphs discovered in ancient Egyptian tombs are the first representations of the process of winemaking and of the fermentation of barley. The art of modern winemaking here was actually developed under British colonisation, but the lack of investors and the conflicts of the 20th century prevented the country from matching the dynamism of the New World winemaking scene.

Now

A handful of companies strive to sustain the Egyptian wine industry, which was still run by the state until the end of the 20th century. The vineyards are concentrated around Lake Mariout, which unites all the best climatic conditions. Proof that wine and beer are always linked: the country's main vineyard belongs to a certain famous brand of beer with a green bottle and a red star.

Main varieties

- Cabernet Sauvignon, Merlot
- Pinot Blanc, <u>Fayoumi</u>

<u>Endemic variety</u>

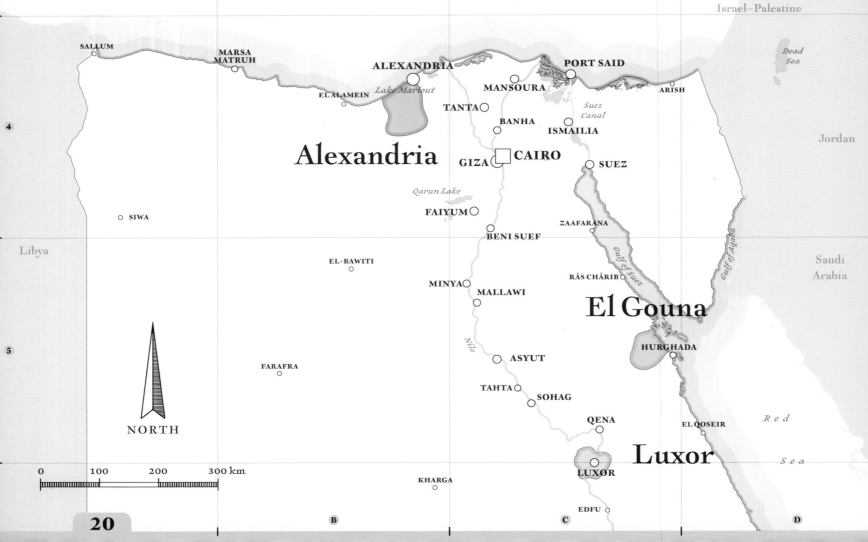

Israel– Palestine

The region can boast of housing both one of the oldest and one of the youngest wine industries in the world. Appearing first in ancient times, winemaking was forgotten for close to 1000 years before being reborn in the hands of determined producers.

Then

Jerusalem, as a holy Jewish, Christian and Muslim city, is the epicentre of great religious conflict. From 637 AD to the end of the First World War, the region was under Arab domination, and its historic vineyards were torn out or abandoned. Wine remains ever-present in Judaism, although its divine character is above all linked to the 'divine' nature of grapes. This meant that when wine was lacking, a ceremony could take place with grape juice. The more recent involvement of foreign investors and wine experts trained in the United States and Italy allowed for remarkable progress in quality.

Now

The country is divided into five wine-growing regions, but the exact provenance of the wines is rarely written on the label because they are often made using a blend of grapes grown in different regions. The renaissance of the Israeli wine industry dates above all to the last decade. The majority of the wines are kosher, catering to the expectations of the global Jewish community: access to a quality wine prepared in accordance with religious rites.

Global ranking (by production)
38

Hectares planted
5500

Annual production (in millions of litres)
26

Proportion of red/white grapes
30%
70%

Harvest period
August to October

Period when wine-growing appeared
3000 BC

Influences
Phoenicians

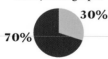

Main varieties

- ● Syrah, Merlot, Cabernet Sauvignon
- ● Chardonnay, Sauvignon Blanc

Galilee
QIRYAT SHEMONA
NAHARIYA
Upper Galilee
Golan Heights
HAIFA
NAZARETH
Sea of Galilee
Lower Galilee
Moint Carmel

MEDITERRANEAN
SEA

HADERA
Shomron
NETANYA
NABLUS
RAMAT GAN
TEL AVIV
HOLON   LOD
RAMALLAH
ASHDOD
JERUSALEM
BEIT SHEMESH
BETHLEHEM
ASHKELON
Jerusalem
Dead Sea
KIRYAT GAT
Samson
Gush Etzion
○ NETIVOT
Judaean Mountains
BEERSHEBA
DIMONA
Jordan
Negev

Negev Highlands

Lebanon
Syria
Jordan
Egypt

NORTH

0   25   50   75 km

Who made wine in 1500 BC?

This period marks the heyday of the Phoenicians. Formidable sailors, these original inhabitants of current-day Lebanon, thirsting for new horizons, are the first to undertake large-scale exploration and conquest of the Mediterranean and its shores.

3300 BC   3000 BC   2700 BC   2400 BC

Israel–Palestine •
Lebanon •
Egypt •
Bulgaria •

• *The Greeks settle the shores of the Aegean*

The idea of appellations is introduced by the Egyptians, who are the first to name a wine after its place of origin

Appearance of the amphora in the Middle East

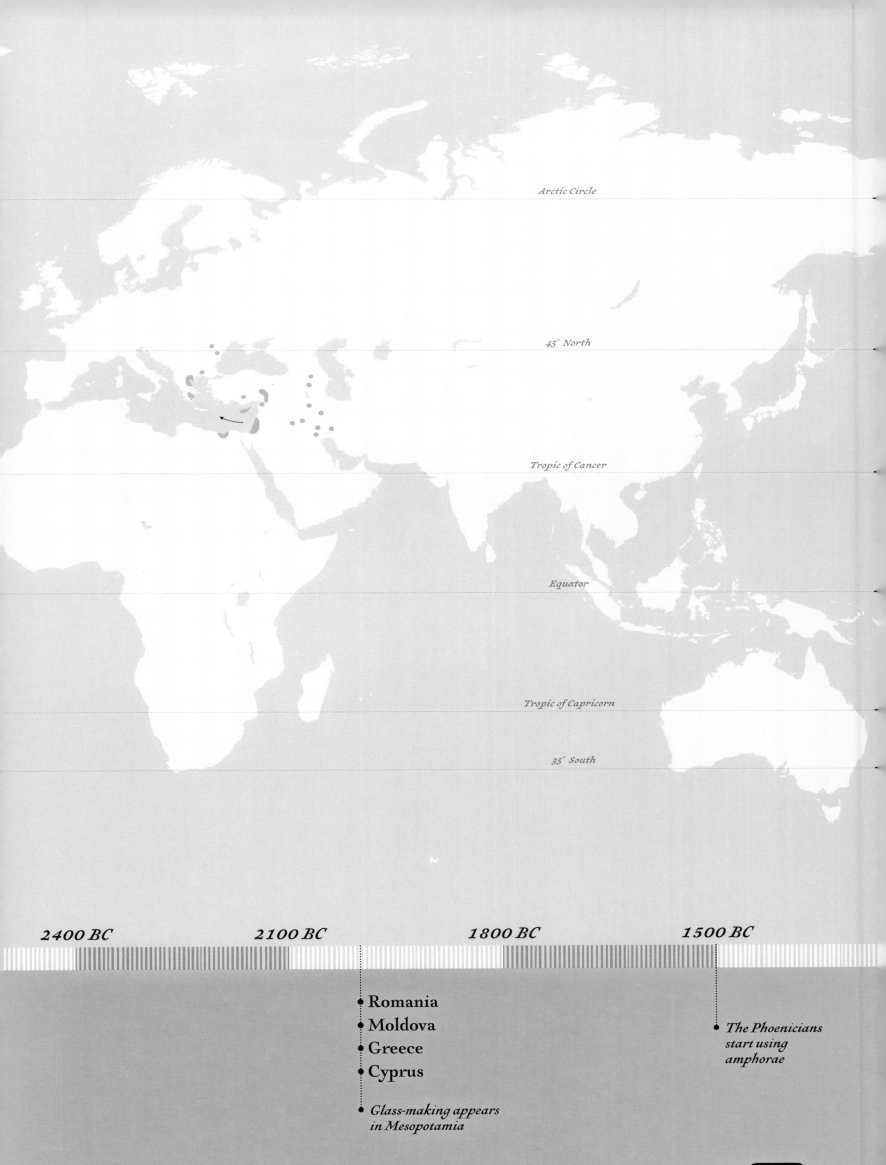

Arctic Circle

45° North

Tropic of Cancer

Equator

Tropic of Capricorn

35° South

2400 BC   2100 BC   1800 BC   1500 BC

- **Romania**
- **Moldova**
- **Greece**
- **Cyprus**

- *Glass-making appears in Mesopotamia*

- *The Phoenicians start using amphorae*

Romania & Moldova

Proportion of red/white grapes

47% — 53%

Harvest period

September

Period when wine-growing appeared

2000
BC

Influences

Greeks

These two producers, both formerly part of the Soviet Union, were a single nation until the 19th century and thus share a common history. The two countries even speak the same language: Romanian. It's difficult to date the appearance of wine-growing in this region. A verse from Homer's *Iliad* indicates that in ancient times the Greeks came to Thrace, now the Balkan Peninsula, in search of wine. We owe the structure of the vineyard to Greek colonists and its development to the Romanians. In the 1980s, when the rest of Europe was enjoying an absolute boom, the anti-alcohol policy of Russia's President Gorbachev checked development in these two countries, which still lag somewhat behind in terms of winemaking infrastructure.

Romania

Global ranking (by production)

13

Hectares planted

191,000

Annual production (in millions of litres)

350

Situated on the Danube and crossed by the alpine belt of the Carpathians, Romania has roughly the same surface area as the United Kingdom. Today it's the sixth biggest producer of wine in the European Union and one of the oldest. In the Middle Ages, the Germans planted Germanic varieties that still exist today, such as welschriesling and riesling. Romanian winemaking has advanced more rapidly than that of Moldova, thanks to significant investment at the end of the 20th century.

5 appellations to start with
Cotnari, Recas, Jidvei, Murfatlar, Dealul Mare

Main varieties

● Merlot, Cabernet Sauvignon, <u>Babeasca Neagra</u>
● <u>Feteasca Alba</u>, <u>Feteasca Regala</u>, Grasevina

<u>Endemic variety</u>

ORADEA

Crisana

Minis

ARAD

Mures

Teremia

TIMISOARA

Recas

Banat

RESITA

Drobeta-T. Severi

Serbia

Moldova

Global ranking / (by production)

19

Hectares planted

142,000

Annual production (in millions of litres)

170

Main varieties

- Cabernet Sauvignon, Merlot, Pinot Noir, Isabelle
- Aligoté, Rkatsiteli, Sauvignon Blanc

3 appellations to start with

Valul lui Traian, Stefan Voda, Codru

Moldova overflows with surprising wine facts. The winemaking tradition is so strong here that on 7 October it celebrates Wine Day, a public holiday. It's also a country that exports the larger part of the wine it produces, with 80 per cent leaving for the rest of the world each year. Another badge of honour: *The Guinness Book of Records* awarded Moldova the record for the largest cellar in the world. The honour lies with the wine producer Milestii Mici, located on the oustkirts of the country's capital, which has a cellar of more than 1.5 million bottles stocked in 55 kilometres of subterranean galleries. It takes a whole day to visit and an eternity to taste everything …

Germany
- Pinot Noir
- Müller-Thurgau

○ STUTTGART

▲ Black Forest

MUNICH ○

France

Italy

Austria
- Riesling, Grüner Veltliner

□ VIENNA

GRAZ ○

Isar

Slovenia

Sava

□ ZAGREB

Poland

Slovakia
- Cabernet Sauvignon
- Chardonnay, Sauvignon

□ BRATISLAVA

□ BUDAPEST

Croatia
- Cabernet Sauvignon
- Welschriesling, Sauvignon, Chardonnay

The Danube
River of the east

From the Black Forest to the Black Sea, the 'Beautiful Blue Danube' links west and east, passing different languages and grapes.

In the majority of the countries it passes through, the concentration of grapevines on the south side of the river has a historical explanation. For a long time, the Danube was a border between the Roman Empire and diverse 'barbarian' populations, so the banks were guarded by Roman legions, and it was necessary to slake the thirst of everyone involved. They thus grew grapevines there, whose nectars needed only to glide along the water to be drunk elsewhere.

For the past twenty years or so, the Danube's terroirs have piqued the curiosity of well-informed wine buffs. The variations in soils, climate and traditions offer such a remarkable palette of wines that you could spend a whole year exploring them without ever getting bored.

The river rises in Germany, but its real link with wine doesn't begin until Austria, on the outskirts of the only European capital city to retain its vineyards: Vienna. The 'Beautiful Blue Danube' then runs on, making its tour of capital cities, as if welcoming the river was a diplomatic obligation. Bratislava, Budapest and Belgrade, cities still scarred by recent conflicts, were torn apart by war but reunited by the river. As the water flows downstream, the climate grows warmer and the grapes change from predominantly white to red. The Danube pays a visit to Bulgarian wines, then returns to Romania via a brief 340-metre visit to Moldova. Unable to choose which country to end its run in, it decides to open up its delta, sharing it between Romania and the Ukraine. After a 2860-kilometre course, it returns here to the origin of wine along the shores of the Black Sea, and the cycle is complete.

0   100   200   300 km

Ukraine

Moldova
- Cabernet Sauvignon, Merlot, Pinot Noir
- Aligoté, Rkatsiteli, Sauvignon Blanc

CHISINAU

ODESSA

Hungary
- Kékfrankos
- Chardonnay, Pinot Gris

Mures

Racaciuni Lake

Romania
- Cabernet Sauvignon, Merlot, Pinot Noir
- Feteasca Alba, Feteasca Regala

BUCHAREST

CRAIOVA

Black Sea

GRADE

Danube

VARNA

Serbia
- Prokupac
- Welschriesling

Bulgaria
- Pamid, Merlot
- Rkatsiteli, Dimyat

Macedonia

Turkey

Greece

NORTH

Characteristics

Length	2860 km
Main source	The Breg (Germany)
Mouth	Black Sea
Countries crossed	Germany, Austria, Slovakia, Hungary, Croatia, Serbia, Romania, Bulgaria, Moldova, Ukraine
Main tributaries	Morava, Tisza, Olt, Siret, Prut, Inn, Sava, Iskar, Yantra

Legend

● Main red variety/ies
● Main white variety/ies

Eastern
Mediterranean

GREECE, MACEDONIA & CYPRUS

The cradle of Europe today offers a less glorious wine industry than in the past. The Greeks were the first to master wine-growing and to propagate that knowledge throughout the Mediterranean Basin, but numerous conflicts have since profoundly affected the civilisations of the region.

BLACK SEA

Cyprus

Syria

Lebanon

MEDITERRANEAN

SEA

0   50   100   150 km

Greece

Greek winemaking reached its peak under the Roman Empire. Through the centuries and changes in fashion, the Greeks never abandoned their ancestral varieties.

Global ranking (by production)

15

Hectares planted

107,000

Annual production (in millions of litres)

265

Proportion of red/white grapes

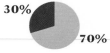

30%

70%

Harvest period

August September

Period when wine-growing appeared

2000 BC

Then

The tales of ancient Greece overflow with references to wine and its pleasures. From the Cyclops of Homer's *Odyssey* to Spartan warriors, numerous historical and legendary figures drank wine. Outside of literature, references to grapevines on coinage prove the importance of wine in the commerce of many cities. Archaeological digs attest to Greek amphorae voyaging as far as the Rhône Valley and the northern coast of the Black Sea, in Crimea. In Greek mythology, Dionysos, son of Zeus, is the God of grapevines, wine, theatre and festivals. That's quite a program!

Now

The grape varieties grown have remained local, and foreign varieties occupy less than 15 per cent of the wine-growing area. To protect this heritage, the 33 Greek Protected Designations of Origin (PDOs) are reserved for wines produced with a majority of endemic varieties. Greece is the only European country whose wine-growing area has shrunk since

Greece is the only European country whose wine-growing area has shrunk.

the 1960s, but improvements in vineyards have allowed increases in yield and have stabilised production.

Retsina, popularised in Europe in the 1960s and synonymous with Greece, is a white wine fermented with traces of pine resin. This traditional method gives the wine a unique taste and distinctive aroma.

5 appellations to start with

Nemea
Naoussa
Mantinia
Muscat of Samos
Patras

Main varieties

- ● Agiorgitiko, Xinomavro
- ● Savatiano, Roditis, Muscat d'Alexandrie

Endemic variety

Cyprus

Global ranking
(by production)

44

Hectares planted

9000

Annual production
(in millions of litres)

14

Proportion
of red/white grapes

40%

60%

Harvest period

September

Period when wine-
growing appeared

2000

BC

Influences

Greeks
Romans

Between the dry plains and the humid
mountains of Cyprus, grapevines and
almond trees withstand the burning sun.

Then

Coveted for centuries for its strategic position,
this island has lived under Roman, Ottoman,
Greek and even British rule. Thanks to its isolation,
it is the only country in Europe to have escaped
the phylloxera plague at the end of the 19th century.

Now

Cyprus is known for producing an exceptional wine:
Commandaria. It's made using two great endemic
varieties, and the grapes are first sun-dried to
concentrate the sugars. The juice is then fortified
with an *eau de vie* or distilled wine. For a long time,
the country sold its fortified wines as sherry, but
international laws now forbid winemakers from
using this Spanish appellation on their labels.

Main varieties

- ● <u>Mavro</u>, Carignan,
  Cabernet Sauvignon
- ● <u>Xynisteri</u>, Sultaniye

<u>Endemic variety</u>

RIZOKARPASO

Morphou Bay

KYRENIA
LAPITHOS
AKANTHOU
PATRIKI

Paphos
KOKKINA
MORPHOU
NICOSIA
ASHA
FAMAGUSTA

GIALIA
LEFKA
AKAKI
DALI

POLIS
GERAKIES
KLIROU

Laona - Akamas
Vouni Panagias -
Ambelitis
Pitsilia
KORNOS
ARADIPPOU

STROUMPI
Commandaria
Lemesos
LARNACA
Larnaca Bay

PAPHOS
PACHNA
LIMNITIS
Limassol

LIMASSOL

Akrotiri Bay

MEDITERRANEAN SEA

0   25   50 km

NORTH

Pcinja–Osogovo

Kosovo

LIPKOVO
KRIVA PALANKA
Bulgaria

TEARCE
KUMANOVO

TETOVO
SKOPJE
SARAJ
Vardar

KOCANI

GOSTIVAR
Treska
Bregalnica

Veles

VELES
○ STIP

Povardarie
RADOVIS

KICEVO
Tikves
Strumica

KAVADARCI
STRUMICA

Black Drin

Pelagonija–Polog
Vardar

PRILEP

Reka Crna
Doiran Lake

STRUGA
GEVGELIJA

OHRID *Ohrid*
Lake Ohrid
BITOLA

Greece

Albania
Lake Prespa

0   25   50   75 km

Global ranking
(by production)

24

Hectares planted

22,300

Annual production
(in millions of litres)

120

Proportion
of red/white grapes

20%

80%

Harvest period

September

Period when wine-
growing appeared

1300
BC

Influences
Greeks

Macedonia

With the recent drawing-up of 16 PDOs, this country
of just 2 million inhabitants aims to make
a serious impact as a Balkan wine producer.

Littered with wars and periods of occupation, history
has had a habit of redrawing the borders of this small
mountainous Balkan country. It's therefore difficult to speak
of a true wine-producing identity
in a nation formed only in 1944.
The first grapevines were planted,
however, in ancient times, in the
Vardar Valley, which has excellent
climatic conditions for wine-
growing. Today this region, known
by the name Povardarie, nurtures

After tobacco,
wine is the most
exported product
of Macedonia.

85 per cent of the country's grapevines. After tobacco, wine
is the most exported product of Macedonia.

NORTH

Main varieties

● Stanušina, Vranac, Merlot

● Smederevka, Chardonnay

Endemic variety

Who made wine in 500 BC?

The ancient world is at its height, Julius Caesar is not yet born and there's still no ferry to link Barcelona and Algeria. With one foot in the Ukraine and the other in Morocco, the grapevine continues to spread.

-1700   -1500   -1300   -1100

Pharaoh Ramses II makes wine accessible to all Egyptians

Macedonia

The Phoenicians invent the alphabet

1352 BC
Tutankhamen buried with his amphorae of wine

Arctic Circle

45° North

Tropic of Cancer

Equator

Tropic of Capricorn

35° South

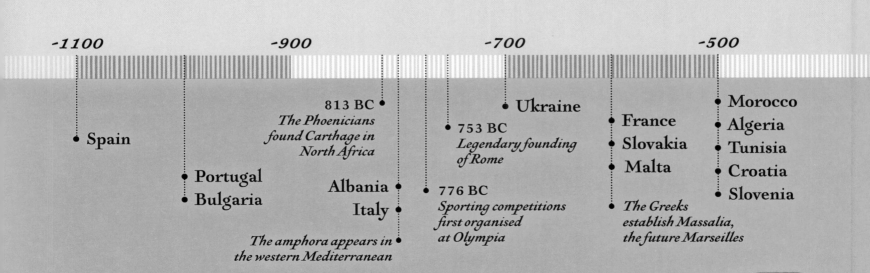

-1100   -900   -700   -500

- Spain

- Portugal
- Bulgaria

- Albania
- Italy

  The amphora appears in
  the western Mediterranean

813 BC •
The Phoenicians
found Carthage in
North Africa

753 BC
Legendary founding
of Rome

776 BC
Sporting competitions
first organised
at Olympia

• Ukraine

• France
• Slovakia
• Malta

  The Greeks
  establish Massalia,
  the future Marseilles

• Morocco
• Algeria
• Tunisia
• Croatia
• Slovenia

Basque Country

GIJÓN
SANTANDER
A CORUÑA
OVIEDO

Bizkaiko Txakolina
SAN SEBASTIÁN
BILBAO
Txakoli de Álava
Getariako Txakolina

Galicia

PAMPLONA
VITORIA-GASTEIZ

Castile
and León
LEÓN
BURGOS
LOGROÑO

Navarre

Ribeira Sacra
Bierzo
Rías Baixas

Rioja

OURENSE
Ribeiro
Valdeorras
VIGO

Tierra de León
Arlanza

Monterrei
Cigales

Campo de Borja
ZARAGOZA

Ribera del Duero
Duero
Ebro

Calatayud
Cariñena

Arribes
VALLADOLID
Toro
Rueda

Aragon

SALAMANCA

Madrid
MADRID
GETAFE

Méntrida
Mondéjar

Portugal
Uclés

Castilla–
La Mancha
La Mancha

Utiel-Requena
VALEN

Extremadura
Manchuela

Tagus

BADAJOZ
ALBACETE
Almansa

Yecla

Valdepeñas
Jumilla
Alican

ALICANT

Segura
Bullas
MURCIA

CÓRDOBA
Guadalquivir

Andalusia

Murcia

Montilla-Moriles
SEVILLE
CARTAGENA

HUELVA
GRENADA

Condado de Huelva
Málaga
ALMERÍA

Gulf of
Càdiz
Sierras de Málaga

Jerez-Xérès-Sherry
JEREZ
MÁLAGA

CÀDIZ
MARBELLA

ATLANTIC
OCEAN

Gibraltar
ALGECIRAS

Strait of Gibraltar

Alboran
Sea

0   100   200   300 km

Morocco

Algeria

France

Andorra

Catalonia

Empordà

montano
Costers del Segre

LLEIDA

Alella

SABADELL

Tarragona

Penedès

BADALONA

BARCELONA

Terra Alta

TARRAGONA

Valencia

Mínorca

Binissalem

Plà i Llevant

PALMA

Majorca

Ibiza

Balearic Islands

Formentera

MEDITERRANEAN SEA

THE AGE OF EXPLORATION
Tempranillo
Jerez
Denominación de Origen
El vino

Spain

A wind of modernity blows over the Iberian Peninsula. After 20 years of investment and the rise of a new generation, the Spanish wine industry is remarkable for its dynamism. Not that this prevents wine-growers from prioritising historic endemic varieties.

Canary Islands

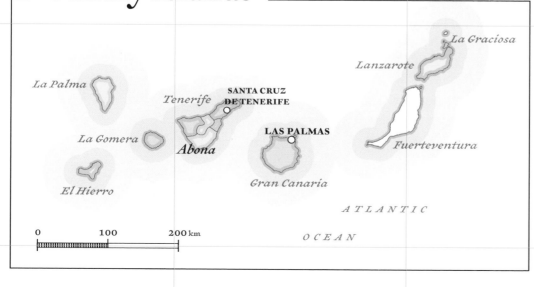

La Graciosa

Lanzarote

La Palma

Tenerife

SANTA CRUZ
DE TENERIFE

LAS PALMAS

La Gomera

Abona

Fuerteventura

El Hierro

Gran Canaria

ATLANTIC

OCEAN

0   100   200 km

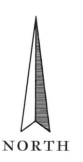

NORTH

Global ranking
(by production)

3

Hectares planted

975,000

Annual production
(in millions of litres)

3780

Proportion
of red/white grapes

45%

55%

Harvest period

September

Period when wine-growing appeared

1100
BC

Influences

Phoenicians
Greeks

Then

It's difficult to impose an enduring culture on a territory occupied successively by the Phoenicians, Greeks, Romans, Visigoths and Arabs. Although Spanish wine-growing is 2000 years old, the industry's organisation began in the 15th century, after the Reconquista – the reconquest by the Christian kingdoms of the peninsular territories and Balearic Islands occupied by Muslims.

Although Spanish wine-growing is 2000 years old, the industry's organisation began in the 15th century.

The Portuguese explorer Ferdinand Magellan was a great fan of the wines from Xérès. History tells that for his circumnavigation of the globe in 1519, he spent more money on wine than on weapons. Finally, a navigator who thought of his sailors' morale!

For a long time, Spain exported its wines to the United Kingdom or Italy. But thanks to the phylloxera plague that struck French vineyards in the 19th century, Spain became *the* supplier for Europe. The misfortunes of some made the fortune of others. While the 19th century was marked by productive wine-growing, it took until the 1990s to see a resurgence in the Spanish wine industry.

Main varieties

- Tempranillo, Grenache, Bobal, Mourvèdre, Cabernet Sauvignon
- Airén, Cayetana Blanca, Macabeo, Palomino, Verdejo

Endemic variety

Now

For the wine buff, Spain is an exciting playground. First, the industry has 63 appellations: just enough to neither get lost nor go around in circles. On the bottles, the appellation is followed by

Spain is an exciting playground.

the letters DO, or Denominación de Origen. In addition to the provenance, the label can indicate, next to the vintage, the degree of ageing in barrels. *Vino de Crianza*: two years, at least one of them in oak casks; *Vino de Reserva*: three years, at least one of them in oak casks; *Vino de Gran Reserva*: five years, two of them in oak casks. The largest wine-growing area in the world is also notable for the great diversity of varieties under cultivation. Although international varieties such as merlot, syrah (shiraz) and chardonnay are progressively establishing themselves, they have the manners to leave the limelight to endemic varieties.

Spain is surely the country with the best match of quality and price. From the intense reds of Andalusia to the effervescent whites of the Basque Country, not to mention the volcanic wines of the Canary Islands, there is something for every taste and budget.

5 appellations to start with

Jerez
Rioja
Priorat
Ribera del Duero
Rías Baixas

Córdoba

CÓRDOBA

Guadalquivir

Seville

SEVILLE

Montilla–Moriles

HUELVA

Condado de Huelva

GRENADA

Jerez–Xérès–Sherry

Málaga
Sierras de Málaga

Málaga

Manzanilla

JEREZ

CÀDIZ

Càdiz

MARBELLA

MÁLAGA

CÀDIZ

ALGECIRAS

0 25 50 km

NORTH

Hectares planted
86,000

Proportion
of red/white grapes
20%

80%

Andalusia

The first Spanish wines were developed here, 3000 years ago. While Portugal has its Porto (port), Spain has its Jerez (sherry). It's a white wine fortified with distilled wine and aged in casks until the alcohol content is at least 18 per cent. The idea of adding distilled wine dates back to when souring of wine had to be prevented during long marine voyages.

Depending on how it's made, Jerez falls into several categories, from driest to sweetest. As Shakespeare put it, a good sherry 'hath a twofold operation in it': 'It ascends me into the brain, dries me there all the foolish and dull and cloudy vapours', and it warms the blood, 'which, before cold and settled, left the liver white and pale, which is the badge of pusillanimity and cowardice'.

Main varieties

| ● | **Grenache**, Cabernet Franc |
| ● | **Palomino**, **Pedro Ximénez**, Moscatel |

Endemic variety

Castilla–La Mancha

Hectares planted
520,000

Proportion
of red/white grapes
15%

85%

The largest vineyard area in the world lies at the gates of Madrid. This 'green lung' of grapes makes up 50 per cent of total national output. Long geared for mass production, the industry of the region reorganised itself at the end of the 19th century. Half the region now boasts a DO.

Main varieties

| ● | **Tempranillo**, **Grenache** |
| ● | **Airén** |

Endemic variety

NORTH

MADRID

Mondéjar

Méntrida

CUENCA

TOLEDO

Uclés

Manchuela

La Mancha

Ribera del Júcar

CIUDAD REAL

ALBACETE

Almansa

Valdepeñas

0 20 40 60 km

Castile & Léon

Hectares planted
68,000

Proportion of red/white grapes

85% 15%

Aside from Arlanza and Bierzo, all the appellations are nestled on the banks of the Duero (Douro) or its confluences. In this region, life isn't easy for vines, which endure both extreme frosts in winter and high heat in summer. But don't they say that the vine has to suffer to make a great wine?

Main varieties

- Tempranillo, Mencía
- Verdejo

Endemic variety

NORTH

Rioja & Navarre

Rioja is like Bordeaux: known throughout the world for its very strong wines made with a blend of grapes, for which old vines are particularly appreciated. And these common points are no accident, given numerous people from Bordeaux invested in the region after the phylloxera plague at the end of the 19th century.

Hectares planted
80,000

Proportion of red/white grapes

92% 8%

Main varieties

- Tempranillo, Grenache, Graciano
- Macabeo, Chardonnay

Endemic variety

Catalonia

Catalonia is known for its Cava, the majority of which is produced in the Penedès DO. This bubbling wine tends to compete with certain champagnes and prosecco, thanks to its excellent combination of quality and price. Catalonia is also notable for its rosés, which benefit from the gentle Mediterranean climate.

Hectares planted
61,000

Proportion of red/white grapes

40% 60%

Main varieties

- Grenache, Syrah
- Macabeo, Parellada, Xarel-Lo

Endemic variety

NORTH

Galicia

Hectares planted
26,000

Proportion of red/white grapes
15%
85%

G alicia is a land of white wines. Thanks to its geographic location, this wine area has more points in common with its Portuguese neighbours than its fellow Spanish regions.

Galicia, and primarily the Rías Baixas DO, has made a name for itself with its leading variety: albariño. It enjoys the oceanic climate and produces wines that are remarkable for their freshness and generous aromatic notes. It's also all the rage in the United States. A new rival for chardonnay perhaps?

Main varieties

- Mencía, Alicante Bouschet
- Albariño, Palomino Treixadura

Endemic variety

NORTH

Rías Baixas

SANTIAGO DE COMPOSTELA

Val do Salnés

Ribeira Sacra

Ribeiro

Valdeorras

OURENSE
RIBADAVIA

VIGO Condado de Tea

Ourense

O Rosal

Monterrei

NORTH

Portugal

0   15   30 km

Navarre

PAMPLONA

ESTELLA

Valdizarbe

Rioja Alavesa

Tierra de Estella

Baja Montaña

LOGROÑO

Rioja Alta

Ebro

Ribera Alta

CALAHORRA

Rioja Baja

Rioja

TUDELA

Ribera Baja

0 10 20 30 km

NORTH

The islands

Hectares planted
18,000

Proportion of red/white grapes
80%   20%

B efore sailing the high seas to the Americas, Spanish sailors were in the habit of stopping off at the Canaries. This is surely one reason for the birth of the islands' vineyards, whose products are still little known. The proof: it's virtually impossible to buy their wines outside the archipelago.

Main varieties

- Listán Negro, Manto Negro
- Palomino, Chardonnay

Endemic variety

0   50 km

Valle de la Orotava

Tacoronte-Acentejo

La Graciosa

Lanzarote

La Palma

Lanzarote

La Palma

Ycoden-Daute-Isora

SANTA CRUZ DE TENERIFE

La Gomera

Abona

LAS PALMAS

Fuerteventura

El Hierro

Tenerife

Valle de Güímar

Gran Canaria

El Hierro

Canary Islands

0   50 km

Binissalem

Minorca

PALMA

Plà i Llevant

Ibiza

Majorca

Balearic Islands

Vinho Verde

Monção
Lima
VIANA DO CASTELO
Cávado
BRAGA
Ave
BOUGADO
Amarante
Sousa
PORTO
Baião
Paiva

Trás-os-Montes

Chaves
Valpaços
MIRANDELA
Planalto Mirandês
VILA REAL
Baixo Corgo
Cima Corgo
Douro Superior

Douro Valley

Basto
Távora–Varosa

Lafões
Dão
VISEU
Pinhel
Castelo Rodrigo
GUARDA

Beira Interior

Bairrada

Dão

Cova da Beira

Beira Atlântico

COIMBRA
FIGUEIRA DA FOZ
Sicó
POMBAL
CASTELO BRANCO

MARINHA GRANDE
Encostas de Aire

Lisboa

Tomar
CALDAS DA RAINHA
Santarém
Óbidos
SANTARÉM
Chamusca

Tejo

Portalegre
PORTALEGRE

TORRES VEDRAS
Cartaxo
Almeirim
Coruche

Alentejo

Borba
Bucelas
AMADORA
Palmela
Redondo
LISBON
Évora
SETÚBAL
ÉVORA
Reguengos

Setúbal

Vidigueira
Moura

BEJA
SINES

Algarve

Portimão
Lagoa
Lagos
Tavira
LAGOS
ALBUFEIRA
FARO
Cape St Vincent

Madeira

ATLANTIC OCEAN
CAMACHA
Porto Santo
MACHICO
RIBEIRA BRAVA
FUNCHAL
Deserta Grande

0   25   50 km

Azores

Western Azores
Graciosa
Central Azores
Biscoitos
ATLANTIC OCEAN
ANGRA
Pico
PONTA DELGADA
Eastern Azores

0   100   200 km

ATLANTIC OCEAN

Spain

0   40   80   120 km

NORTH

Portugal

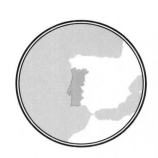

At the extreme south-west of Europe, this land is lapped by a single ocean: the Atlantic. Yet given its climate, and diversity of grape varieties and terroirs, Portugal is just like a Mediterranean country.

Global ranking
(by production)

11

Hectares planted

204,000

Annual production
(in millions of litres)

670

Proportion of red/white grapes

30%

70%

Harvest period

September

Period when wine-growing appeared

1000
BC

Influences

Phoenicians

Then

Well before modern-day nations and borders saw the light of day, the Iberian Peninsula belonged to the Roman Empire. Numerous authors, however, attribute the appearance of wine-growing to the Phoenicians, around 1000 BC. With its ports open to the world, Portugal was a special place throughout the Age of Discovery of the 15th to 18th centuries. Thanks to its colonies, it figured among the most powerful countries on the planet.

With its ports open to the world, Portugal was a special place throughout the Age of Discovery.

It was with its famous port that Portugal made a name for itself in the world of wine. During the Hundred Years' War of the 14th and 15th centuries, the British ceased importing French wine. The demand for port became so strong that the wine-growers increased their yield, to the detriment of quality. Because of this, the Marquis of Pombal decided to restrict the production of port to a single region and to categorise the winemakers in a hierarchy based on quality. It was in 1757 that one of the oldest appellations in the world was born. However, the dictatorship of Antonio Salazar from 1932 to 1974 curbed the development of the country's wine industry.

Now

Portugal is an extraordinary museum of grape varieties. To give an idea, 48 varieties can be involved in the production of port.

Portugal is an extraordinary museum of varieties.

There are more than 50 varieties cultivated in the Douro Valley, and 250 in the entire country. New generations have understood well that each region deserves its own variety and each variety its region. In a country only a sixth the size of France, the diversity of terroirs and traditions is fascinating. The wine map of Portugal is reminiscent of that of Italy, where the regions touch one another and occupy more or less the entire country. Among the reds, tempranillo is king. In the south it's called Aragonez and in the north Tinta Roriz. Portugal is surely the European country that has made the most progress with its wines during the past 20 years.

Main varieties

- Tempranillo,* <u>Touriga Nacional,</u> <u>Trincadeira, Castelão, Touriga Franca</u>
- <u>Fernão Pires, Siria, Arinto</u>

* locally called Tinta Roriz or Aragonez

<u>Endemic variety</u>

5 appellations to start with

Vinho Verde
Madeira
Óbidos
Douro
Daõ

Alentejo

Squeezed between the Tagus River and the Algarve, Alentejo is one of the most sun-soaked wine-growing areas in Portugal. It is notable for its red wines, which are excellent in maturity. The climatic conditions lead certain estates to irrigate their vines. International varieties that endure the heat well, such as syrah (shiraz) and cabernet sauvignon, have appeared here in the past few decades.

Hectares planted
22,000

Proportion of red/white grapes
20%
80%

Main varieties

- Alicante Bouschet, Tempranillo,* <u>Trincadeira</u>
- <u>Siria</u>, <u>Encruzado</u>

locally called Aragonez

<u>Endemic variety</u>

PORTALEGRE

Portalegre

Borba

Évora

Redondo

ÉVORA

Reguengos

Granja–Amareleja

Vidigueira

BEJA

Moura

Spain

0 10 20 30 km

NORTH

Vinho Verde

Hectares planted
34,000

Proportion of red/white grapes
10%
90%

The name of this region comes from thr name of its wine. Vinho Verde is a white wine characterised by its freshness, acidity and low alcohol content. A slight effervescence can also reinforce its vivacity. The region competes with the Douro Valley with whites of surprising clarity, for drinking when they are still young.

Main varieties

- <u>Vinhão</u>
- <u>Albariño</u>, <u>Arinto</u>, <u>Loureiro</u>

<u>Endemic variety</u>

Monção

PAREDES DE COURA

Lima

PONTE DE LIMA

VIANA DO CASTELO

Spain

Ave

Cávado

BRAGA

RIBEIRA DE PENA

GUIMARÃES

Basto

VILA DO CONDE

Amarante

Sousa

PORTO

BAIÃO

Douro

Baião

Paiva

0 10 20 km

NORT

0   10   20 km

Tâmega

Tua

MIRANDELA

MURÇA

Sabor

VILA REAL

ALIJÓ

Douro Valley

PINHÃO

MESÃO FRIO

Baixo Corgo

Douro

ARMAMAR

MONCORVO

Cima Corgo

NORTH

Spain

Main varieties

- ● <u>Touriga Franca</u>, <u>Touriga Nacional</u>, Tempranillo*
- ○ <u>Malvoisie</u>, <u>Viosinho</u>, <u>Gouveio</u>

* locally called Tinta Roriz

<u>Endemic variety</u>

Douro Valley

Hectares planted
45,500

Proportion of red/white grapes
10%
90%

A nd here is Portugal's jewel in the crown. As much for its wines as its countryside, the Douro Valley well deserves its inclusion on UNESCO's World Heritage List. The vertiginous hills plunging into the Douro River forced wine-growers to plant their grapes on terraces supported by stone walls. Although the region produces truly great white and red wines, it is known historically for its Port: a fortified wine whose fermentation is halted by the addition of alcohol in order to retain the residual sugars and take the alcohol content to around 20 per cent. The French recently overtook the British as the main consumers of port.

SOURE

POMBAL

Encostas d'Aire

LEIRIA

NAZARÉ

FÁTIMA

Hectares planted
30,741

Proportion of red/white grapes
40%
60%

CALDAS DA RAINHA

PENICHE

Tagus

Óbidos

Lourinhã

TORRES VEDRAS

SANTARÉM

Lisboa

K nown in ancient times by the name Extremadura, this region is the great pride of Lisbonites. The influence of the Atlantic confers a gentler climate than in Alentejo. The white varieties therefore dominate. Óbidos produces excellent sparkling wines.

Alenquer

Torres Vedras

Arruda

Colares

Bucelas

Main varieties

- ● Alicante Bouschet, <u>Castelão</u>, Tempranillo*
- ○ <u>Arinto</u>, <u>Fernão Pires</u>

* locally called Aragonez

<u>Endemic variety</u>

SINTRA

AMADORA

ESTORIL

☐ LISBON

Carcavelos

BARREIRO

NORTH

0   10   20 km

Spain

Toro
● Tempranillo

VALLADOLID

Vinho verde
● Alvarinho, Arinto, Loureiro

Planalto Mirandês
● Touriga Nacional, Touriga Franca
● Malvoisie, Viosinho

○ BRAGA

● VILA REAL

MATOSINHOS

○ PORTO

LAMEGO

Douro Valley
● Touriga Nacional, Touriga Franca
● Malvoisie, Viosinho

Arribes
● Tempranillo
● Verdejo

○ SALAMANCA

OVAR

ATLANTIC

OCEAN

Portugal

Characteristics

Length	895 km
Main source	Picos de Urbión (Spain)
Mouth	Atlantic Ocean
Countries crossed	Spain, Portugal
Main tributaries	Pisuerga, Tâmega, Esla, Tormes, Côa

Legend

● Main red variety/ies
● Main white variety/ies

NORTH

0   25   50   75 km

BURGOS

Pícos de Urbión
2160 m

Ribera del Duero
● Tempranillo

Douro

Rueda
● Verdejo

2

MADRID

The Douro
Iberian river

3

Two countries and thus two names: Duero on the Spanish side and Douro on the Portuguese. The Mediterranean climate obliges the grapevines to share the riverbanks with olive and almond trees. It really is southern Europe …

The history of the Douro begins with its name. Some believe that it comes from the Latin *duris – duro* in Portuguese – in reference to the river's strength and endurance. Others prefer to believe in an Iberian El Dorado, casting gilded stones on its banks; *ouro* means gold in Portuguese. No one knows if you can still make your fortune by following the river's course, but we can be sure of its jewel-like vineyards.

As a sort of welcome, the first region the river flows through carries the name of its visitor. Ribera del Duero follows the river, from its high plateau, for more than 115 kilometres. We are in the heart of Spain, and the severe nature of the climate is reflected in its wine.

In this region, perched at an altitude of 700–850 metres, snow is rare but frosts are frequent. In its descent, the river meets the remarkable Rueda, which, in a region where tempranillo is king, prefers to devote 85 per cent of its vines to the white variety verdejo. As if hesitant to change countries, the river follows the border for 122 kilometres before becoming Portuguese.

New language, new name: the Duero becomes the Douro. It's also here that the river becomes navigable. Portuguese vineyards are already present, but we must wait until the splendid Douro Valley to contemplate the terraced mountains accommodating the great wines that take their name from the city where they set to sea: Porto. On its back, the river carries the *barcos rabelo*, flat-bottomed watercraft with high sails that once transported wine from the vineyards to the country's largest city.

Like a transition between the heat of Porto and the freshness of the ocean, the Douro ends its course by letting loose with the vivacity of the whites of Vinho Verde.

4

5

THRACE
The Balkans
Black Sea
Danube
Sofia

Bulgaria

Overlooked by the west, this is surely the most Mediterranean of the Eastern European countries. At the same latitude as prestigious Tuscany (Italy) and Rioja (Spain), Bulgaria profits from its rich and varied terroirs.

Global ranking (by production)

23

Hectares planted

67,000

Annual production (in millions of litres)

130

Proportion of red/white grapes

63%   37%

Harvest period

September

Period when wine-growing appeared

1000
BC

Influences

Thracians

Then

The Bulgarians say that at the creation of the world, God forgot them. And to apologise, he offered them an ideal climate, fertile plains, access to the Black Sea, and majestic wines.

Rich in knowledge gleaned from their many voyages, it was the Greeks who really provided structure for Bulgarian wine-growing and improved the quality of Bulgarian wines in ancient times.

From 1396 to 1878, the Ottoman occupation signified, in the name of Islam, a period of 'wandering in the desert' for winemaking, but at the end of the 19th century, the Treaty of San Stefano handed back Bulgaria its autonomy and its wine industry. Thereafter Bulgarian wines reached new heights, and by 1980, the country was one of the five largest wine producers in the world. Their best client? Sir Winston Churchill. History tells that the former British Prime Minister ordered close to 500 litres of Bulgarian wine per year.

By 1980, the country was one of the five largest wine producers in the world.

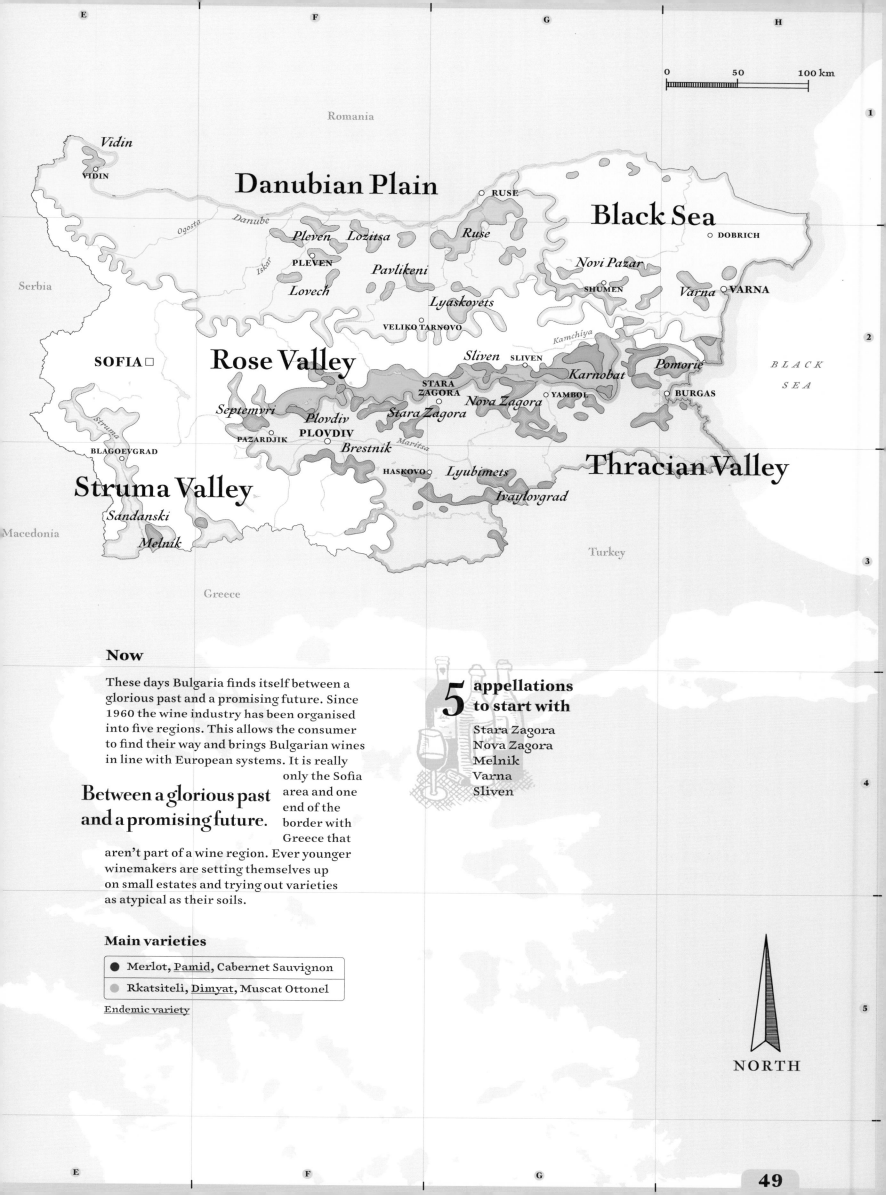

Romania

Vidin

VIDIN

Danubian Plain

○ **RUSE**

Black Sea

○ DOBRICH

Pleven *Lozitsa* *Ruse*

Serbia

PLEVEN *Pavlikeni* *Novi Pazar*

Lovech **SHUMEN** *Varna* **VARNA**

Lyaskovets

VELIKO TARNOVO

Sliven SLIVEN

BLACK

SOFIA □ # Rose Valley *Karnobat* *Pomorie* *SEA*

**STARA
ZAGORA** *Nova Zagora* □ YAMBOL

Septemvri *Stara Zagora* **BURGAS**

Plovdiv

PLOVDIV

PAZARDJIK *Maritsa*

BLAGOEVGRAD *Brestnik* # Thracian Valley

HASKOVO ○ *Lyubimets*

Struma Valley

Macedonia

Sandanski *Ivaylovgrad*

Melnik Turkey

Greece

Now

These days Bulgaria finds itself between a glorious past and a promising future. Since 1960 the wine industry has been organised into five regions. This allows the consumer to find their way and brings Bulgarian wines in line with European systems. It is really only the Sofia area and one end of the border with Greece that aren't part of a wine region. Ever younger winemakers are setting themselves up on small estates and trying out varieties as atypical as their soils.

Between a glorious past and a promising future.

5 appellations to start with

Stara Zagora
Nova Zagora
Melnik
Varna
Sliven

Main varieties

- ● Merlot, <u>Pamid</u>, Cabernet Sauvignon
- ● Rkatsiteli, <u>Dimyat</u>, Muscat Ottonel

<u>Endemic variety</u>

NORTH

Italy

According to legend, it was Dionysos – aka Bacchus, God of Wine – who revealed to humanity the secret of this revered beverage in Sicily. With its varied climates, diverse terroirs and multitude of varieties, it would take a lifetime to explore the wines of Italy.

Global ranking (by production)

1

Hectares planted

682,000

Annual production (in millions of litres)

4880

Proportion of red/white grapes

47%   53%

Harvest priod

August to October

Period when wine-growing appeared

800

BC

Influences

Etruscans Greeks

Then

At the height of Antiquity, the Greeks gave Italy, and more specifically the region of Calabria, located at the toe of the boot, the nickname 'Oenotria', meaning 'Wine Country'. Italy has always produced wine for itself and others, whether for the pleasure of Florentine painters or the thirst of the Roman armies.

The first vineyards were planted in the south of the country, in Sicily and Calabria, before spreading towards the north, until there were vines in every region. Due to its strategic position for commerce in the Mediterranean, Italy has been involved in numerous wars and invasions. The history of Italian winemaking alternates therefore between hours of glory – the Roman Empire and the Renaissance – and dark periods – the invasion of the Goths, the fall of the Medicis and the Second World War.

> ## Italy has always produced wine for itself and others.

Now

The production of wine stretches over the 20 regions of Italy, without exception: from the clay soils of the Aosta Valley to the volcanic earth of Sicily. Italy is the only country where wine is produced in every region. While Italy is actually the world leader in terms of production, ahead of its French and Spanish neighbours, the gap between the three is nevertheless slight, and between them they produce 47 per cent of the wine on the planet. Each region of Italy has its particular character, but we can distinguish two main types of terroir: those that line the Mediterranean, and those situated in the heart of the country on the Appenine mountain range, a diagonal that links Milan to Naples.

> ## It's the only country where wine is produced in every region.

Following the example of the Appellations d'Origine Contrôlée (AOC) in France, the Denominazione di Origine Controllata (DOC) protects 300 wine appellations, thanks to exact specifications for each one. It's impossible to define 'Italian wine': its richness is born of an exceptional, constantly evolving diversity. As in France, the wine industry is subject to numerous internal debates, where generations clash over questions of ecology and taste.

France

DOCG	Denominazione di origine controllata e garantita
DOC	Denominazione di origine controllata
IGT	Indicazione geografica tipica
Vino da tavola	(table wine)

Italian wines are classed in four appellation levels. The most prestigious are the DOC and DOCG, representing 34 per cent of the country's total wine production.

Main varieties

● Sangiovese, Montepulciano, Merlot, Barbera, Nero d'Avola

● Catarratto Bianco, Trebbiano Toscano, Chardonnay, Glera

Endemic variety

E | F | G | H

Liechtenstein
Switzerland
Austria
Slovenia
Croatia
Monaco
Corsica
Bosnia–Herzegovina

5 appellations to start with

Etna
Barolo
Amarone della Valpolicella
Brunello di Montalcino
Taurasi

Trentino–Alto Adige

Friuli
Collio Goriziano

TRENTO

Aosta Valley

Lombardy

BRESCIA
VICENZA

Piedmont
NOVARA
MILAN
VERONA
VENICE

TURIN

Barbaresco
Barolo

Po

PARMA
Lambrusco
Veneto

TRIESTE

Gulf of Venice

BOLOGNA

GENOA

Emilia–Romagna

RIMINI
San Marino

Gulf of Genoa
Cinque Terre

Liguria

FLORENCE
ANCONA

LIVORNO

Ligurian Sea

Tuscany

Chianti

Marche

Elba

Umbria

Abruzzo

TERNI
PESCARA

Trebbiano d'Abruzzo

Tiber

Adriatic Sea

ROME

Corsica

Lazio
Molise

LATINA
Liri

FOGGIA

Puglia

Castel del Monte

Vermentino di Gallura

Campania
BARI

SASSARI

NAPLES

Aglianico del Vulture

TARANTO

Basilicata

Gulf of Taranto

Sardinia

Tyrrhenian Sea

CAGLIARI

Calabria

Cirò

Aeolian Islands

Aegadian Islands

PALERMO
MESSINA

Contea di Sclafani
REGGIO CALABRIA

Marsala

Sicily

CATANIA

Ionian Sea

Strait of Sicily

SYRACUSE

Moscato di Siracusa

NORTH

Tunisia

0   100   200   300 km

Malta

E | F | G

51

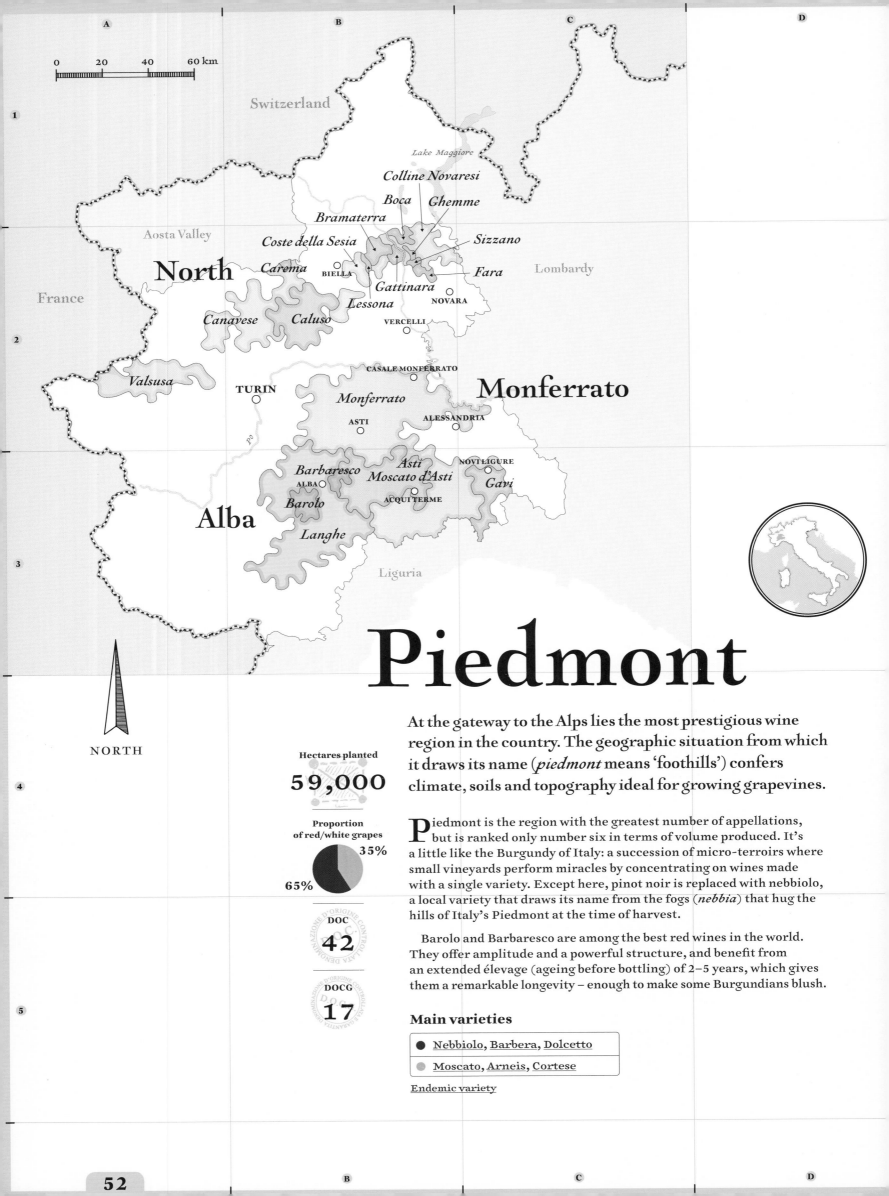

Map labels

Switzerland

Lake Maggiore

Colline Novaresi

Boca · Ghemme

Bramaterra

Coste della Sesia · Sizzano

Aosta Valley

Carema · Fara

North

BIELLA

Gattinara

Lombardy

Lessona

NOVARA

France

Canavese · Caluso

VERCELLI

Valsusa

CASALE MONFERRATO

TURIN

Monferrato · **Monferrato**

Po

ASTI · ALESSANDRIA

NOVI LIGURE

Barbaresco · Asti

ALBA · Moscato d'Asti · Gavi

Alba · Barolo · ACQUI TERME

Langhe

Liguria

NORTH

Piedmont

At the gateway to the Alps lies the most prestigious wine region in the country. The geographic situation from which it draws its name (*piedmont* means 'foothills') confers climate, soils and topography ideal for growing grapevines.

Piedmont is the region with the greatest number of appellations, but is ranked only number six in terms of volume produced. It's a little like the Burgundy of Italy: a succession of micro-terroirs where small vineyards perform miracles by concentrating on wines made with a single variety. Except here, pinot noir is replaced with nebbiolo, a local variety that draws its name from the fogs (*nebbia*) that hug the hills of Italy's Piedmont at the time of harvest.

Barolo and Barbaresco are among the best red wines in the world. They offer amplitude and a powerful structure, and benefit from an extended élevage (ageing before bottling) of 2–5 years, which gives them a remarkable longevity – enough to make some Burgundians blush.

Hectares planted

59,000

Proportion of red/white grapes

35%

65%

DOC

42

DOCG

17

Main varieties

| ● Nebbiolo, Barbera, Dolcetto |
| ○ Moscato, Arneis, Cortese |

Endemic variety

Lombardy

Along with Piedmont, this is the favourite region for nebbiolo, which prefers mild but sunny summers. Production revolves around quality, since 50 per cent of this wine region is classed as DOC or DOCG.

Hectares planted

26,300

Proportion of red/white grapes

40%

60%

DOC

22

DOCG

5

Maggiore, Garda, Iseo and Como lakes give this region a temperate continental climate. These conditions, allied with the varied topography, allow wine-growers to produce all styles of wine: from red to white, passing via rosé or bubbles. It's thanks to the reds of Valtellina, however, that the region has made a name for itself among wine buffs the world over.

We often describe prosecco as 'Italian champagne', but it's not at all. If the most sparkling of French wines must have a trans-alpine cousin, it's here in Lombardy, with the DOCG Franciacorta. This appellation produces remarkable effervescence by respecting the méthode champenoise and using a mixture of pinot noir and chardonnay grapes. Reims and Milan – fighting the same battle?

Main varieties

- ● Nebbiolo, Pinot Noir
- ● Chardonnay, Verdicchio, Pinot Blanc

Endemic variety

Switzerland

Trentino–Alto Adige

Valtellina

Valtellina

SONDRIO

Lake Maggiore   *Lake Como*

LECCO

COMO

Brescia

Valcalepio   *Lake Iseo*

BERGAMO   *Franciacorta*   *Garda*   *Lake Garda*

Colleoni   *Botticino*

LEGNANO   MONZA   *Cellatica*   Veneto

BRESCIA

MILAN   *Capriano del Colle*   *Garda Bresciano* *Lugana*

Garda Colli Mantovani

Piedmont

Pavia   *Adda*   *Oglio*

PAVIA   *San Colombano al Lambro*   CREMONA   MANTUA

Oltrepò Pavese   *Lambrusco Mantovano*

Mantua

NORTH

0   20   40 km

Emilia–Romagna

Trentino–Alto Adige

Hectares planted
13,700

Proportion
of red/white grapes
40% 60%

DOC
8

With a majority of white wines made using
international varieties, the South Tyrol is the least
'Italian' of the country's regions. A large part of its
production is exported to Germany.

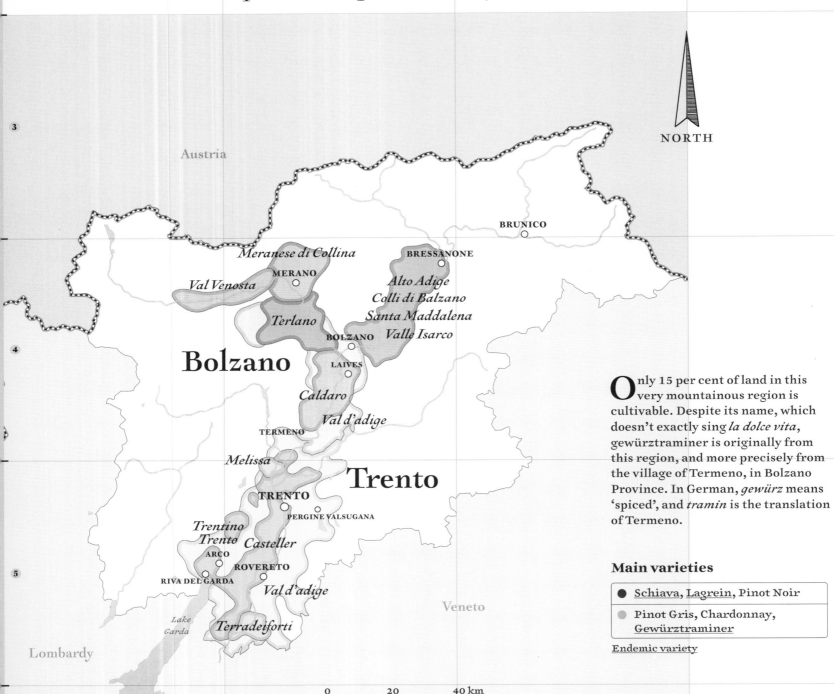

NORTH

Austria

BRUNICO

Meranese di Collina   BRESSANONE

Val Venosta   MERANO

Terlano   *Alto Adige*
              Colli di Balzano
              Santa Maddalena
      BOLZANO   *Valle Isarco*

Bolzano

      LAIVES

Caldaro

Val d'adige

TERMENO

Melissa   **Trento**

  TRENTO

      PERGINE VALSUGANA

*Trentino
Trento*   *Casteller*
  ARCO

    ROVERETO

RIVA DEL GARDA

      Val d'adige   Veneto

Lake
Garda   *Terradeiforti*

Lombardy

Only 15 per cent of land in this
very mountainous region is
cultivable. Despite its name, which
doesn't exactly sing *la dolce vita*,
gewürztraminer is originally from
this region, and more precisely from
the village of Termeno, in Bolzano
Province. In German, *gewürz* means
'spiced', and *tramin* is the translation
of Termeno.

Main varieties

- Schiava, Lagrein, Pinot Noir
- Pinot Gris, Chardonnay, Gewürztraminer

Endemic variety

0   20   40 km

NORTH

Trentino–Alto Adige

Friuli–Venezia Giulia

Colli di Conegliano

Prosecco di Conegliano Valdobbiadene

Treviso

Verona

Breganze

Montello e Colli Asolani

Vini del Piave

Lison–Pramaggiore

Lake Garda

Lessini Durello

Vicenza

TREVISO

Bardolino

Valpolicella

VICENZA

San Martino della Battaglia

VERONA

Soave

Colli Berici

PADUA

VENICE

Bianco di Custoza

Colli Euganei

Gulf of Venice

Padua

Adige

ADRIATIC

SEA

Lombardy

Po

Emilia–Romagna

0   20   40 km

Veneto

Recently becoming the leading wine producer in Italy, the region around Venice is known primarily for its prosecco, the most famous of Italy's sparkling wines.

The town of Prosecco, 5 kilometres from the Slovenian border (in the Trieste Province), lends its name to this white variety and to the wine made with it. In order to avoid complete confusion, the government decided in 2009 to rechristen the variety 'glera'. In 2013, prosecco overtook champagne for the first time in terms of bottles exported throughout the world.

Another source of regional pride is amarone. This red wine is distinctive for its unique method of production, which consists of leaving the grapes to become overripe on the vines, then drying them out naturally: a method called *passerillage*. Once the grapes are harvested, they are laid on beds of straw for three months. This allows the fruit to lose part of its water and concentrates the sugar before pressing and fermentation, to give a full-bodied wine that can have an alcohol content of up to 16 per cent.

Hectares planted

76,900

Proportion of red/white grapes

40%

60%

DOC
27

DOCG
14

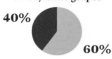

Main varieties

- ● <u>Corvina</u>, <u>Rondinella</u>, <u>Molinara</u>
- ● <u>Garganega</u>, <u>Glera</u>, <u>Trebbiano di Romagna</u>

<u>Endemic variety</u>

Emilia–Romagna

As we move down the country, the climate becomes warmer.

Emilia–Romagna, as its name suggests, is divided into two sub-regions: Emilia and Romagna. The former is known for its sparkling wines, the most festive and famous of which is still lambrusco, a foamy, generally sweet red. The latter region is noted for its sangiovese vintages, which have a Tuscan air, and its remarkable whites of the Albana di Romagna appellation, the oldest white wine DOCG in Italy. There is a significant trend towards international varieties, such as sauvignon, chardonnay and cabernet sauvignon.

Main varieties

- ● Sangiovese, Lambrusco
- ● Albana, Malvoisie, Trebbiano

Endemic variety

Hectares planted

60,000

Proportion of red/white grapes

50% ◐ 50%

DOC
18

DOCG
2

NORTH

Lombardy · Veneto

Emilia

PIACENZA

Colli Piacentini

FIDENZA

Lambrusco Salamino di Santa Croce

PARMA

Lambrusco di Sorbara

FERRARA

Bosco Eliceo

COMACCHIO

Reggiano

REGGIO EMILIA

MODENA

Colli di Parma

Lambrusco Grasparossa di Castelvetro

Colli Bolognesi

Colli di Scandiano e di Canossa

Reno

BOLOGNA

Colli di Imola

RAVENNA

FAENZA

Colli di Faenza

Romagna

Colli di Rimini

RIMINI

Liguria

LIGURIAN

SEA

Tuscany

Romagna

ADRIATIC

SEA

Marche

0   20   40   60 km

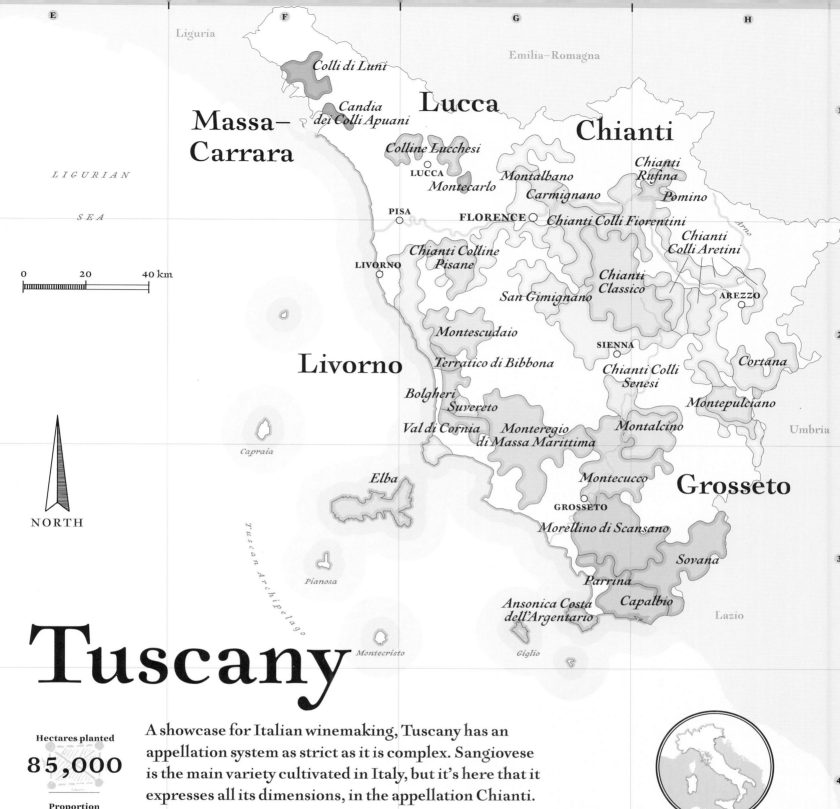

Liguria

Emilia–Romagna

Colli di Luni

Massa–Carrara

Candia
dei Colli Apuani

Lucca

Chianti

Colline Lucchesi

Montalbano

Chianti
Rufina

LUCCA

Montecarlo

Carmignano

Pomino

PISA

FLORENCE

Chianti Colli Fiorentini

Chianti
Colli Aretini

LIGURIAN

Chianti Colline
Pisane

Chianti
Classico

SEA

LIVORNO

San Gimignano

 AREZZO

Montescudaio

SIENNA

Cortana

Livorno

Terratico di Bibbona

Chianti Colli
Senesi

Bolgheri

Montepulciano

Suvereto

Val di Cornia

Monteregio
di Massa Marittima

Montalcino

Umbria

Capraia

Montecucco

Grosseto

Elba

GROSSETO

Tuscan Archipelago

Morellino di Scansano

Sovana

Pianosa

Parrina

Capalbio

Ansonica Costa
dell'Argentario

Lazio

Montecristo

Giglio

0   20   40 km

NORTH

Tuscany

A showcase for Italian winemaking, Tuscany has an appellation system as strict as it is complex. Sangiovese is the main variety cultivated in Italy, but it's here that it expresses all its dimensions, in the appellation Chianti.

Tuscany. The simple act of pronouncing this word takes you on a voyage. And those who have had the luck of visiting know that the cliches (stone walls, cicadas, olive trees) are not exaggerations. Tuscany. And with it an eternal companion: Chianti. This jewel of local winemaking has made a name for itself the world over.

In the Middle Ages, the villages of Gaiole, Castellina and Radda, lying south of Florence, decided to form the 'League of Chianti' in order to limit production and thus competition.

Today, it can be produced in eight appellation areas, the most prestigious of which remains Chianti Classico.

During the 1970s, Tuscan wine-growing was in crisis. A handful of growers decided to plant Bordeaux grapes, as well as cabernet sauvignon and merlot. They couldn't use the appellation Chianti, which requires sangiovese grapes, but the quality of their wines was irreproachable. They took the name 'Super Tuscans', which now personify the resurgence of wine-growing diversity.

Hectares planted

85,000

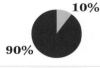

Proportion
of red/white grapes

10%

90%

DOC
41

DOCG
11

Main varieties

- Sangiovese, Merlot, Cabernet Sauvignon
- Trebbiano, Vermentino, Trebbiano Toscano

Endemic variety

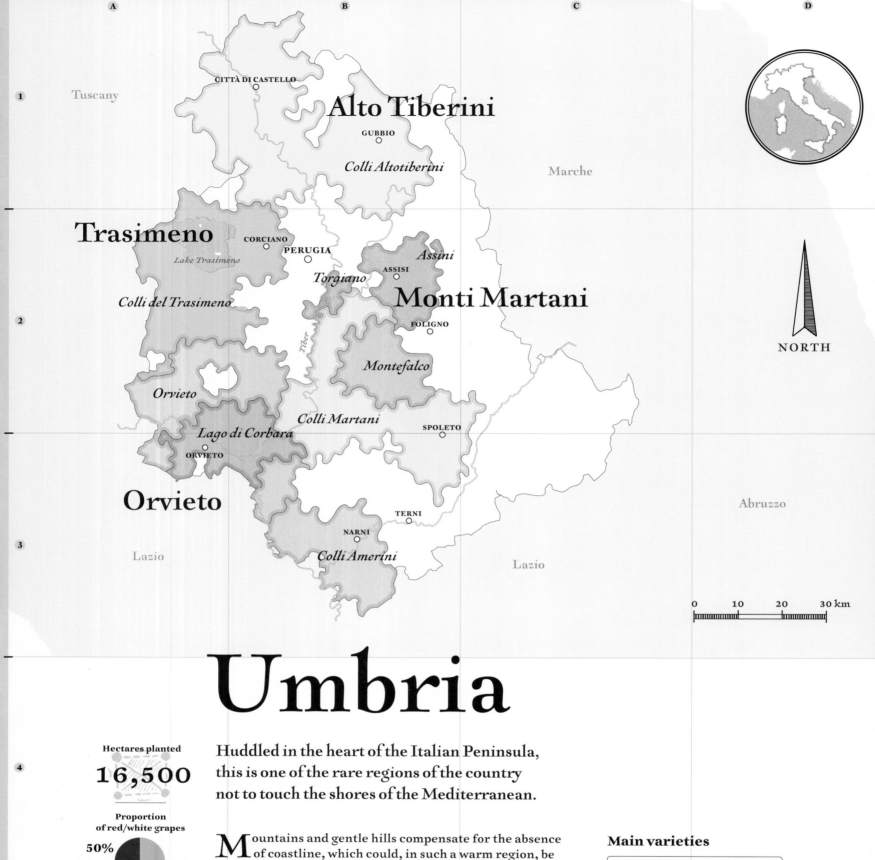

Tuscany

CITTÀ DI CASTELLO

Alto Tiberini

GUBBIO

Colli Altotiberini

Marche

Trasimeno

CORCIANO

PERUGIA

Lake Trasimeno

Assini

ASSISI

Torgiano

Monti Martani

Colli del Trasimeno

FOLIGNO

Tiber

Montefalco

Orvieto

Colli Martani

SPOLETO

Lago di Corbara

ORVIETO

Orvieto

Abruzzo

TERNI

Lazio

NARNI

Colli Amerini

Lazio

NORTH

0   10   20   30 km

Umbria

Hectares planted

16,500

Proportion of red/white grapes

50%

50%

DOC
13

DOCG
2

Huddled in the heart of the Italian Peninsula, this is one of the rare regions of the country not to touch the shores of the Mediterranean.

Mountains and gentle hills compensate for the absence of coastline, which could, in such a warm region, be fatal to grapevines. Long made for consumption within the family, the region's wines are getting better and better, much to the joy of wine buffs looking to leave the beaten track.

The region won its patents of nobility thanks to its orvieto. A white wine made using a mixture of varieties, for centuries it has enjoyed admirable success overseas. The soils, most often limestone, have given whites the starring role, but the two DOCG of the Umbrian wine region are for reds, in the appellations Sagrantino di Montefalco and Torgiano Rosso Riserva.

Main varieties

- ● Sangiovese, Sagrantino, Ciliegiolo
- ● Trebbiano,* Grechetto

* locally called Procanico

Endemic variety

Sicily

The largest island in the Mediterranean has the most extensive wine-growing area in the country. Sicily has even more vines than South Africa, the world's seventh-largest wine producer.

These vines are far from the snowy slopes of the Aosta Valley … and besides, we're closer to Tunisia than to Rome. Here, one is Sicilian first and Italian second, and Mount Etna is a more important landmark than the Colosseum.

Sicily is known for its fortified wine: marsala. It remains less popular among wine buffs, however, than its Portuguese and Spanish cousins, porto and jerez. Production is still dominated by cooperatives, which produce 90 per cent of the volumes, but the wines of the smaller producers are becoming increasingly attractive.

Hectares planted

140,000

Proportion of red/white grapes

30%

70%

DOC

23

DOCG

1

NORTH

Main varieties

- ● Nero d'Avola, Nerello Mascales
- ● Catarratto Bianco, Trebbiano

Endemic variety

Aeolian Islands

Malvasia delle Lipari

MESSINA

Messina

Faro

PALERMO

Palermo

TRAPANI

Monreale

Marsala

Alcamo

Etna

MARSALA

Delia Nivolelli

Contessa Entellina

Contea di Sclafani

Santa Margherita di Belice

Sambuca di Sicilia

CATANIA

Menfi

Sciacca

CALTANISSETTA

Trapani

Syracuse

AGRIGENTO

Moscato di Siracusa

GELA

Cerasuolo di Vittoria

SYRACUSE

VITTORIA

RAGUSA

Moscato di Noto

AVOLA

Aegadian Islands

Eloro

Pantelleria

0   20   40   60 km

Austria

A   B   C   D

0   10   20 km

TOLMEZZO

Ramandolo

MANIAGO

Udine

Colli Orientali del Friuli

Picolit

UDINE

Friuli Grave

Rosazzo

Gorizia

Collio

PORDENONE

Slovenia

SACILE

Friuli Isonzo

Lison

Friuli Latisana

Friuli Annia

Friuli Aquileia

MONFALCONE

Trieste

Pordenone

LATISANA

Carso

Veneto

Gulf of Trieste

TRIESTE

ADRIATIC SEA

NORTH

Friuli–Venezia Giulia

Hectares planted

19,000

Wedged between Austria, Slovenia and the shores of the Adriatic Sea, Friuli-Venezia Giulia claims a multicultural heritage that is expressed in both its cooking and its wines.

Before the phylloxera plague, this region grew more than 350 different grape varieties! Although the selection has been refined for the benefit of quality, diversity is still to be found in more than 30 varieties, both local and imported. Locals believe that they produce the best pinot gris in the country – perhaps even the world.

For some time, wine-growers have shown interest in picolit and verduzzo: two old white varieties that were cultivated in the region and prized during the time of the Austro–Hungarian Empire. The reds, long restricted to young and fruity wines, are causing a stir with blends and barrel ageing.

Proportion of red/white grapes

23%

77%

DOC

10

DOCG

4

Main varieties

- ● Merlot, <u>Refosco</u>, Cabernet Franc
- ● Pinot Gris, <u>Friulano</u>, <u>Glera</u>

<u>Endemic variety</u>

Marche

This region can't choose between lively northern whites and generous southern reds. Luckily, its diverse terroirs and temperate climate allow it to produce both.

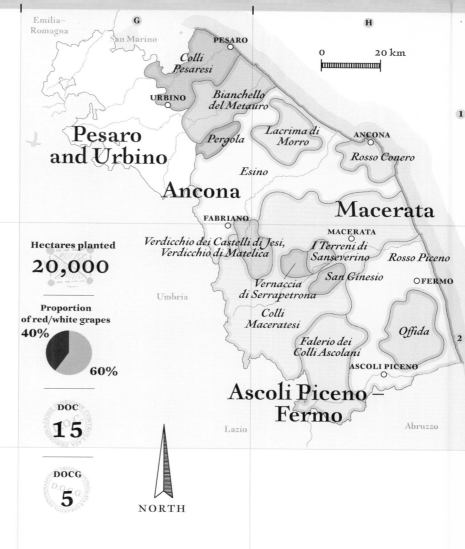

Marche has most notably established itself as a terroir of choice for verdicchio, which has been grown on these soils for more than 600 years. This variety, which takes its name from the green highlights on its grapes, was widespread in Italy before it lost ground to international varieties. Here, however, it managed to retain its leading position and has become the region's calling card. Its acidic base also allows it to produce good sparkling wines.

Hectares planted
20,000

Proportion of red/white grapes
40%
60%

DOC
15

DOCG
5

NORTH

Main varieties

- ● Montepulciano, <u>Sangiovese</u>
- ● <u>Verdicchio</u>

<u>Endemic variety</u>

Abruzzo

Inland from the golden beaches of the Abruzzo coast, this region is one-third hills and two-thirds mountains. In other words, ideal conditions for wine-growing!

Abruzzo is not weighed down by appellations – not that this takes anything away from the fine quality of the wines. Often underestimated, the montepulciano variety (not to be confused with the town in Tuscany of the same name) is the most representative of the region, which allows perfect expression of its intensity. When it comes to whites, trebbiano d'Abruzzo is the local variant of trebbiano.

Main varieties

- ● Montepulciano, <u>Sangiovese</u>
- ● <u>Trebbiano d'Abruzzo</u>, Chardonnay

<u>Endemic variety</u>

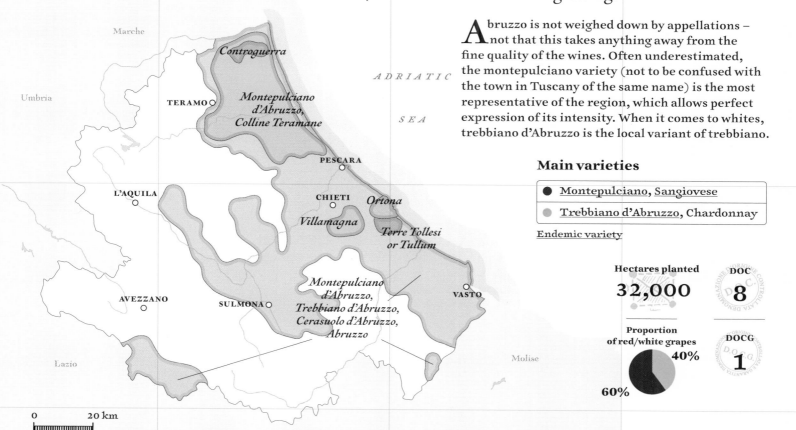

Hectares planted
32,000

DOC
8

Proportion of red/white grapes
40%
60%

DOCG
1

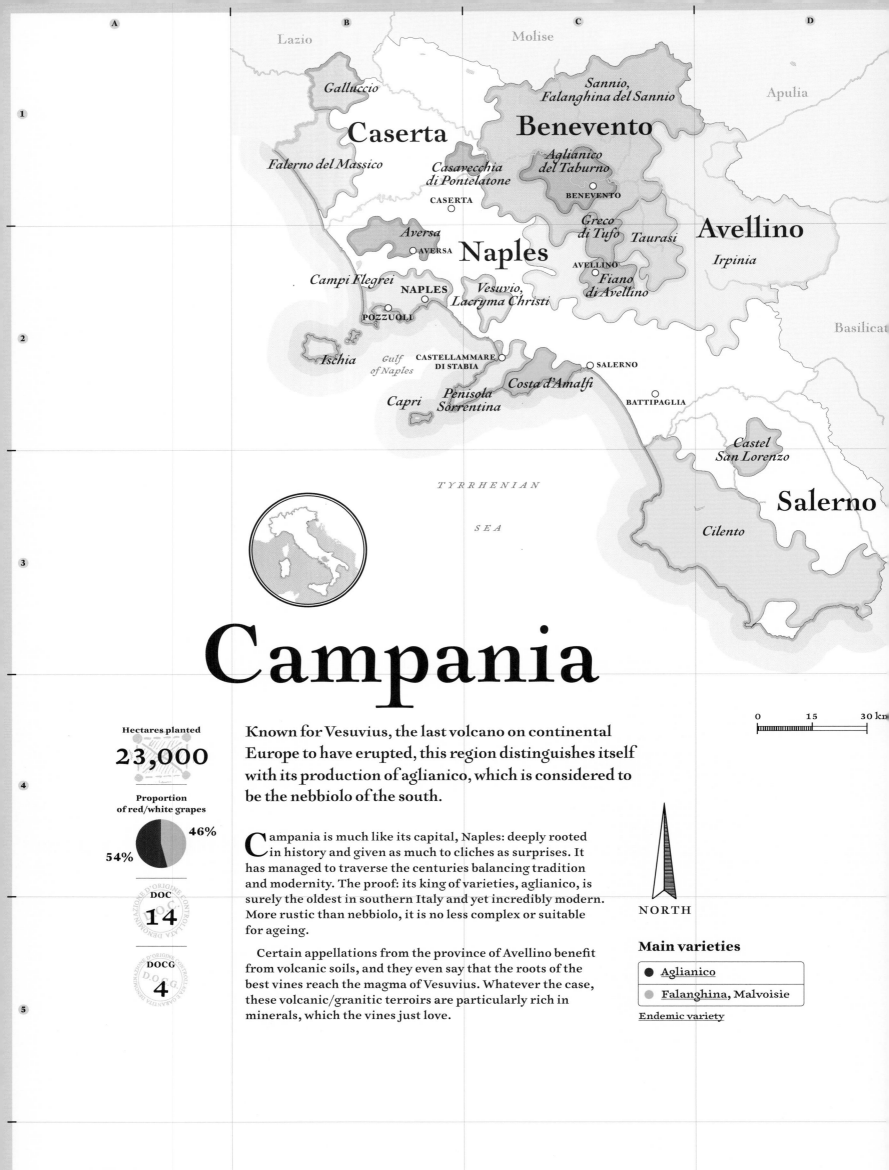

Campania

Known for Vesuvius, the last volcano on continental Europe to have erupted, this region distinguishes itself with its production of aglianico, which is considered to be the nebbiolo of the south.

Campania is much like its capital, Naples: deeply rooted in history and given as much to cliches as surprises. It has managed to traverse the centuries balancing tradition and modernity. The proof: its king of varieties, aglianico, is surely the oldest in southern Italy and yet incredibly modern. More rustic than nebbiolo, it is no less complex or suitable for ageing.

Certain appellations from the province of Avellino benefit from volcanic soils, and they even say that the roots of the best vines reach the magma of Vesuvius. Whatever the case, these volcanic/granitic terroirs are particularly rich in minerals, which the vines just love.

Hectares planted
23,000

Proportion of red/white grapes

46%
54%

DOC **14**

DOCG **4**

NORTH

0   15   30 km

Main varieties

- ● Aglianico
- ● Falanghina, Malvoisie

Endemic variety

Puglia

Internationally, the heel of Italy's boot is better known for its picturesque villages and olive trees than its wines. But its winemakers haven't yet had their last word!

Main varieties

- ● Sangiovese, Negroamaro, Primitivo
- ● Trebbiano

Endemic variety

Being one of the flattest and sunniest Italian regions, Puglia was long devoted to productive agriculture for items such as olive oil – of which Puglia accounts for half the country's national production. The local wine-growing scene shares a similar history to that of Languedoc–Roussillon in France: a vast region bathed in sunlight and devoted to the production of blended wines of mediocre quality. But since the end of the 1990s, with precise market demands and the advent of a new generation of wine-growers, the region has continued to distinguish itself through betting on quality and building a strong identity. This change of focus gave the region its first DOCG in 2010: Primitivo di Manduria Dolce Naturale.

Hectares planted

82,000

Proportion of red/white grapes

20%

80%

DOC **28**

DOCG **4**

San Severo

Foggia

FOGGIA

Foggia

Orta Nova

Rosso di Cerignola

BARLETTA

Bari

Rosso Barletta, Rosso Canosa, Castel del Monte, Moscato di Trani

BARI

ADRIATIC

SEA

MONOPOLI

Gravina

Gioia del Colle

ALTAMURA

Campania

Locorotondo

Martina Franca

Ostuni

Brindisi

BRINDISI

Brindisi

Squinzano

Salice Salentino

LECCE

Basilicata

TARANTO

Primitivo di Manduria

Lizzano

Taranto

Copertino

Leverano

Nardò

Lecce

Galatina

Alezio

Matino

NORTH

0   20   40 km

Gulf of Taranto

Calabria

Albania

Global ranking (by production)

41

Hectares planted

10,000

Annual production (in millions of litres)

17.5

Proportion of red/white grapes

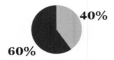

40%

60%

Period when wine-growing appeared

800

BC

Influences

Greeks
Romans

The majority of the country's vineyards are located more than 300 metres above sea level, enjoying the gentler climate. After 1912 and the establishment of the first Albanian government, the wine industry was reborn. The potential for growth is limited in this small mountainous country, but all the necessary conditions combine to produce beautiful wines with a Balkan accent.

Main varieties

- Merlot, <u>Shesh i zi</u>, Cabernet Sauvignon, <u>Kallmet</u>
- <u>Shesh i bardhe</u>, Chardonnay

<u>Endemic variety</u>

Montenegro

Kosovo

Macedonia

Drin

Lake Skadar

Vau i Dejës Lake

Lake Fierza

SHKODËR

Kallmet

TIRANA

DURRËS

□ **TIRANA**

Tirana

Shesh

○ **ELBASAN**

Lake Ohrid

Fier

FIER ○

Semani

Vlosh

Pulës

Lake Prespa

Serina

○ **KORÇË**

VLORË ○

Vjosë

Korçë

Përmet

Leskovik

Greece

ADRIATIC

SEA

Corfu

Albania & Montenegro

Harvest period

August September

These two countries share a similar history to their Balkan neighbours: they have lived through successive influxes of people from the great Mediterranean civilisations. Wine was produced here before the arrival of the Romans, but they were responsible for organising the industry and trade of Albanian and Montenegrin wines, which Pliny the Elder (23–79 AD) described as 'sweet and tasty'.

The Ottoman occupation banned wine-growing in the name of Islam for close to 500 years, and it wasn't until the 20th century that a return to winemaking occurred. In 1992, the fall of Communism encouraged expatriates to return to the region and kickstart the wine industry.

Ionian Sea

NORTH

0   40   80 km

E F G H

Bosnia–Herzegovina

Serbia

NORTH

1

PLJEVLJA

Lake
Piva

Tara

Komarnica

BIJELO POLJE

MOJKOVAC

ROZAJE

2

BERANE

NIKSIC

Savina

DANILOVGRAD

Podgorica

Lake
Plav

PLAV

Kosovo

HERCEG
NOVI

TIVAT

CETINJE

PODGORICA

KOTOR

Lake Skadar

A D R I A T I C

BUDVA

Crmnica

*Lake
Skadar*

Albania

3

S E A

BAR

**Global ranking
(by production)**

43

Hectares planted

4400

**Annual production
(in millions of litres)**

16

**Proportion
of red/white grapes**

25%

75%

**Period when wine-
growing appeared**

200

BC

Influences

Romans

ULCINJ

Ulcinj

4

0   20   40   60 km

Montenegro

T he last European state to obtain its independence
in 2006, the youngest nation in this atlas is a
significant producer of wine. The creation of the first
wine trails in 2007 underlines the government's desire
to bank on wine tourism as a way of showing off the
country. Numerous families produce wine for private
consumption, with neither label nor selling price.

Main varieties

● Vranac, Zinfandel,*
Cabernet Sauvignon

● Krstac, Chardonnay

* locally called Kratošija

5

E F G

Ukraine

Not deeply rooted in the country's culture, wine has depended on the determination of Swiss, French and Georgian winemakers to take its place on the shores of the Black Sea.

Global ranking (by production)
21

Hectares planted
69,000

Annual production (in millions of litres)
150

Proportion of red/white grapes
20%
80%

Harvest period
September

Period when wine-growing appeared
700
BC

Influences
Greeks

Then

The discovery of wine presses has confirmed that wine was already produced here in ancient times. Between 1985 and 1987, Ukraine was subject, like all members of the Soviet Union, to Mikhail Gorbachev's anti-alcohol policy ordering that a large proportion of the vineyards be torn out. With the best terroir of the country and rich in resort towns, Crimea has always set the pace.

Now

Of all the former Soviet bloc countries, Ukraine is among the most dynamic, producing quality wines made with grapes grown on site, and adopting a modest but promising AOC-style system. Crimea, at the heart of political tensions between Russia and Ukraine, leaves an element of doubt regarding the nationality of the wines produced on the peninsula.

Main varieties

- Cabernet Sauvignon, Merlot
- Rkatsiteli, Chardonnay, Aligoté, Sauvignon Blanc

NORTH

Slovakia

Global ranking (by production)
36

Hectares planted
15,000

Annual production (in millions of litres)
31

Proportion of white / red grapes
40%

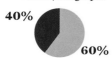

60%

Harvest period
September

Period when wine-growing appeared
600
BC

The country lost half its vineyards in 20 years due to economic shifts, but efforts to concentrate on quality are starting to bear fruit.

Then

O ver time, each grape variety has found its own playing field in Slovakia. The stony soils of the east delight the whites, while the warmer earth of the south is better suited to reds. More favourable for skiing than wine-growing, the northern part of the country is taken up by the Carpathian mountain range. Gaining independence from the Czech Republic in 1993, Slovakia decided to adopt a protectionist policy, taking the French and German AOC systems as inspiration for the creation of the DSC: Districtus Slovakia Controllatus.

Now

As for most Eastern European countries, it's important to distinguish between two types of producer. On the one hand there are the large enterprises that buy the majority of their grapes and aim at exporting their wines. On the other are the hundreds of farming families that produce their wines for personal consumption and for their neighbours.

Main varieties

- Cabernet Sauvignon
- Grüner Veltliner, Riesling, Sylvaner, Welschriesling

NORTH

Poland

ŽILINA
Váh

Little Carpathians

MARTIN

POPRAD

PREŠOV

Hornád

Eastern Slovakia

Topľa

TRENČÍN

PRIEVIDZA

BANSKÁ BYSTRICA

Nitra

Hron

Central Slovakia

KOŠICE

TRNAVA

NITRA

Nitra

BRATISLAVA

Morava

Váh

Southern Slovakia

Danube

Hungary

Tokaj

Ukraine

ustria

| 0 | 50 | 100 km |

France

The history of French wine is written along its rivers. These waterways allowed each winemaker to transport their precious nectars to Lutèce (Roman Paris), Rome or England. Throughout the world, France is considered *the* wine country. The diversity of its soils and climates creates a remarkable mosaic of terroirs.

BREST

QUIMPER

Global ranking (by production)

2

Hectares planted

786,000

Annual production (in millions of litres)

4556

Proportion of red/white grapes

36%
64%

Harvest period

September

Period when wine-growing appeared

600
BC

Influences

Romans

5 appellations to start with

Gigondas
Saint-Julien
Meursault
Chinon
Pic Saint-Loup

Then

The majority of French people would be surprised to learn that the Georgians and Egyptians produced wine before the French did. Grapevines were introduced by the Greeks around 600 BC in the region of Marseille, but it was the Romans who planted virtually all the French wine-growing areas. The Roman legions adored Alsace riesling, and the monks at Châteauneuf-du-Pape found the wines of the Rhône so fulfilling that they categorically refused to return to the Vatican. The development of French wines is intimately linked with religion. At the end of the 10th century, each church had its own grapevines, and while wars and the Crusades were at their height, monks were the guardians of the wine-growing traditions.

The development of French wines is intimately linked with religion.

In the middle of the 19th century, a phylloxera plague struck the industry. This minuscule aphid caused appalling devastation in every region. The decision was then made to use more resistant American rootstocks, and a new wine industry was born.

Now

France is known for its micro-terroirs. For example, Burgundy has more wine appellations than the whole of Spain, which is neverthless the world's third-biggest wine producer. Besides, 'terroir' has no translation in any other language. In 1936 the Appellation d'Origine Contrôlée (AOC) system was introduced to protect the know-how of each region. This has lifted the entire profession to the highest possible standard.

'Terroir' has no translation in any other language.

The country is now in a period of deep soul-searching in order to regain its place as world leader, all while adapting to new markets. Thanks to the appeal of its regions to tourists, France has established itself as the pioneer of wine tourism in Europe.

Main varieties

- Cabernet Sauvignon, Pinot Noir, Gamay, Merlot, Grenache, Syrah
- Chardonnay, Sauvignon Blanc, Chenin Blanc, Ugni Blanc

Endemic variety

Champagne

Montagne de Reims

Côte des Blancs

Lorraine

Alsace

Loire

Chablisien

Burgundy

Côte de Nuits

Côtes de Beaune

Jura

Bugey

Beaujolais

Savoie

Touraine

Anjou–
Saumur

Chinon

Muscadet

Bordeaux

Médoc

Libournais

Graves

Bergerac

Sauternais

Cahors

Rhône

Châteauneuf
du Pape

South-West

Gaillac

Jurançon

Faugères

Minervois

Corbières

Languedoc–
Roussillon

Provence

Patrimonio

Corsica

UNITED KINGDOM

Netherlands

Belgium

Germany

Switzerland

Italy

Spain

Andorra

English Channel

Strait of Dover

Bay of
Biscay

Gulf of Lion

MEDITERRANEAN

SEA

NORTH

Jersey

Ré

Oléron

Yeu

Noirmoutier

Lake
Geneva

DUNKIRK

CALAIS

LILLE

AMIENS

LE HAVRE

ROUEN

CAEN

SAINT-MALO

RENNES

NANTES

ANGERS

LE MANS

ORLÉANS

TOURS

BOURGES

PARIS

NANTERRE

VERSAILLES

REIMS

TROYES

METZ

NANCY

STRASBOURG

COLMAR

MULHOUSE

DIJON

BESANÇON

POITIERS

NIORT

LA ROCHELLE

LIMOGES

CLERMONT-
FERRAND

LYON

SAINT-
ÉTIENNE

ANNECY

GRENOBLE

VALENCE

BORDEAUX

MONTAUBAN

TOULOUSE

PAU

PERPIGNAN

NÎMES

AVIGNON

ARLES

MONTPELLIER

AIX-EN-
PROVENCE

MARSEILLE

TOULON

NICE

CANNES

AJACCIO

Seine

Seine

Mayenne

Loire

Loire

Indre

Cher

Creuse

Yonne

Aube

Meuse

Moselle

Rhine

Dordogne

Garonne

Lot

Tarn

Gers

Allier

Rhône

Durance

0   100   200 km

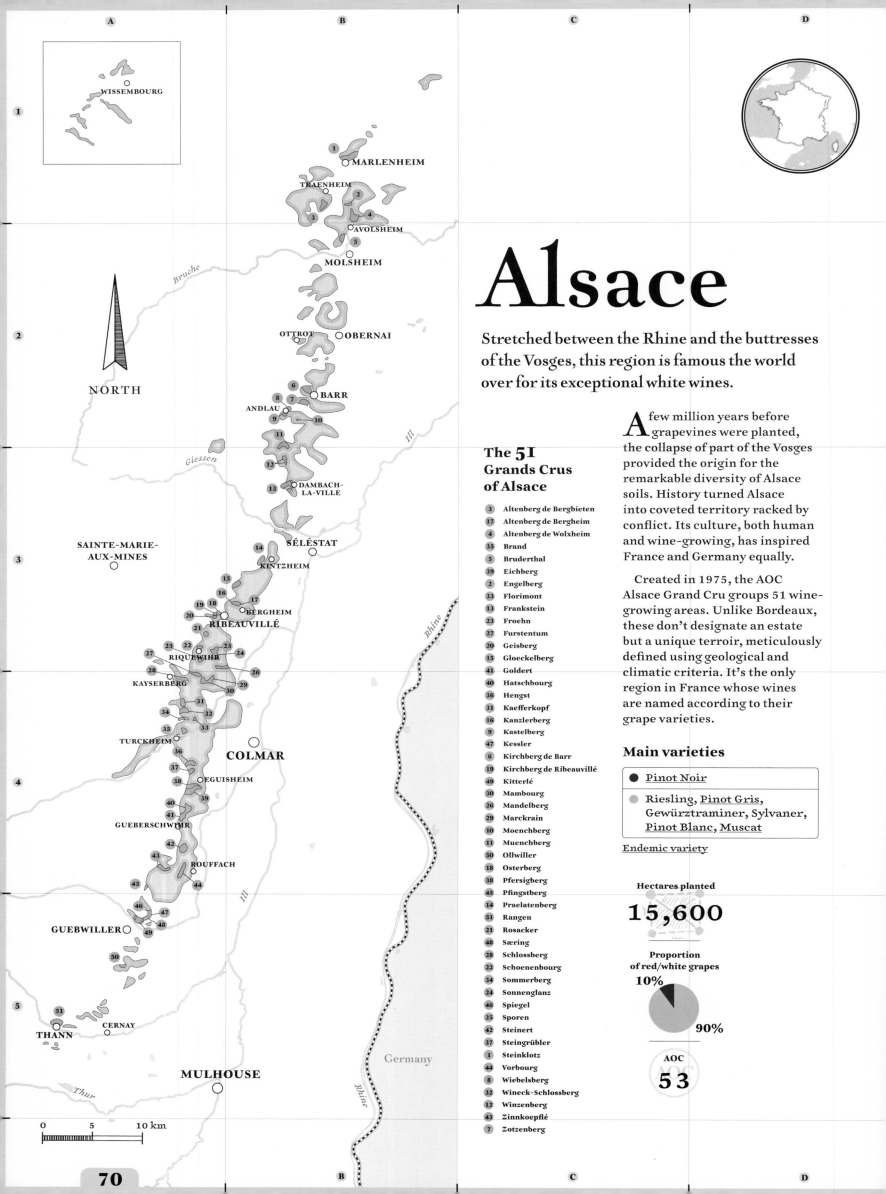

Alsace

Stretched between the Rhine and the buttresses of the Vosges, this region is famous the world over for its exceptional white wines.

A few million years before grapevines were planted, the collapse of part of the Vosges provided the origin for the remarkable diversity of Alsace soils. History turned Alsace into coveted territory racked by conflict. Its culture, both human and wine-growing, has inspired France and Germany equally.

Created in 1975, the AOC Alsace Grand Cru groups 51 wine-growing areas. Unlike Bordeaux, these don't designate an estate but a unique terroir, meticulously defined using geological and climatic criteria. It's the only region in France whose wines are named according to their grape varieties.

The 51 Grands Crus of Alsace

3	Altenberg de Bergbieten
17	Altenberg de Bergheim
4	Altenberg de Wolxheim
35	Brand
5	Bruderthal
39	Eichberg
2	Engelberg
33	Florimont
13	Frankstein
23	Froehn
27	Furstentum
20	Geisberg
15	Gloeckelberg
41	Goldert
40	Hatschbourg
36	Hengst
31	Kaefferkopf
16	Kanzlerberg
9	Kastelberg
47	Kessler
6	Kirchberg de Barr
19	Kirchberg de Ribeauvillé
49	Kitterlé
30	Mambourg
26	Mandelberg
29	Marckrain
10	Moenchberg
11	Muenchberg
50	Ollwiller
18	Osterberg
38	Pfersigberg
45	Pfingstberg
14	Praelatenberg
51	Rangen
21	Rosacker
48	Saering
28	Schlossberg
22	Schoenenbourg
34	Sommerberg
24	Sonnenglanz
46	Spiegel
25	Sporen
42	Steinert
37	Steingrübler
1	Steinklotz
44	Vorbourg
32	Wineck-Schlossberg
12	Winzenberg
43	Zinnkoepflé
7	Zotzenberg

Main varieties

● **Pinot Noir**

● Riesling, **Pinot Gris**, Gewürztraminer, Sylvaner, **Pinot Blanc**, **Muscat**

Endemic variety

Hectares planted

15,600

Proportion of red/white grapes

10%

90%

AOC
53

5 appellations to start with
Saint-Amour
Morgon
Juliénas
Brouilly
Moulin-à-Vent

Hectares planted
17,300

Proportion of red/white grapes
3%

97%

AOC
12

Beaujolais

At a remove from the great conurbations, this gamay paradise has managed to keep its countryside as pristine as it is bucolic.

Gamay is a Burgundian variety distinctive for its intense fruit and vivid appearance. Banished from its native Burgundy by Duke Philip the Bold, it found itself in Beaujolais, a region it favoured.

Although not all wines are ready to be tasted early on, it is the case for gamay. Since the 1950s, the people of Lyon have celebrated the Beaujolais Nouveau on the third Thursday of November. The wine is bottled immediately after fermentation and is destined to be consumed in the weeks that follow. This phenomenon has enjoyed a resounding success: each year, the wine is exported to 110 countries in two weeks. But while the operation is a marketing coup, this youthful drop often tarnishes the image of its elders. Contrary to popular belief, the ten Beaujolais crus can offer complex wines that are remarkably well suited to ageing.

Juliénas *Saint-Amour*
Chénas
Moulin-à-Vent
Fleurie
Chiroubles
Morgon
Régnié
BELLEVILLE
Côte-de-Brouilly
Brouilly

Beaujolais Villages

VILLEFRANCHE-
SUR-SAÔNE

Beaujolais

Saône

Main varieties

| ● | Gamay |
| ● | Chardonnay |

Endemic variety

NORTH

0 5 10 km

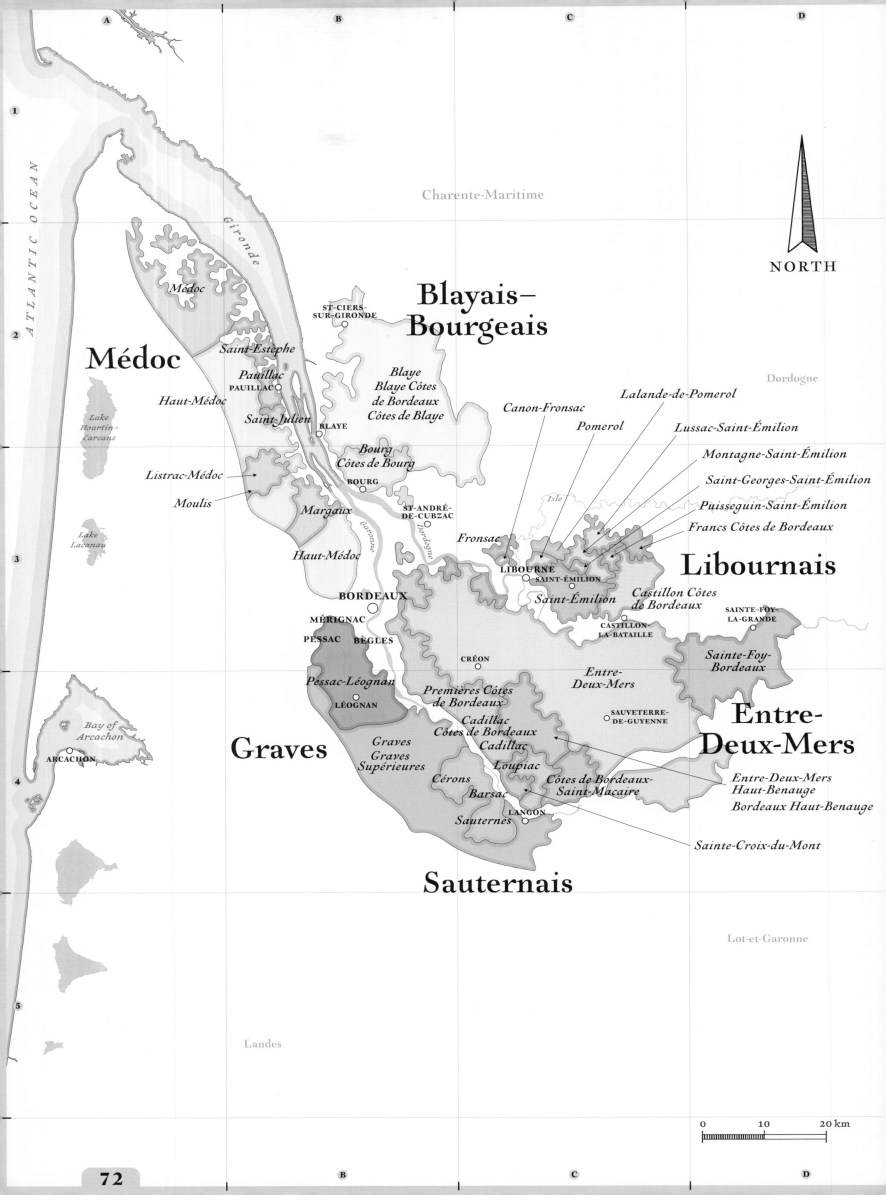

ATLANTIC OCEAN

Gironde

Charente-Maritime

Dordogne

Médoc

Médoc

Lake Hourtin-Carcans

Saint-Estèphe

Pauillac
PAUILLAC

Haut-Médoc

Saint-Julien
BLAYE

ST-CIERS-
SUR-GIRONDE

Blayais–
Bourgeais

Blaye
*Blaye Côtes
de Bordeaux
Côtes de Blaye*

*Bourg
Côtes de Bourg*
BOURG

Listrac-Médoc

Lake Lacanau

Moulis

Margaux

ST-ANDRÉ-
DE-CUBZAC

Garonne

Dordogne

Isle

Canon-Fronsac

Pomerol

Lalande-de-Pomerol

Lussac-Saint-Émilion

Montagne-Saint-Émilion

Saint-Georges-Saint-Émilion

Puisseguin-Saint-Émilion

Francs Côtes de Bordeaux

Haut-Médoc

Fronsac

LIBOURNE
SAINT-ÉMILION

Saint-Émilion

Libournais

*Castillon Côtes
de Bordeaux*

SAINTE-FOY-
LA-GRANDE

CASTILLON-
LA-BATAILLE

BORDEAUX

MÉRIGNAC

PESSAC   BÈGLES

CRÉON

*Sainte-Foy-
Bordeaux*

*Premières Côtes
de Bordeaux*

*Entre-
Deux-Mers*

Pessac-Léognan
LÉOGNAN

Graves

*Cadillac
Côtes de Bordeaux
Cadillac*

SAUVETERRE-
DE-GUYENNE

Entre-
Deux-Mers

*Graves
Graves
Supérieures*

Loupiac

Cérons

Barsac

*Côtes de Bordeaux-
Saint-Macaire*

*Entre-Deux-Mers
Haut-Benauge*

Bordeaux Haut-Benauge

LANGON

Sauternes

Sainte-Croix-du-Mont

Bay of Arcachon

ARCACHON

Sauternais

Landes

Lot-et-Garonne

NORTH

0   10   20 km

Bordeaux

The cradle for a good number of the greatest red wines in history,
Bordeaux is the largest wine-growing AOC in the world.

Hectares planted

119,000

**Proportion
of red/white grapes**

10%

90%

AOC
60

Bordeaux was one of the most important French ports. Allegiance to the English crown for three centuries reinforced demand for and circulation of wine.

Apart from the Landes Forest, grapevines virtually invaded the entire region. Influenced by a capricious oceanic climate, it's surely the wine area most marked by the vintage effect: the quality of the grapes is rarely constant from one year to the next. It's one of the reasons Bordeaux wines are made with blends of varieties. Depending on the harvest and the desired style, the winemakers determine each year the exact proportions of each variety in their wines.

During the 19th century, at the World's Fair in Paris, a classification system for the wines of Bordeaux's châteaux was commanded by Emperor Napoleon III. The courtiers were charged with tasting and ranking the greatest vintages of the region, and thus the famous Classification of 1855 was born, in whose name, from that day to this, much ink has been spilt.

La rive gauche (left bank) designates the estates situated to the west of the River Garonne. Over millennia, the streaming river has deposited tonnes of gravel beside the riverbed, which captures the daytime heat and releases it each night. This phenomenon allows a long maturation time for the cabernet sauvignons, which explains why the greatest vintages come from Médoc and Graves, which lie close to the river. For the record, the Bordeaux suburbs of Pessac and Talence are today stitting on the best gravel terroirs in the region. Thanks, urbanisation!

It was in the south of this region so dominated by reds that the most famous white dessert wine in the world was born: Sauternes. In autumn, the cool waters of the Ciron, flowing in from Landes, meet the warmer waters of the Garonne, triggering a fog whose mists creep up to the hills, promoting the growth of the vine fungus Botrytis cinerea. This dries out the fruit, which becomes wrinkled in the sunshine. Called the 'noble rot', this phenomenon gives the liquorous Sauternes its strength, aroma and exceptional cellaring potential.

From landscape to climate, you need only pass through Dordogne and Garonne to discover a different wine area: la rive droite (right bank). There, merlot is king. Fruitier and less austere than cabernet sauvignon, this variety yields wines that are more accessible when young but just as noble with age. Saint-Émilion has its own classification system, which is scheduled for revision every ten years.

Main varieties

- Merlot, Cabernet Sauvignon, Cabernet Franc
- Sauvignon Blanc, Semillon

Endemic variety

5 appellations to start with

Saint-Estèphe
Pessac-Léognan
Fronsac
Loupiac
Moulis-en-Médoc

Châtillonnais

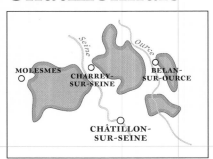

MOLESMES
CHARREY-
SUR-SEINE
BELAN-
SUR-OURCE
CHÂTILLON-
SUR-SEINE

Seine
Ource

Chablis & Grand Auxerrois

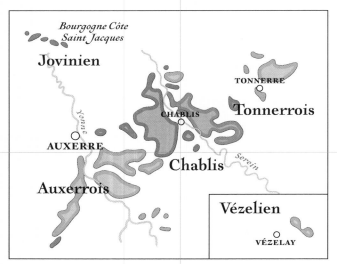

*Bourgogne Côte
Saint Jacques*

Jovinien

TONNERRE

Tonnerrois

CHABLIS

AUXERRE

Chablis

Yonne

Serein

Auxerrois

Vézelien

VÉZELAY

Burgundy – General view

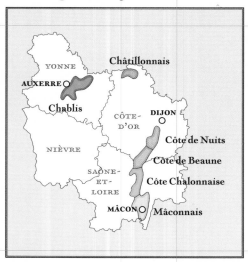

YONNE

Châtillonnais

AUXERRE

Chablis

CÔTE-
D'OR

DIJON

NIÈVRE

Côte de Nuits

Côte de Beaune

SAÔNE-
ET-
LOIRE

Côte Chalonnaise

MÂCON

Mâconnais

Côte de Nuits

DIJON

*Marsannay-
la-Côte*

Fixin

Gevrey-Chambertin

Morey-St-Denis

Chambolle-Musigny

Vougeot

Vosne-Romanée

HAUTES
CÔTES DE NUITS

NUIT-ST-
GEORGES

Pernand-Vergelesses

Savigny-lès-Beaune

Ladoix-Serrigny

Aloxe-Corton

HAUTES
CÔTES DE BEAUNE

Pommard

BEAUNE

St-Romain

Volnay

Monthélie

*Auxey-
Duresses*

Meursault

Côte
de Beaune

St-Aubin

*Puligny-
Montrachet*

Chassagne-Montrachet

Santenay

Sampigny-lès-Maranges

Bouzeron

CHAGNY

Rully

Mercurey

CHALON-
SUR-SAÔNE

Givry

Saône

Doubs

Côte Chalonnaise

Montagny-lès-Buxy

Canal du Centre

Mâconnais

Mancey

TOURNUS

Chardonnay

Bray

Uchizy

Lugny

Viré

Péronne

Cluny

Clessé

Senozan

Berzé-la-Ville

Bussières

Hurigny

Prissé

Vergisson

MÂCON

Serrières

Pouilly-Fuissé

Chasselas

Loché

St-Véran

Vinzelles

Saône

NORTH

0   5   10   15 km

Romanèche-Thorins

Burgundy

The combination of microclimates and ancestral know-how makes Burgundy an exceptional place, considered by many experts to be *the* model of winemaking ingenuity.

The region follows a geological fault line that has created an exceptional concentration of sedimentary deposits. The segmentation of the wine area is in part due to Napoleon I's laws imposing equal division of inheritances between male descendants: the average size of an estate is no bigger than 7 hectares.

Despite its smaller list of varieties, Burgundy is surely the most complex and difficult to grasp of regions. Each AOC designates an area close to the village to which it owes its name. It's an indication of identity, but not of quality. For that, the Burgundians have instituted another system that classes the parcels of land within each appellation according to their soil and orientation. Depending on the provenance of its grapes and the way it's made, a wine will be labelled *Village*, *Premier Cru* or, as a mark of supreme distinction, *Grand Cru*.

We can't talk about Burgundy without mentioning its *climats*. This term, recently inscribed on UNESCO's World Heritage List of Cultural Landscapes, designates a parcel of land that has been meticulously studied and defined for its terroir. Often cultivated by several winemakers, a *climat* can vary from a few hundred square metres to several dozen hectares. There are more than 1500 Burgundy *climats* in existence, and, like the Grands Crus, the great majority are concentrated on the hills, the Côte de Nuits and Côte de Beaune.

While chardonnay is one of the most commonly planted varieties in the world, it's in its native Burgundy that it expresses its full unmatched potential, particularly in Chablis, Côte de Beaune, and the Mâconnais.

Chablis, known as Burdundy's 'golden gate', was long restricted to providing Paris with table wine. But the advent of the railways allowed Mediterranean wines to reach the capital, and encouraged the winemakers of the Yonne area to reposition themselves as producers of quality wines.

The Hospices de Beaune almshouse was founded in 1443 with the idea of taking in invalids without the means to care for themselves. As a sort of thank you, some families of cured winemakers donated a piece of their land to the institution. During the centuries, this ancestor of the public hospital put together an extraordinary wine estate made up of the best Burgundian terroirs. Today, its wines are auctioned to finance the hospital's operation in the famous annual Hospices de Beaune Wine Auction.

The wine-growers of the Mâconnais abandoned gamay to offer an excellent playing field to chardonnay, which occupies 90 per cent of the wine-growing area. The Pouilly-Fuissé appellation has established itself as the emblem of the Mâconnais wine region.

The mystery remains when it comes to a scientific explanation of this region's incredible richness of micro-terroirs, and thus of its wines. But isn't it in enigma that magic is born?

Hectares planted

28,800

Proportion of red/white grapes

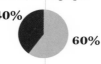

40%

60%

AOC

100

Main varieties

●	Pinot Noir
○	Chardonnay

Endemic variety

5 appellations to start with

Chablis
Gevrey-Chambertin
Pommard
Pouilly-Fuissé
Savigny-lès-Beaune

Vesle

Massif de Saint-Thierry

REIMS

Montagne de Reims

Vallée de l'Ardre

Vallée de la Marne

CHÂTILLON-SUR-MARNE

Vesle

NORTH

CHÂTEAU-THIERRY

ÉPERNAY

CHÂLONS-EN-CHAMPAGNE

Vitry-le-François

Côte des Blancs

Marne

VITRY-LE-FRANÇOIS

Côte de Sézanne

Lake Der-Chantecoq

Aube

Seine

Main varieties

- ● Pinot Noir, Pinot Meunier
- ● Chardonnay

Endemic variety

Seine

Lake Amance

Montgueux

Lake Auzon-Temple

Seine Reservoir

BAR-SUR-AUBE

TROYES

Côte des Bar

In all the four corners of the globe, this most sparkling of French regions has become the uncontested invitee to great events. Each minute, worldwide, 578 champagne corks are popped.

Although far from the coast, Champagne is subject to the influence of oceanic air currents that bring rain no mountain range can stop. The chalk that makes up the Champagne region's subsoil is notable for its double advantage of absorbing excess water and retaining heat. Thanks to its cold autumns, which allow slow maturation of the grapes, the region brings together all the necessary conditions for obtaining the acidity for making great sparkling wines.

Until the 17th century and the discoveries of Pierre Pérignon, known as Dom Pérignon, to whom we owe the mastery of effervescence and the systematic use of reinforced bottles and cork stoppers, it wasn't unknown for bottles to explode in cellars or at the table.

Champagne isn't a terroir wine. The grapes used to make it come from different parcels of land within the region, and often from different years. Contrary to popular belief, the majority of champagnes are made using red grapes. But as these are fermented without their skins, where the colour resides, the juices remain white.

BAR-SUR-SEINE

Aube

0   10   20   30 km

Hectares planted

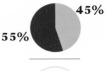

34,500

Proportion of red/white grapes

45%

55%

AOC
3

Champagne

Languedoc–Roussillon

Facing the sea and its destiny, the largest wine-growing region in France always looks forward.

Despite its indisputable Mediterranean location, the Languedoc–Roussillon wine region receives, in its most westerly part, the cooling influence of the Atlantic Ocean. This phenomenon allows it to produce the oldest sparkling wine in the world: blanquette de Limoux.

Growing grapevines here dates back to the Roman era, but we must look forward to a more contemporary epoque to undestand this region. The development of the ports, the creation of the Midi Canal and the establishment of a railway linked to the capital allowed the region to provide to the whole of France what we might call 'très ordinaires' table wines. After the Second World War, the French wine industry was at its lowest ebb and the Languedoc,

planted with high-yield varieties, immediately became the official producer of table wines.

The era of the 'rough red' has now passed. By the end of the 1980s, the motivation provided by the creation of appellations, the planting of noble varieties and the arrival of young winemakers turned this region into one of the most dynamic and promising in the country.

Hectares planted

228,000

Proportion of red/white grapes

20%

80%

AOC
26

Main varieties

- ● Carignan, Grenache, <u>Syrah</u>, Mourvèdre
- ● <u>Roussanne</u>, <u>Marsanne</u>, <u>Viognier</u>, Grenache Blanc

<u>Endemic variety</u>

Languedoc

Roussillon

Hérault

Sommières   NÎMES

Pic Saint-Loup

Terrasse du Larzac
LODÈVE

Grès de Montpellier
MONTPELLIER

Clairette du Languedoc
Faugères   Grès de Montpellier
Pézénas

Saint-Chinian   Picpoul de Pinet   SÈTE
BÉZIERS   Étang de Thau

Cabardès
Minervois   Terrasse de Béziers   AGDE

Canal du Midi

Malepère   CARCASSONNE   La Clape
NARBONNE

Corbières   Quatourze

Limoux
LIMOUX

Fitou

Côtes-du-Roussillon
PERPIGNAN

Côtes du Roussillon Villages

COLLIOURE
Collioure
Banyuls

Spain

MEDITERRANEAN SEA

Gulf of Lion

NORTH

5 appellations to start with
Saint-Chinian
Faugères
Minervois
Banyuls
Pic Saint-Loup

0   20   40 km

Loire Valley

From Muscadet to Sancerrois, you need only travel up France's longest river to pass through centuries and wine styles.

Unlike most regions of France, here grapevines don't monopolise the countryside. They cohabit with the remarkable flora of the Loire Valley, which is nicknamed 'The Garden of France'. Since the French Revolution in 1789, the vineyards have been broken up, and it's now rare for an estate to exceed 15 hectares.

Three different scenes, three different ambiances. In the west, in the realm of Muscadet, the salty mists bring an inimitable vivacity to the melon de Bourgogne grapes. In the centre of the region, Anjou, Saumur and Touraine transform the royal chenin blanc and cabernet franc. And then, in the east, around Sancerre, sauvignon blanc has found its stomping ground. Now we can better understand what motivated the French kings to construct their châteaux in this corner of the country …

Main varieties

- ● Cabernet Franc, Gamay, Pinot Noir
- ● Chenin Blanc, Sauvignon Blanc, Melon de Bourgogne

Endemic variety

Hectares planted
72,000

Proportion of red/white grapes
56%
44%

AOC 86

5 appellations to start with
Sacerre
Montlouis
Bourgueil
Jasnières
Muscadet

NORTH

Map

Pays Nantais

ST-NAZAIRE
NANTES
ANCENIS
Gros-Plant du-Pays-Nantais
Muscadet
Île de Noirmoutier
Île d'Yeu
LA ROCHE-SUR-YON
Fiefs Vendéens
ATLANTIC OCEAN

Coteaux d'Ancenis
ANGERS
Coteaux-de-l'Aubance
Quarts-de-Chaume
Anjou
Bonnezeaux
Coteaux-du-Layon
Serre Nantaise
Vins du Thouarsais

Anjou & Saumur

La Coulée de Serrant
Savennières
Saint-Nicolas-de-Bourgueil
Bourgueil
SAUMUR
Saumur
Chinon
Saumur Champigny
Haut-Poitou
POITIERS

Jasnières
Coteaux-du-loir
Loir
Coteaux-du-Vendômois
VENDÔME
BLOIS
Vouvray
Mesland
Amboise
TOURS
AMBOISE
Montlouis
Azay-le-Rideau
Touraine
Vienne
CHÂTEAUROUX
Indre

Touraine

ORLÉANS
Orléanais
GIEN
Coteaux-du-Giennois

Centre

Cour Cheverny
Cheverny
Sancerre
Menetou-Salon
Cher
Quincy
BOURGES
Reuilly
Valençay
Pouilly-fumé
Pouilly-sur-Loire
Châteaumeillant

0   20   40   60 km

Map Labels

Italy

Languedoc

Rhône

Haute-Provence

Côtes de Provence

Bouches-du-Rhône

Coteaux de Pierrevert

Var

Bellet

Durance

Les Baux-de-Provence

SALON-DE-PROVENCE

Coteaux d'Aix-en-Provence

Coteaux Varois

Var

GRASSE

Monaco

ARLES

ISTRES

AIX-EN-PROVENCE

Palette

NICE

Camargue

Étang de Berre

Côtes de Provence Sainte-Victoire

CANNES

Côte d'Azur

Côtes de Provence

FRÉJUS

Côtes de Provence Fréjus

Gulf of Lion

MARSEILLE

Cassis

PIERREFEU-DU-VAR

Côtes de Provence

0 20 40 km

TOULON

Côtes de Provence La Londe

MEDITERRANEAN

Bandol

SEA

Côtes de Provence Pierrefeu

Porquerolles

Île du Levant

Îles d'Hyères

Hectares planted

26,000

Proportion of red/white grapes

4%

96%

AOC
8

Provence

Between lavender fields and cicada song, this region flooded with sunlight produces the best rosés in the world.

Counting from the moment when the first amphorae left the Port of Marseille, this wine region has blown out 2600 birthday candles. And for blowing, the winemakers can count on their champion: the mistral. Despite the inumerable hills of the hinterland, this wind doesn't hesitate to shake the vineyards. It's said that its breath sends you mad, but one thing is sure: it protects the vines from humidity-related diseases.

Squeezed between mountain and sea, this area is not subject to great seasonal temperature differentials. The rosés are lively, the reds intense and the whites clean. There's no doubting that we're really in the Mediterranean!

NORTH

5 appellations to start with
Bandol
Cassis
Baux-de-Provence
Bellet
Palette

Main varieties

- Syrah, Grenache, Cinsault, Mourvèdre

- Ugni Blanc, Rolle, Grenache Blanc, Clairette

Endemic variety

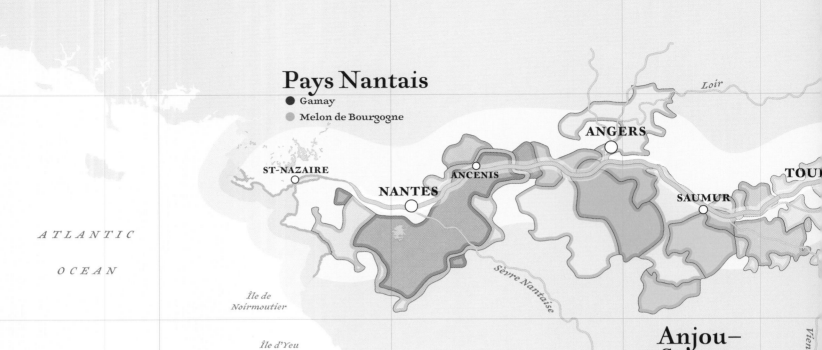

Pays Nantais
● Gamay
● Melon de Bourgogne

ANGERS

Loir

ST-NAZAIRE

ANCENIS

NANTES

SAUMUR

TOU

Anjou–Saumur
● Cabernet Franc
● Chenin Blanc

ATLANTIC

OCEAN

Île de Noirmoutier

Île d'Yeu

Serre Nantaise

Vienne

The Loire

Royal river

Managed but never tamed, the Loire was for a long time the best way to travel through France.

The longest and wildest river in the country rises in the Massif Central and flows into the waters of the Atlantic Ocean at the ports of Brittany. The generous Loire has also nurtured the wines of neighbouring regions, such as Languedoc, Beaujolais and Burgundy. In the 17th century, the Briare and Orléans canals joined the Loire and the Seine, and opened up the ports of the capital to the wines of France. Crossing the Auvergne, Charolais, Berry, Touraine, Anjou and the south of Brittany, it's surely the most gastronomic route in the world. In 2000, the Loire became the first river to be incribed on UNESCO's World Heritage List.

What a beautiful adventure from Saint-Étienne to Saint-Nazaire!

The first vineyards adorn the foothills of the Madeleine Mountains, west of Roanne where gamay is king. At Nevers, the river is swelled by the waters of the Allier and increases in intensity. We arrive at Pouilly-sur-Loire and see the village of Sancerre, proudly perched on its rock at an altitude of 310 metres. Half the voyage is completed, but the true wine trail has only just begun. Here, we speak of sauvignon blanc and pinot noir of freshness and precision. After Blois, the banks become the repositories of an epoque of opulence: the Renaissance, the apogee of the French kings whose châteaux seem to flourish as the current flows. Chaumont, Chambord, Amboise, Villandry … And for the court, an undethronable variety was required: chenin blanc. Just as magical when sweet or dry, still in Saumur or sparkling in Vouvray. To end its promenade, the Loire greets its last château, that of the dukes of Brittany at Nantes, and runs towards the ocean while embracing the lands of Muscadet and its white variety, melon de Bourgogne. The wines of the Loire are definitely above all wines of France.

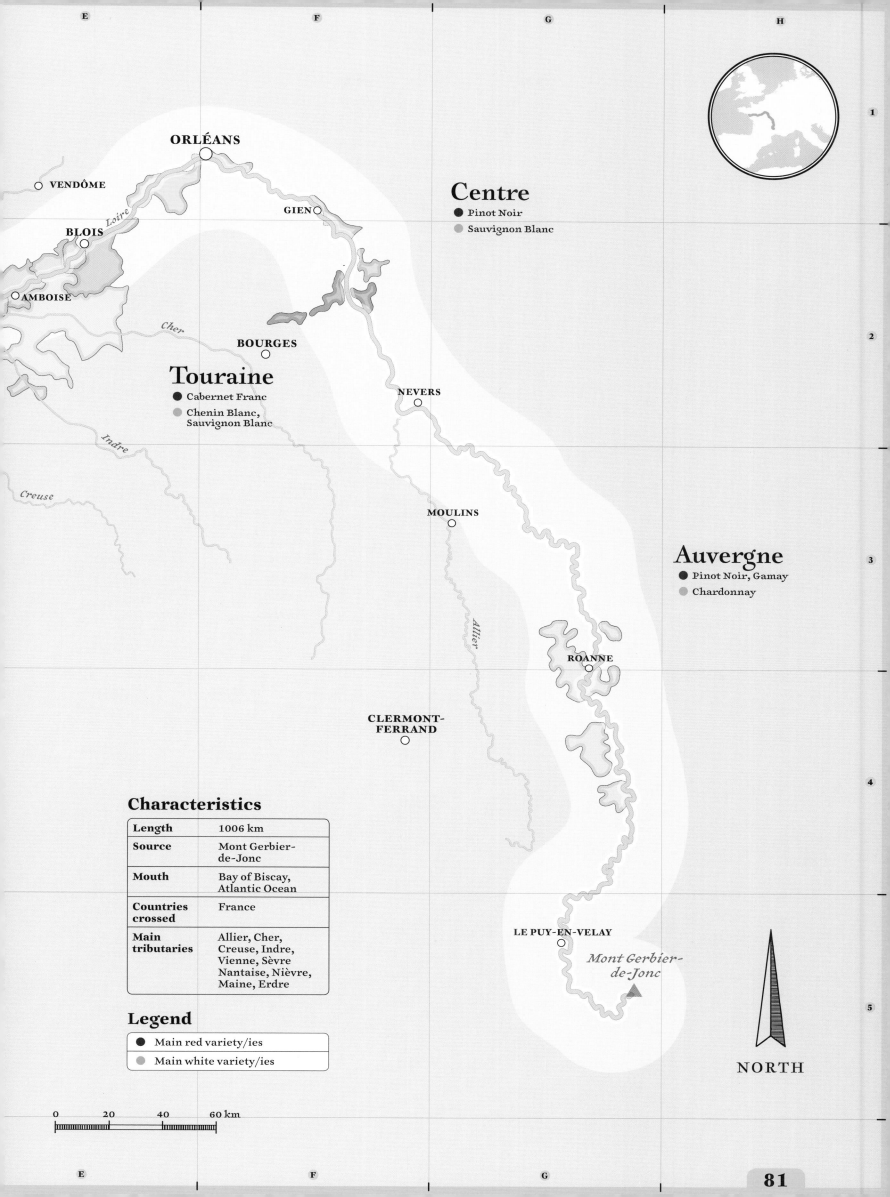

Centre
- Pinot Noir
- Sauvignon Blanc

Touraine
- Cabernet Franc
- Chenin Blanc,
  Sauvignon Blanc

Auvergne
- Pinot Noir, Gamay
- Chardonnay

VENDÔME

ORLÉANS

GIEN

BLOIS

AMBOISE

Loire

Cher

BOURGES

Indre

NEVERS

Creuse

MOULINS

Allier

ROANNE

CLERMONT-
FERRAND

LE PUY-EN-VELAY

*Mont Gerbier-
de-Jonc*

Characteristics

Length	1006 km
Source	Mont Gerbier-de-Jonc
Mouth	Bay of Biscay, Atlantic Ocean
Countries crossed	France
Main tributaries	Allier, Cher, Creuse, Indre, Vienne, Sèvre Nantaise, Nièvre, Maine, Erdre

Legend
- Main red variety/ies
- Main white variety/ies

NORTH

0   20   40   60 km

Hectares planted

79,000

Proportion of red/white grapes

20%

80%

AOC
32

Rhône

The vines that cover the flanks of the perilous Rhône Valley terraces are among the most famous in all of France.

Apart from Hermitage, all the great wines of the northern Rhône come from the right bank of the river, making the most of the ideal eastern sunshine. Although these days they are planted throughout the world, it's on the banks of the Rhône that syrah (shiraz) and viognier grew their first leaves. And they rapidly yielded very good wines. So good that in 1446, the Duke of Burgundy forbade wines from the Rhône in his own region, fearing they would win the favour of the capital and dethrone Burgundian wines. The wine lobby, already!

The only thing the central Rhône shares with its neighbour to the north is the river. The wines here are blends, the countryside less rugged and the climate Mediterranean. With their direct access to the sea, the wines of the Rhône have always found favour with the lucrative Mediterranean market.

Main varieties

- **Syrah**, Grenache, Carignan, Mourvèdre, **Cinsault**
- **Viognier**, **Roussanne**, Marsanne

Endemic variety

Map labels

VIENNE

Côte-Rôtie
Château Grillet
Condrieu

NORTH

Saint Joseph

Côtes du Rhône

Hermitage
Crozes-Hermitage

Isère

Cornas

○ VALENCE

Saint Péray

Diois

Côtes du Rhône

Northern
Rhône

CREST ○

Clairette de Die
Coteaux de Die

Châtillon en Diois

MONTÉLIMAR

Grignan-les-adhémar

Ardèche

Côtes du Vivarais

Grignan-les-adhémar

Côtes
du Rhône
Village

Côtes
du Rhône
Village

Aigue

Ouvèze

Vinsobres
Rasteau
Gigondas
Vacqueyras
Beaumes de Venise

Côtes
du Rhône
Village

ORANGE ○

Côtes du Rhône

Châteauneuf-
du-Pape

Lirac

Tavel

CARPENTRAS

Ventoux

Duché d'Uzès

Côtes du Rhône
Village

AVIGNON ○

NÎMES ○

CAVAILLON ○

Clairette
de Bellegarde

Luberon

Costières-
de-Nîmes

Southern
Rhône

Durance

ARLES ○

Rhône

MEDITERRANEAN SEA

5 appellations to start with

Saint-Joseph
Cornas
Châteauneuf-du-Pape
Clairette de Die
Costières-de-Nîmes

0   20   40 km

South-West

In the shadow of Bordeaux lies a wine area of pleasing diversity.

This wine-growing area – an inevitable stop on the pilgrimage to Santiago de Compostela – was developed in part to meet the needs of the numerous abbeys and monasteries welcoming pilgrims. The pilgrims themselves were recognised as distributors of varieties between regions.

It's a scattered wine region, stretching from the Atlantic to the Mediterranean ports, and is notable for its surprising grapevine biodiversity. Of the 300 varieties planted in the region, 120 are endemic, including the famous cabernet franc and merlot. During the 1960s, the return of French colonists from Algeria after Algerian independence stimulated the reconstruction of an industry still bearing the scars of the great phylloxera plague of the 19th century.

Main varieties

- ● Malbec,* Tannat, Négrette, Fer Servadou
- ● Colombard, Petit Manseng, Gros Manseng, Mauzac

* locally called Côt

Endemic variety

Hectares planted

47,000

Proportion of red/white grapes

40%

60%

AOC

29

5 appellations to start with
Cahors
Gaillac
Monbazillac
Madiran
Fronton

ATLANTIC OCEAN

Dordogne / Bergerac

BORDEAUX

Rosette
Montravel   Pécharmant
Saussignac   Bergerac
BERGERAC
Monbazillac
Côtes de Duras

Côtes du Marmandais

Garonne

Dordogne

Aveyron

Entraygues / Fel

Estaing

Mareillac

RODEZ

Cahors   CAHORS

Lot

Garonne

Côtes de Buzet   AGEN

Lavilledieu

Côtes de Brulhois   MONTAUBAU

Côtes du Frontonnais

Gaillac   ALBI

GAILLAC

MILLAU

Côtes de Millau

Tarn

MONT-DE-MARSAN

Côtes de Saint-Mont

Tursan

Madiran

AUCH

TOULOUSE

Gascogne

BAYONNE

Béarn   PAU

Irouléguy

Jurançon   TARBES

Béarn / Basque Country

NORTH

Spain

0   25   50 km

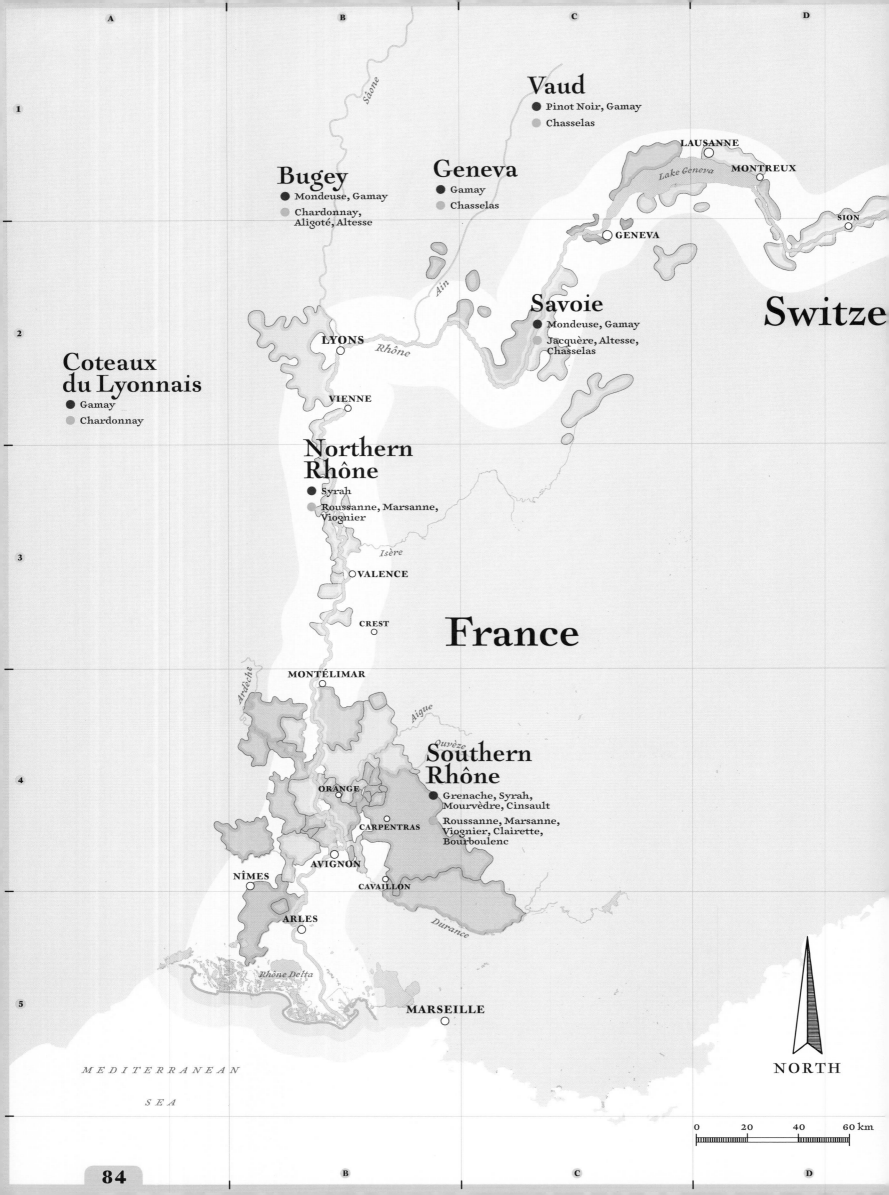

Vaud
- Pinot Noir, Gamay
- Chasselas

Bugey
- Mondeuse, Gamay
- Chardonnay, Aligoté, Altesse

Geneva
- Gamay
- Chasselas

Savoie
- Mondeuse, Gamay
- Jacquère, Altesse, Chasselas

Switze

Coteaux du Lyonnais
- Gamay
- Chardonnay

Northern Rhône
- Syrah
- Roussanne, Marsanne, Viognier

France

Southern Rhône
- Grenache, Syrah, Mourvèdre, Cinsault
- Roussanne, Marsanne, Viognier, Clairette, Bourboulenc

LAUSANNE
MONTREUX
SION
GENEVA

LYONS
VIENNE
VALENCE
CREST
MONTÉLIMAR
ORANGE
CARPENTRAS
AVIGNON
NÎMES
CAVAILLON
ARLES
MARSEILLE

Saône
Ain
Rhône
Lake Geneva
Isère
Ardèche
Aigue
Ouvèze
Durance
Rhône Delta

MEDITERRANEAN SEA

NORTH

0   20   40   60 km

*Rhône
Glacier*

Rhône

Valais
● Pinot Noir,
Gamay
● Chasselas

d

The Rhône

Roman river

From Lake Geneva to the Camargue, vines follow the river on its way to the sea.

The Gauls knew about wine, but preferred the mead-like hydromel or the beer ancestor cervoise, a barley wine. The first Rhône wines were thus transported to Rome, where there was no shortage of wine buffs. To feed the Roman trade and quench the thirst of the people of Lyon and of the popes, there was only the water flowing under Avignon Bridge.

The use of the Rhône as a waterway reached its zenith at the beginning of the 19th century, with the invention of steamboats that could transport goods upstream. With the inauguration of the Paris–Lyon–Marseille railway line in 1856, then the advent of motorways, river transportation gradually fell away, without ever being abandoned altogther.

You could say that the Swiss look down on the Rhône. First because its source lies in Helvetian territory, at about 1900 metres altitude, with the Rhône (or Furka) Glacier. And secondly

because the vineyards perched on the heights of Lausanne can almost see the reflection of their vines in Lake Geneva, the slopes are so steep.

Crossing the Jura range makes the river aggressive and its navigation impracticable. It calms down again and widens at Lyon, swollen by the Saône and bolstered in energy by the capital of gastronomy's embankments and bridges.

Then comes the Rhône Valley, formed by the downward displacement of earth between the Massif Central and the Alps. The spectacular hillsides of the northern Rhône, with variable soils and optimal sunlight, are home to the great terroirs of Condrieu, Côte-Rôtie, Cornas, Château Grillet …

In the south, the Rhône opens its arms to the Camargue and its Mediterranean climate. The vineyards, freed from the course of the river, then spread out over the hills of Provence until the ports of Languedoc.

Characteristics

Length	812 km
Source	Rhône Glacier (Switzerland)
Mouth	Gulf of Lion, Mediterranean Sea
Countries crossed	Switzerland, France
Main tributaries	Isère, Durance, Drôme, Ain, Saône, Ardèche, Gardon

Legend

● Main red variety/ies
● Main white variety/ies

The Maghreb

MOROCCO, ALGERIA & TUNISIA

Although wine has always been produced by those who drink it, The Maghreb is the exception that proves the rule. In North Africa, as in the rest of the Arab world, the Koran forbids the faithful from consuming fermented beverages. And yet, since Antiquity, winemaking has never ceased here.

Spain

ALBORAN SEA

Strait of Gibraltar

ATLANTIC OCEAN

MOSTAGANEM

TANGIER
CEUTA
TÉTOUAN
ORAN
RELIZANE

MELILLA
NADOR
SIDI BEL ABBÈS
SAÏDA

OUEZZANE
Berkane
TLEMCEN

Morocco

KENITRA
FEZ
TAZA
Za

RABAT
MEKNES

CASABLANCA
Moulouya

SETTAT
KHOURIBGA
KHENIFRA

Oum er-Rbia

SAFI
BENI-MELLAL

ERRACHIDIA

EL KELAA
DES SRAGHNA

Tensift
BÉCHAR

ESSAOUIRA
MARRAKESH

OUARZAZATE

Sous

AGADIR
BÉNI ABBÈS

1

2

NORTH

MEDITERRANEAN

SEA

Algeria

Tunisia

Galite Island

Strait of Sicily

BIZERTE

Zembra Island

3

ALGIERS   TIZI
OUZOU   **TUNIS** LA MARSA

BÉJAÏA   BÉJA

MEDITERRANEAN

BLIDA   SKIKDA   ANNABA

HAMMAMET

SEA

CF   *Gulf
of Hammamet*

SÉTIF   CONSTANTINE   SOUSSE

BIRINE   BATNA   KAIROUAN   MONASTIR

MOKNINE

Chelif   TÉBESSA

BISKRA   KASSERINE

DJELFA   SFAX   *Sharqui Island*

Kerkennah Islands

Gharbi Island

AFLOU   GAFSA   4

Gulf of Gabès

LAGHOUAT   GABÈS   HOUMT SOUK

EL HAMMA   *Djerba Island*

Chott el Djerid   *Gulf of Bou Grara*

EL OUED   ZARZIS   *Bahiret el Bibane*

TOUGGOURT   MEDENINE   BEN GARDANE

TATAOUINE

GHARDAÏA

OUARGLA

Libya

5

0   50   100   150 km

NORTH

Portugal

Spain

Mediterranean
Sea

Strait of Gibraltar
CEUTA
TANGIER
TÉTOUAN

Oriental

NADOR

Berkane
Angad

OUJDA

OUEZZANE

Gharb

Meknès

Guerrouane

KENITRA

FEZ

TAZA

Za

Guerrouane

Benslimane

RABAT

MEKNÈS

Coteaux de l'Atlas

Beni M'tir

KHEMISSET

Guerrouane

CASABLANCA

Zaïre
Zenata

AZROU

Moulouya

EL JADIDA

SETTAT

KHOURIBGA

KHENIFRA

ATLANTIC

Doukkala
Boulaouane

Oum er-Rbia

BENI-MELLAL

OCEAN

SAFI

ERRACHIDIA

Doukkala

Tensift

El-Abid

ESSAOUIRA

MARRAKESH

Val d'Argan

Dadès

Essaouira

OUARZAZATE

Algeria

AGADIR

Sous

Draa

GUELMIM

TAN-TAN

Draa

Western Sahara

0   75   150   225   300 km

Meknès
Guerrouane
THE MAGHREB
Coteaux de l'Atlas

Morocco

Between olive trees and date palms, grapevines weave along the coastal plains. Its topography and climate, tempered by the Atlantic, makes Morocco the most promising Maghreb country.

Then

Wild grapevines already grew here before the arrival of the Phoenicians. The vines climbed up the trees and the Berbers dried the grapes before eating them. During Antiquity, the vineyards were concentrated around Volubilis, in the region of the modern-day city of Meknès. It's to the Romans that we owe the development of wine-growing and the establishment of a trade route taking the wines to Rome at a time when the north of the country formed Mauretania Tingitana, an African province of the Roman Empire. The Muslim conquest favoured table grapes, but didn't spell the disappearance of wine-growing.

> ### Wild grapevines already grew here before the arrival of the Phoenicians.

Main varieties

- ● Cinsault, Carignan, Alicante Bouschet
- ● Grenache Blanc, Clairette, Muscat

Now

In the 1990s, to kickstart winemaking activity, the government encouraged French estates to invest in the country by providing land concessions and financial advantages. This operation

> ### The majority of the wine produced is consumed on the spot by tourists.

led to a restructuring of the wine industry and modernisation of the equipment used. Since 1977, an appellation of origin system has guaranteed the protection of terroirs and varieties, and controlled the yield per hectare.

In the past few years, the political climate has tended to restrict the consumption of wine by Moroccans themselves and increase taxes on the local market. Exports are minimal, so the majority of the wine produced is thus consumed on the spot by tourists. It's an unusual distribution model but it has a bright future, given Morocco is the most visited of African countries.

Global ranking
(by production)
35

Hectares planted
49,000

Annual production
(in millions of litres)
40

Proportion of red/white grapes

25%

75%

Harvest period
August September

Period when wine-growing appeared
500
BC

Influences
Phoenicians Romans

5 appellations to start with
Coteaux de l'Atlas
Guerrouane
Beni M'Tir
Zaër
Doukkala

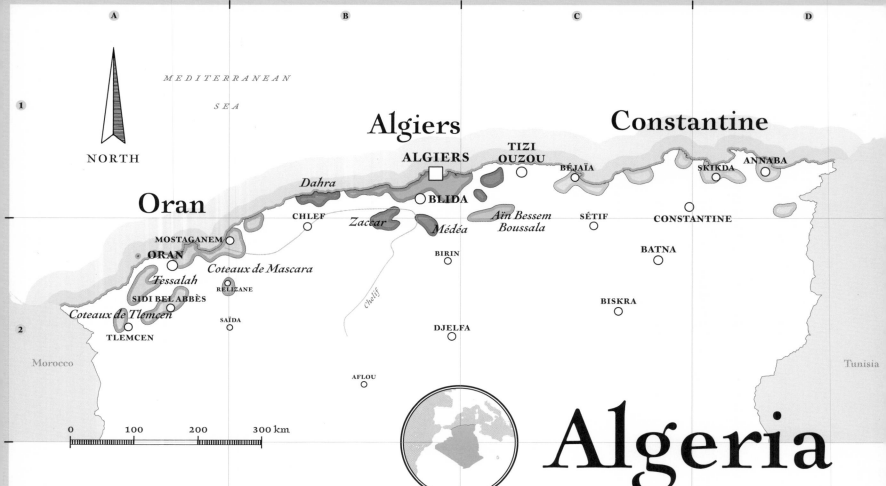

MEDITERRANEAN SEA

NORTH

Algiers

Constantine

Oran

Dahra

ALGIERS

TIZI OUZOU

BÉJAÏA

SKIKDA

ANNABA

BLIDA

CHLEF

Zaccar

Médéa

Aïn Bessem Boussala

SÉTIF

CONSTANTINE

MOSTAGANEM

ORAN

Coteaux de Mascara

BIRIN

BATNA

Tessalah

RELIZANE

Chelif

SIDI BEL ABBÈS

BISKRA

Coteaux de Tlemcen

SAÏDA

DJELFA

TLEMCEN

AFLOU

Morocco

Tunisia

0   100   200   300 km

Algeria

Algeria & Tunisia

After gaining its independence in 1962 and the Treaty of Rome in 1967 banning the 'cutting' of European Community wines with those of foreign countries, Algeria lost 80 per cent of its wine-growing area – but it remains, after South Africa, the second-largest wine producer on the African continent. The best nectars are found around Algiers and Oran. Algerian wine-growing is faced with an uncertain future, but after some dark years, tourism is taking off again. In fact, the country is now one of the five most visited in Africa – perhaps an opportunity for its wines.

Harvest period

August to September

Period when wine-growing appeared

500

BC

Influences

Phoenicians Greeks Romans

At the end of the 19th century, the phylloxera plague that struck European vineyards forced France to turn towards other horizons. To meet the demand for wine, which never slumped, France developed vineyards in its nearest colonies and organised the biggest bulk importation of wine in history, using tankers called *pinardiers*. Millions of hectolitres were transported by boat, to be watered down and breathe life into the most mediocre French wines. By 1930, virtually the whole wine trade was run by the French government, and Algeria was among the most important wine producers on the planet. In 1956 and 1962, Tunisia and Algeria gained their independence from France, and the end of the 20th century marked the departure of the colonists and a return to Islamic principles.

● Carignan, Cinsault, Grenache
● Clairette, Ugni Blanc, Aligoté

Global ranking (by production)

30

Annuelle production (in millions of litres)

62

Hectares planted

77,000

Proportion of red/white grapes

35%

65%

3 appellations to start with

Coteaux de Mascara
Coteaux de Tlemcen
Dahra

Tunisia

Five wine regions were recognised in Tunisia in 1975 and there are seven AOCs. Of The Maghreb countries, Tunisia uses the largest proportion of its grapes for winemaking. The industry is monopolised by two cooperatives and one private company, which together account for 97 per cent of national production, exporting half. As well as the French influence, Tunisian wine-growing has benefited from the knowledge of its Italian community, which has lived in the region for centuries.

Global ranking (by production)
39

Hectares planted
21,000

Annual production (in millions of litres)
24

Proportion of red/white grapes
10%
90%

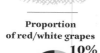

- Carignan, Mourvèdre, Cinsault
- Muscat, Chardonnay, Pedro Ximénez

3 appellations to start with
Coteaux d'Utique
Grand Cru Mornag
Sidi Salem

NORTH

Galite Island

Bizerte

BIZERTE

MENZEL BOURGUIBA · *Coteaux d'Utique*

MATEUR

Coteaux de Tebourba

TABARKA

Zembra Island

Gulf of Tunis

Cap Bon

Kelibia

Tunis

BÉJA

ARIANA · TUNIS · LA GOULETTE

LE BARDO · BEN AROUS

HAMMAM-LIF

KELIBIA

Mornag

KORBA

Grand Cru Mornag · *Sidi Salem*

JENDOUBA · *Thibar* · TEBOURSOUK

NABEUL

Béja–Jendouba

EL FASHS

HAMMAMET

M E D I T E R R A N E A N

EL KEF

SILIANA

Gulf of Hammamet

S E A

HERGLA

TAJEROUINE

MAKTAR

SOUSSE

MASAKIN · MONASTIR

KAIROUAN

0 25 50 75 km

Who made wine in 500 AD?

With Rome at its apex, the grapevine conquers Europe and its civilisations. The Roman legions take care to carry vines with them, and are the first to know how to spot a favourable terroir for wine-growing.

Arctic Circle

45° North

Tropic of Cancer

Equator

Tropic of Capricorn

35° South

700 BC   **500 BC**   **300 BC**   **100 BC**

- Morocco
- Algeria
- Tunisia
- Croatia
- Slovenia

Austria •
Uzbekistan •

- Bosnia–Herzegovina
- Montenegro
- Switzerland
- China

Start of the Roman conquests
The barrel dethrones the amphora

The Silk Road

Christianity

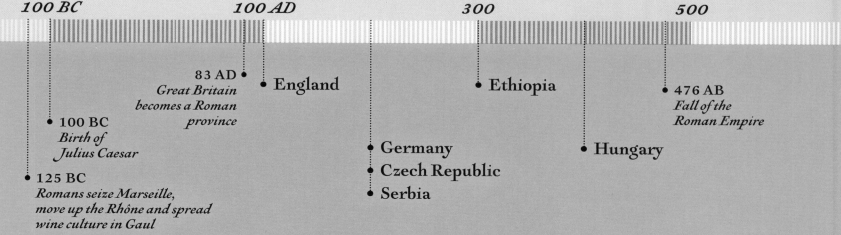

100 BC   100 AD   300   500

83 AD
*Great Britain
becomes a Roman
province*

● **England**

● **Ethiopia**

476 AB
*Fall of the
Roman Empire*

● **100 BC**
*Birth of
Julius Caesar*

● **Germany**

● **Hungary**

● **Czech Republic**

● **125 BC**
*Romans seize Marseille,
move up the Rhône and spread
wine culture in Gaul*

● **Serbia**

In this corner of south-eastern Europe, the two world wars and the Communist regime winded both the people and the land. Since the wars of the 2000s and the successive integration of each country into the European Union, the wine sector has been undergoing a revival.

Romania

SUBOTICA

SOMBOR

EK*

UZLA

Tisa

ZRENJANIN

NOVI SAD

Danube

Sava

BELGRADE   PANCEVO

ŠABAC

SMEDEREVO

Danube

VALJEVO

Serbia

KRAGUJEVAC

CACAK

UŽICE

KRALJEVO   *Rasina*

KRUŠEVAC

Uvac

NIŠ

Bulgaria

Toplica   *South Morava*

NOVI PAZAR

PODUJEVO

Montenegro

PRISTINA

PEJAC

UROŠEVAC   VRANJE

PRIZREN

Kosovo

NORTH

Albania   Greece

0   50   100 km

Global ranking
(by production)

33

Hectares planted

16,000

Annual production
(in millions of litres)

54

Proportion
of red/white grapes

30%

70%

Harvest period

July to October

Period when wine-growing appeared

500

BC

Influences

Celts

Slovenia

Having always lain on human migration routes, this region is a contact point between cultures and can boast, for example, of its Greek, Celtic, Roman and Etruscan heritage. It was the first former Yugoslavian country to gain independence and to rebuild its wine industry.

From the soils to the sunshine, the country's rolling foothills offer all the ideal conditions for viticulture. The wine-growing area is particularly fragmented, given 29,000 producers share the 16,000 hectares of the country. Primorska, the westernmost of the regions, is highly influenced by the Mediterranean. This climate allows it to produce reds drenched with sunlight, while Podravaska, cooled by the proximity of the Alps, is a land of whites.

Main varieties

● <u>Refosco</u>,* Merlot, <u>Zametovka</u>

● Welschriesling,** Chardonnay, Sauvignon Blanc

* locally called Refošk
** locally called Laški Rizling

<u>Endemic variety</u>

Austria

Slovenia

Zagorje-Medimurje

Inner Croatia

○ SESVETE

Plešivica

ZAGREB

Prigorje-Bilogora

Hungary

Drava

Slavonia

OSIJEK ○

Kupa

Prokuplje

Moslavina

Istria–Kvarner

RIJEKA ○

Istria

North Coast

KRK

Sava

Danube

Slavonia & Danube

Podunavlje

SLAVONSKI BROD ○

RAB

CRES

Kvarner

PAG

LOŠINJ

DUGI OTOC

ZADAR ○

North Dalmatia

Dalmatia

Bosnia–Herzegovina

Dalmatian Hinterland

Cetina

↑ NORTH

* A D R I A T I C   S E A*

ŠIBENIK ○

SPLIT ●

BRAC

HVAR

Central and Southern Dalmatia

VIS

DUBROVNIK ○

Montenegro

KORCULA

LASTOVO

MLJET

Global ranking (by production)

31

Hectares planted

30,000

Annual production (in millions of litres)

60

Proportion of red/white grapes

35%

65%

Harvest period

September to October

Period when wine-growing appeared

500 BC

Influences

Greeks

Croatia

With its diversity and modernity, Croatia is probably the most promising of the Balkan countries for wine.

Then

The youngest country in the region shares a similar history to its neighbours. Weakened by years of war before gaining independence in 1991, Croatia embarked on a major campaign for land privatisation. As numerous private owners took control of land belonging to the state, the wine industry began an era of reconstruction.

Now

The islands of Croatia have retained a remakable collection of endemic grape varieties that have virtually disappeared from the Continent. A distinction has to be drawn between the wines produced on the Adriatic coasts, famous for their diversity, and those of the hinterland, which are more uniform. The winemakers can rely on tourism to make their wines known: each year the country welcomes twice as many visitors as it has inhabitants.

Main varieties

- ● **Plavac Mali**, Merlot, Cabernet Sauvignon
- ● Welschriesling,* Malvasia Istriana, Chardonnay

* *locally called* Graševina

Endemic variety

A   **B**   **C**   **D**

VELIKA
KLADUŠA

KOSARSKA DUBICA

Sava

BROD

CAZIN

PRIJEDOR

Vrbas

Bosna

GRADACAC

BRCKO

BOSANSKA KRUPA

Una

DOBOJ

GRACANICA

BIJELJINA

BIHAC

BANJA LUKA

Serbia

BOSANSKI
PETROVAC

Sana

Spreca

TUZLA

ZAVIDOVICI

ŽIVINICE

Drina

Unac

JAJCE

Krivaja

KLADANJ

DRVAR

TRAVNIK

ZENICA

Croatia

NORTH

BUGOJNO

KAKANJ

VISOKO

LIVNO

*Rama
Lake*

SARAJEVO ☐

GORAŽDE

*Lac
Buško*

KONJIC

Drina

FOCA

ADRIATIC

Neretva

MOSTAR

SEA

CITLUK

NEVESINJE

LJUBUŠKI

STOLAC

Montenegro

BILECA

TREBINJE

**Global ranking
(by production)**

49

**Annual production
(in millions of litres)**

5.5

**Proportion
of red/white grapes**

45%

55%

Harvest period

July to
October

**Period when wine-
growing appeared**

200
BC

Bosnia–
Herzegovina

Before being annexed by the Austro–
Hungarian Empire at the end of
the 19th century, Bosnia–Herzegovina
was under Ottoman rule. Alcohol was
forbidden then in the name of Islam,
and wine-growing activity virtually
disappeared. The civil war resulting
in the break-up of Yugoslavia destroyed
the majority of the wine-growing area.

0   25   50   75   100 km

Hungary

SUBOTICA

Subotica–Horgoš

SOMBOR

Vojvodina

Croatia

ZRENJANIN

Srem

NOVI SAD

Danube

Sava

BELGRADE   PANCEVO

ŠABAC

Banat

Danube

SMEDEREVO

Pocerina

Šumadija

VALJEVO

Central Serbia

Bosnia–
Herzegovina

ČAČAK   KRAGUJEVAC

Timok

UŽICE

KRALJEVO

Rasina

KRUŠEVAC

Uvac

West Morava

NIŠ

NOVI PAZAR

Toplica

South Morava

Nišava

Montenegro

Kosovo

PODUJEVO

PRISTINA

PEJA

Bulgaria

UROŠEVAC

VRANJE

PRIZREN

NORTH

Macedonia

0   50   100   150 km

Global ranking
(by production)

16

Hectares planted

69,000

Annual production
(in millions of litres)

230

Proportion
of red/white grapes

35%

65%

Harvest period

July to October

Period when wine-
growing appeared

200

Influences

Romans

Serbia

Located at the same latitude as Bordeaux and Rhône,
the Serbian wine-growing area is broken into nine regions
and gives pride of place to endemic varieties.

Then

Ancient texts report that
grapevines were planted by
Emperor Probus around the city of
Sirmium, now
called Sremska
Mitrovica.
As in Bosnia,
the Muslim
Turks tried
to eradicate
grapevines.

The Austro–
Hungarian Empire was the golden
age for the wine industry, which
faded during the regional conflicts
of the Yugoslavian Wars. For 200
years, Serbian wines have crossed the
country's borders and even the Atlantic.
Bermet, a dessert wine produced
in the north of the country, was even
on the menu of the ill-fated *Titanic*.

The Austro–Hungarian Empire was the golden age for the wine industry.

Now

Lacking a sea coast, Serbia owes its wine
industry to the Danube, which tempers
the climate.

Weakened by the Communist era,
the country must make a place for itself
on the international market: only 5 per
cent of its wine production is exported.
The industry's outlook is improving
thanks to numerous small family estates
devoted to quality.

Main varieties

●	**Prokupac**, Cabernet Sauvignon, Vranac
●	Welschriesling, Chasselas

Endemic variety

**Global ranking
(by production)**

37

Hectares planted

127,000

**Annual production
(in millions of litres)**

30

Harvest period

**September
October**

**Period when wine-
growing appeared**

300

BC

Aral Sea

KUNGRAD

NUKUS

BER

URGENCI

Turkmenistan

NORTH

Then

The region was ruled by the Persians for a large part of Antiquity, but they weren't great winemakers. We have very little in writing about the origins of wine-growing in Central Asia, but its appearance coincides with the opening up of the largest trade route in history: the Silk Road. This connection between East and West,

Wine was brought by the Greeks and Romans via the Silk Road.

initially destined for the transport of precious fabrics whose secrets were known only to the Chinese, would sustain dozens of peoples for close to 2000 years, until the explorations of the New World.

In the seventh century, the Arab conquests condemned the wine industry to producing table grapes.

Now

After the Russian invasion of the 19th century, wine production began again, but only from a very small proportion of the grapes grown. Uzbek wine production hasn't stopped shrinking. Typically Continental, the climate brings important seasonal temperature fluctuations, so the major part of the wine-growing area must be covered in winter to stop it freezing.

Main varieties

- ● Aleatico, Mourvèdre, Saperavi
- ● Riesling, Rkatsiteli

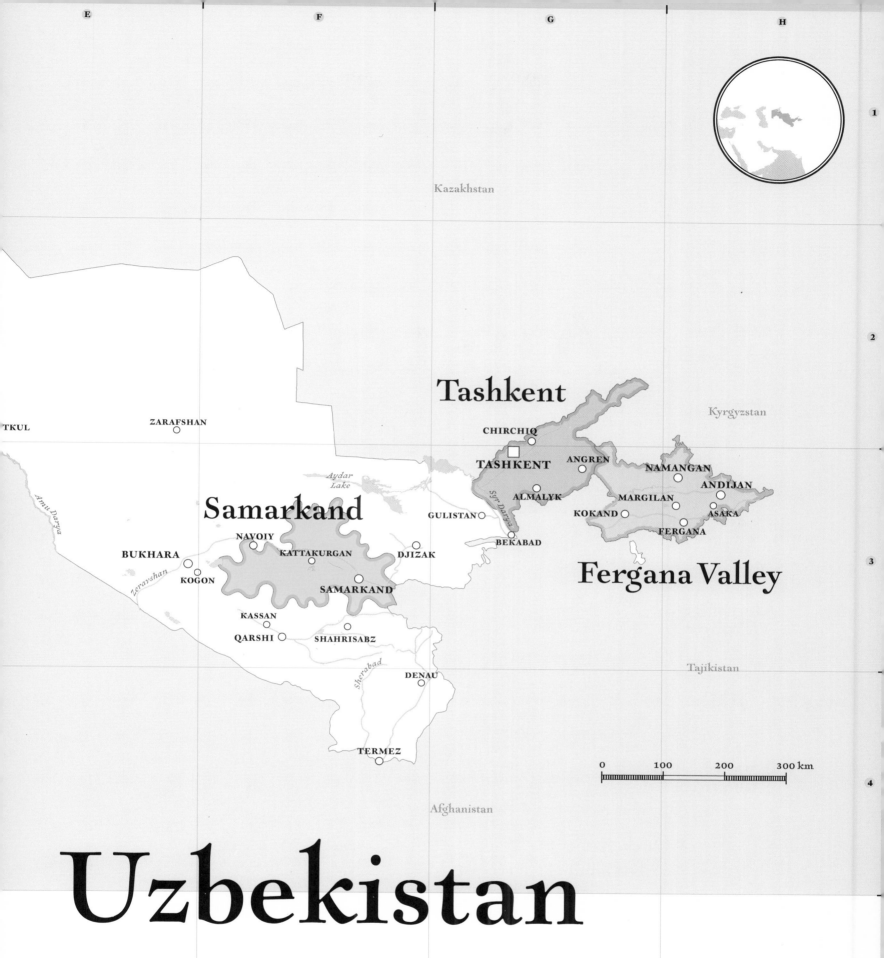

Kazakhstan

TKUL

ZARAFSHAN

Tashkent

CHIRCHIQ

Kyrgyzstan

Aydar
Lake

TASHKENT ANGREN

Samarkand

ALMALYK

NAMANGAN

ANDIJAN

Amu Darya

NAVOIY

GULISTAN

MARGILAN

ASAKA

BUKHARA

KATTAKURGAN

DJIZAK

Syr Darya

KOKAND

FERGANA

Zeravshan

KOGON

SAMARKAND

BEKABAD

Fergana Valley

KASSAN

QARSHI

SHAHRISABZ

Tajikistan

Sherabad

DENAU

0   100   200   300 km

TERMEZ

Afghanistan

Uzbekistan

Lying on the Silk Road, this country has seen its fair share
of travelling merchants, and thus of amphorae …

Austria

In Austria you will find the oldest traces of liqueur wines; in the 16th century they were already harvesting the grapes when overripe. Lower Austria accounts for 60 per cent of national production and is the pride of the nation thanks to its grüner-veltliner, a first cousin of riesling.

Global ranking (by production)

17

Hectares planted

43,540

Annual production (in millions of litres)

230

Proportion of red/white grapes

35%

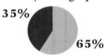

65%

Harvest period

August to October

Period when wine-growing appeared

300

BC

Influences

Celts
Romans

Then

The Celts were the first to cultivate grapevines in the region, but the Romans were responsible for the true expansion of the industry. On the banks of the Danube, the grapevines have not known a tranquil river. Between successive invasions and phylloxera plagues, the Austrian wine area has come back from oblivion. In the 1980s, poor climatic conditions prevented winegrowers from producing their famous liqueur wines. To meet the strong demand of the German market,

> **On the banks of the Danube, the grapevines have not known a tranquil river.**

some producers had the idea to add diethylene glycol (antifreeze) to the wine to achieve the desired body and sweetness. This fraudulent practice, uncovered by the authorities in 1985, put Austria at the heart of one the biggest wine-growing scandals in history. In a few weeks, numerous countries banned Austrian bottles and its exports fell by 90 per cent.

Now

After the scandal of wines adulterated with antifreeze, the government undertook a huge campaign to control and restructure the wine industry by creating a very strict system of appellations. And it's bearing fruit: winemakers are concentrating on quality, and Austria has recovered its prime position among the best European producers. As well as its region and variety, each label indicates the wine's sweetness: *trocken* (sec/dry), *halbtrocken* (demi-sec/medium-dry), *lieblich* (semi-doux/semi-sweet) and *süp* (doux/sweet).

Fun fact: Vienna is the only metropolis in the world with a wine-growing area of 700 hectares right in the city.

Lake Constance

Liechtenstein

Switzerland

Italy

INNSBRUC

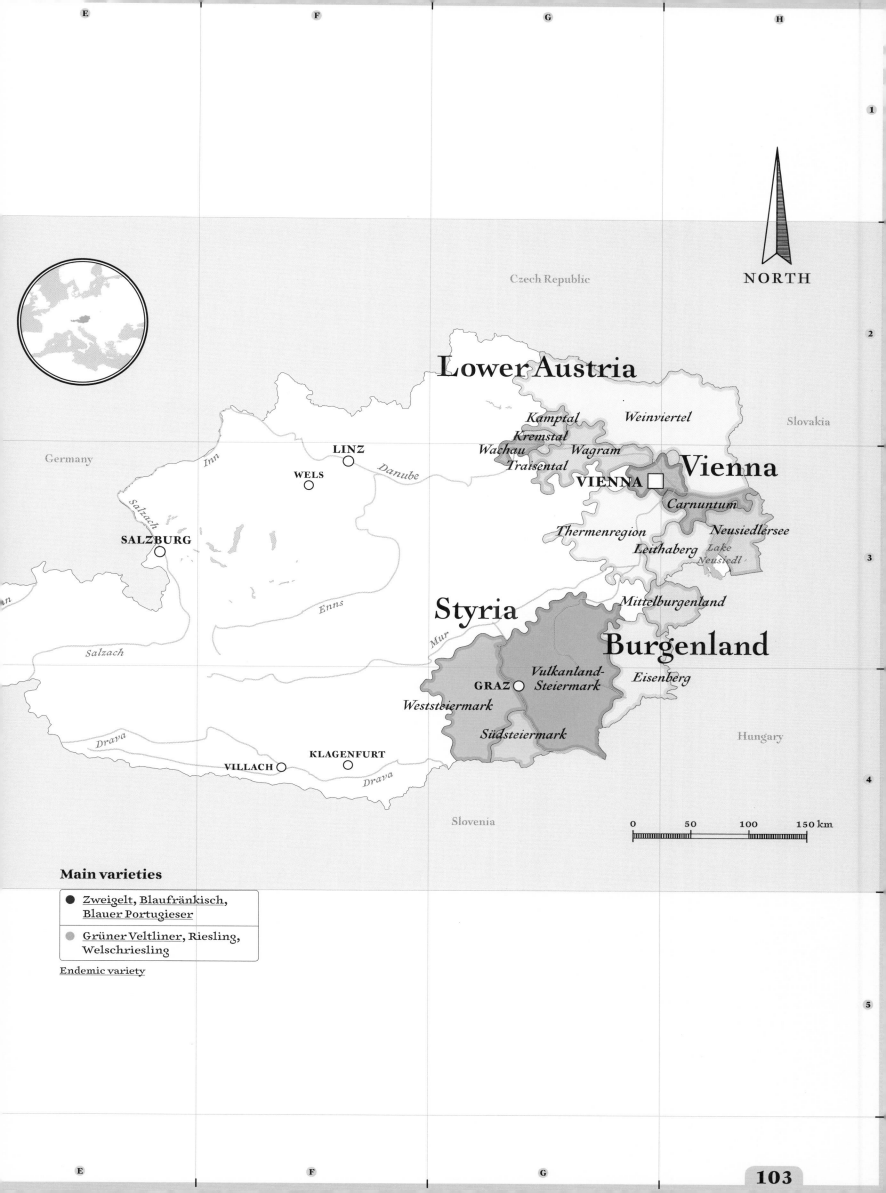

Czech Republic

NORTH

Lower Austria

Kamptal
Weinviertel
Kremstal
Wachau   Wagram
Traisental
VIENNA   **Vienna**
Carnuntum
Thermenregion   Neusiedlersee
Leithaberg   Lake
Neusiedl

Slovakia

LINZ
WELS
Germany

Inn
Danube

Salzach
SALZBURG

Enns

Styria   Mittelburgenland

Burgenland

Mur
Vulkanland-   Eisenberg
GRAZ   Steiermark
Weststeiermark
Südsteiermark   Hungary

Drava
VILLACH   KLAGENFURT
Drava

Slovenia

0   50   100   150 km

Main varieties

● Zweigelt, <u>Blaufränkisch</u>,
<u>Blauer Portugieser</u>

● <u>Grüner Veltliner</u>, Riesling,
Welschriesling

<u>Endemic variety</u>

Switzerland

Summits
LAKE GENEVA
Chasselas
Trilingual

The Swiss wine industry is like its country: atypical.
Tormented by the Alps and the Jura, its vines
have managed to climb along the valleys to bring
us surprising diversity.

**Global ranking
(by production)**

25

Hectares planted

14,793

**Annual production
(in millions of litres)**

100

**Proportion
of red/white grapes**

40%

60%

Harvest period

September
October

**Period when wine-
growing appeared**

200

BC

Influences

Romans

France

BASEL
GRENZACH-WYHLEN
Ba

Jura

Neuchâtel

LA CHAUX-DE-FONDS   BIEL
Lac de Bienne

NEUCHÂTEL   BERN

Bonvillars   *Vully*

YVERDON   FRIBOURG   *Bern*
THUN

Côtes de l'Orbe

Vaud

LAUSANNE
La Côte   *Lavaux*
Lake Geneva   MONTREUX

Chablais

VERNIER   SION
GENEVA

Geneva   ## Valais

0   25   50   75 km

**5 appellations
to start with**

Valais
Graubünden
Ticino
Geneva
Lac de Bienne

NORTH

SCHAFFHAUSEN

Schaffhausen

WALDSHUT-TIENGEN

Thur

Thurgau

Lake Constance

Aargau

FRAUENFELD

WINTERTHUR

ST GALLEN

DIETIKON

ZÜRICH

St Gallen

Zürich

USTER

Lake Zürich

Appenzell

Luzern

BAAR

Zug

ZUG

Lake Walen

Liechtenstein

LUCERNE

EMMEN

Lake Zug

Glarus

KRIENS

Lake Lucerne

East Switerland

Austria

CHUR

Graubünden

Rhine

Inn

Ticino

Sopraceneri

Lake Maggiore

Sottoceneri

LUGANO

Italy

Main varieties

- ● Pinot Noir, Gamay, Merlot
- ● <u>Chasselas</u>, <u>Müller-Thurgau</u>, Chardonnay, Sylvaner

<u>Endemic variety</u>

Then

The country's 26 cantons formed the Helvetic Confederation, one of the oldest nations in the world. Although Switzerland is without a sea coast, it has no lack of water; it's even nicknamed Europe's 'water castle'. In fact, water from this country flows into the North Sea via the Rhine, reaches the Black Sea thanks to the Danube, and dives into the Mediterranean by following the Rhône. The surface planted with grapevines is equivalent to that of Alsace, but more than 50 varieties are grown, which for the most part are endemic. From one valley to the next, the soil and climate change. Geological upheavals are largely responsible for this surprising diversity of terroirs. The village of Visperterminen, in Valais, has the highest vineyard in Europe, with vines growing at an altitude of 1100 metres.

Now

The Swiss consume more wine than they produce. This explains why it's so difficult to find a Swiss wine: they export less than 1 per cent of their own products. And on top of being rare, Swiss wine is not exactly cheap. As the vines are often grown on terraces, the vineyards can't be mechanised; this is very good for the grapes, but a little less so for the price of a bottle. In the 1980s, whites made up 60 per cent of the wines produced, but that trend has reversed, and reds now dominate. Moving beyond the cliche of the fruity white, Swiss winemakers stick hard to terroir wines, staking a claim to their ancestral know-how.

The Swiss consume more wine than they produce.

Kyrgyzstan

○ KASHI

GHUI

India

China

Wine-growing by this Eastern giant dates back more than 2000 years, but not everyone is aware of its presence on the global scene. Nevertheless, China is on its way to becoming the number-one wine producer in the world.

Global ranking (by production)

6

Hectares planted

847,000

Annual production (in millions of litres)

1140

Proportion of red/white grapes

20%
80%

Harvest period

July to October

Period when wine-growing appeared

200
BC

Then

Recent studies place China as the source of humanity's first fermented drinks, with traces of beer and wine from cereals dating back more than 6000 years. Thanks, however, to the words of *Shiji*, the most famous book in Chinese history, we estimate that the first winemaking using

We estimate that the first winemaking using grapes from *Vitis vinifera* dates back 2000 years.

grapes from *Vitis vinifera* dates back 2000 years. This work indicates that General Zhang Qian, envoy to Central Asia in 126 BC, returned with grapevines originally from a region of the Persian Empire corresponding to modern-day Uzbekistan. The history of winemaking in China, which remained small and not deeply embedded in the culture, was turned on its head, like the history of the country, in 1949 when the proclamation of the People's Republic of China released the population from a long civil war.

Now

Since opening up their economy in 1992, the Chinese have become healthy wine-buyers. But recently they also appear to have become formidable producers, and the evolution of their wines has much surprised the experts. In 2000, Chinese vineyards represented 4 per cent of the grapevines planted worldwide. Today that number has tripled. With a population increasingly interested in wine, and a country almost the same size as the whole of Europe, their progress isn't set to end any time soon! Like all 'new' entrants to the wine industry, the Chinese understand that they need a signature, a flagship, and that could well be the cabernet gernischt variety. It was long considered an adaptation of cabernet franc, but scientists have shown that its DNA is roughly identical to that of carménère – a French variety that had been almost forgotten until it became the emblem of Chilean wines.

Main varieties

●	Cabernet Sauvignon, Merlot, <u>Cabernet Gernischt</u>
●	<u>Long Yan</u>, Chardonnay

<u>Endemic variety</u>

E   F   G   H

Russia

1

Mongolia

Hulun Lake

QIQIHAR

HARBIN

Lac Khanka

URUMQI   SHIHEZI

CHANGCHUN   JILIN

North-East

Shihezi

SHENYANG

Turpan

○ HAMI

Gansu   **Ningxia**

Hebei

ANSHAN

KORLA

BEIJING

DALIAN

North Korea

Sea of
Japan

2

Xinjiang

Wuwei   Helan

TIANJIN

Shandong

Qinghai

YINCHUAN

SHIZUISHAN

Baie de Bohai

Shanxi

TAIYUAN

South
Korea

XINING ○

LANZHOU

JINAN

QINGDAO

Japan

ZHENGZHOU

Yellow

Shaanxi

XI'AN

Jiangsu

Sea

Yellow

Xiaojin

CHENGDU

Yangtze

NANJING

Sichuan

WUHAN

SHANGHAI

Brahmaputra   Salween

○ LHASA

HANGZHOU

East

CHONGQING

NANCHANG

China

Nepal

CHANGSHA

Bhutan

Sea

Bangladesh

GUIYANG

FUZHOU

Mekong

KUNMING

Yunnan

Xi   GUANGZHOU

Taiwan

3

Myanmar
(Burma)

NANNING

PACIFIC

MACAU

Laos

FANGCHENG GANG

HONG KONG

OCEAN

Bay of
Bengal

Vietnam

Thailand

4

NORTH

5

0   300   600   900   1200 km

Malta

Right in the heart of the Mediterranean, between East and West, the smallest country in this atlas nurtures a wine industry as modest as it is promising.

Then

With such a strategic position, it was difficult for Malta to fade into the background. Falling under the domination of the Phoenicians, Greeks, Romans, Vandals, Ostrogoths, Arabs and British, the island's heritage is the most varied of all the Mediterranean nations. Before Malta joined the European Union in 2004, it mainly produced table grapes, using the unsold portion to make wine. For this reason, Maltese wine has been saddled with a reputation for being very rustic.

Now

The two local varieties are still in the majority, but are certainly yielding space to international grapes, which have been planted in huge numbers in the past decade. On the strength of its tourism, the island plans on becoming a serious wine producer. Aside from the motivation, the climate suits

The island's heritage is the Mediterranean's most varied.

grapevines, with plentiful sunshine and mild winters that still allow the vines to enter dormancy: a vital stage in their vegetative cycle. They make beautiful wines in Sicily and Tunisia, so why not here? It's very difficult to get hold of a bottle of Maltese wine outside the island, so the best way to try their wines is to go there!

Global ranking (by production)
56

Hectares planted
750

Annual production (in millions of litres)
0.6

Harvest period
September

Period when wine-growing appeared
600 BC

Influences
Phoenicians

NORTH

Main varieties

- ● Gellewza, Cabernet Sauvignon, Syrah
- ● Ghirgentina, Sauvignon Blanc, Vermentino

Endemic variety

0   5   10 km

Ireland

NORTH

0   100   200 km

LIVERPOOL   MANCHESTER

SHEFFIELD

DERBY   NOTTINGHAM

East Anglia

Norfolk   NORWICH

LEICESTER

BIRMINGHAM   COVENTRY

Suffolk

WORCESTER   NORTHAMPTON   CAMBRIDGE   IPSWICH

GLOUCESTER   OXFORD   LUTON   COLCHESTER

CHELMSFORD

SWANSEA   **Surrey**

CARDIFF   BRISTOL   **Hampshire**   LONDON   SOUTHEND-ON-SEA

Bristol Channel   *Thames*   **Kent**

Somerset   *Wiltshire*   CRAWLEY

Devon   SOUTHAMPTON   *West Sussex*   *East Sussex*   *Strait of Dover*

EXETER   *Dorset*   BRIGHTON

BOURNEMOUTH   France

Cornwall   PLYMOUTH   *Isle of Wight*   **Sussex**

South-West   *English Channel*

Alderney

England

Lacking the ideal conditions for wine-growing, England has tasted the world's wine for centuries thanks to its domination of the oceans, and now plans, in turn, to send its wines across the seas.

Then

Grapevines have been grown here for centuries but England made a real mark in the history of wine through its trade. When Bordeaux was annexed by the English crown in the 12th century, the nectars of the Girond were so cheap that the English drank nothing but médoc and saint-émilion. A decree of 1321 ordered that each wine arriving in the Port of London be declared either 'good' or 'ordinary' before its price was set. The English were therefore the first to establish a system of wine classification based on quality. Their modest wine industry was entirely destroyed by the 'Little Ice Age' of the 17th century, and its renaissance only occurred in 1945, just after the Second World War.

Now

The south of England enjoys the same chalky soils as the Champagne region in France, and global warming promises a good future for sparkling wines. The grapes used in the famous bubbly (chardonnay, pinot noir and pinot meunier) already make up half the vines planted, and continue to gain ground. Will there be a war of the bubbles? In any case, the great French Champagne houses have already bought land across the Channel. They are clairvoyant, those folk from Champagne …

Main varieties

●	Pinot Noir, Pinot Meunier
●	Chardonnay, Seyval Blanc

Global ranking
(by production)

52

Hectares planted

1000

Annual production
(in millions of litres)

4

Proportion
of red/white grapes

20%

80%

Harvest period

September
October

Period when wine-growing appeared

100
AD

Influences

Romans

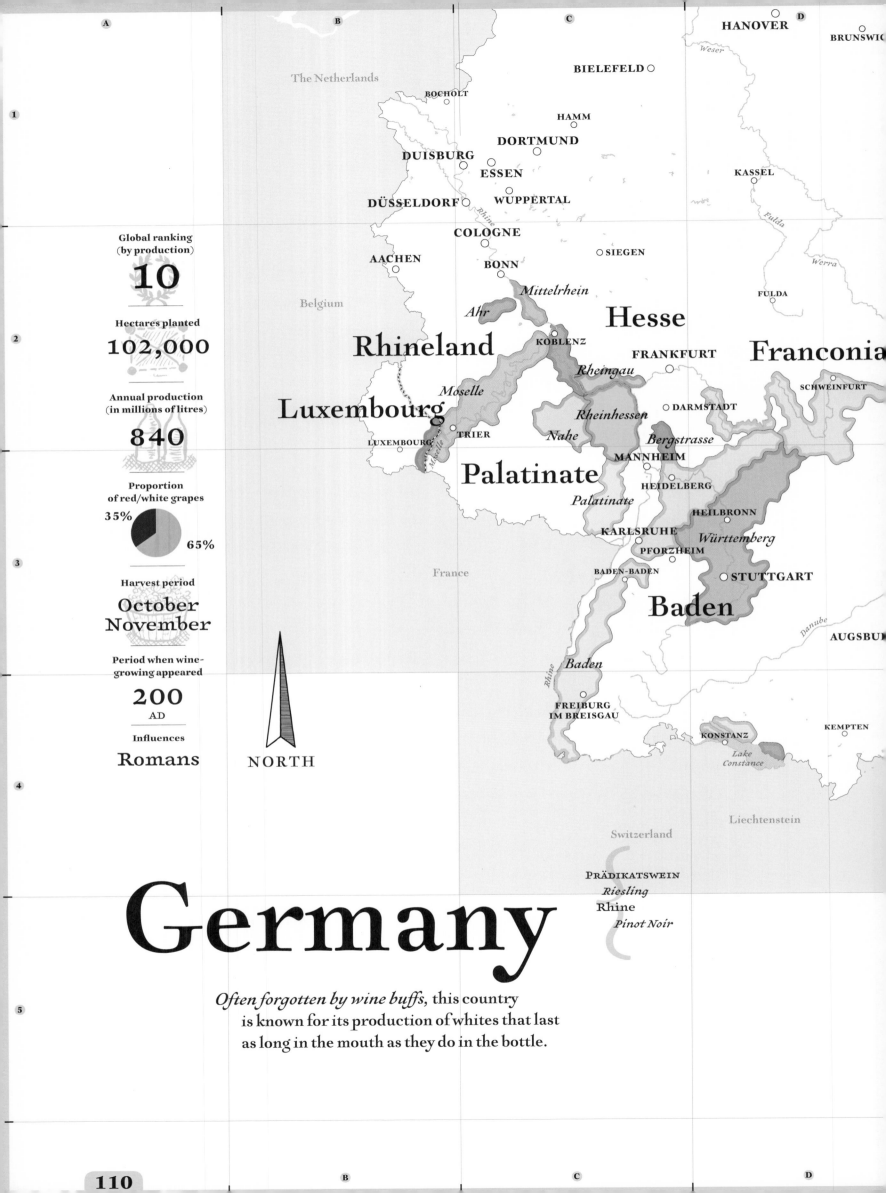

HANOVER

BRUNSWICK

Weser

The Netherlands

BIELEFELD

BOCHOLT

HAMM

DORTMUND

DUISBURG
ESSEN

KASSEL

DÜSSELDORF
WUPPERTAL

Rhine

COLOGNE

SIEGEN

Fulda

AACHEN
BONN

FULDA

Werra

Mittelrhein

Ahr

Hesse

Belgium

Rhineland

KOBLENZ

FRANKFURT

Franconia

Rheingau

SCHWEINFURT

Moselle

Luxembourg

Rheinhessen

DARMSTADT

LUXEMBOURG

TRIER

Nahe

Bergstrasse

Moselle

MANNHEIM

Palatinate

HEIDELBERG

Palatinate

HEILBRONN

KARLSRUHE

Württemberg

PFORZHEIM

France

BADEN-BADEN

STUTTGART

Baden

Danube

AUGSBURG

Rhine

Baden

KEMPTEN

FREIBURG
IM BREISGAU

KONSTANZ

*Lake
Constance*

Liechtenstein

Switzerland

PRÄDIKATSWEIN

Riesling

Rhine

Pinot Noir

Germany

Often forgotten by wine buffs, this country
is known for its production of whites that last
as long in the mouth as they do in the bottle.

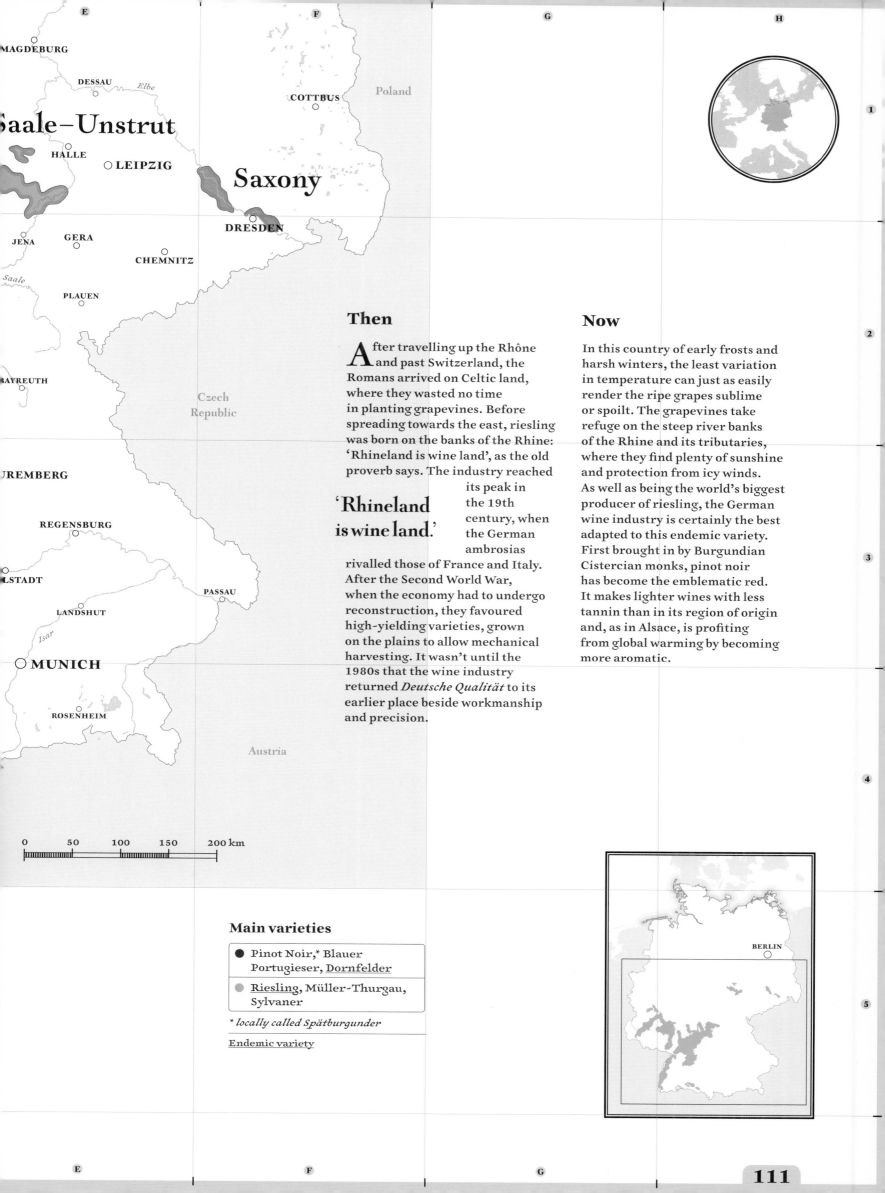

MAGDEBURG

DESSAU   *Elbe*

COTTBUS

Poland

Saale–Unstrut

HALLE   LEIPZIG

Saxony

JENA   GERA

DRESDEN

CHEMNITZ

Saale

PLAUEN

BAYREUTH

Czech
Republic

UREMBERG

REGENSBURG

LSTADT

PASSAU

LANDSHUT

Isar

MUNICH

ROSENHEIM

Austria

0   50   100   150   200 km

Then

After travelling up the Rhône and past Switzerland, the Romans arrived on Celtic land, where they wasted no time in planting grapevines. Before spreading towards the east, riesling was born on the banks of the Rhine: 'Rhineland is wine land', as the old proverb says. The industry reached its peak in the 19th century, when the German ambrosias rivalled those of France and Italy. After the Second World War, when the economy had to undergo reconstruction, they favoured high-yielding varieties, grown on the plains to allow mechanical harvesting. It wasn't until the 1980s that the wine industry returned *Deutsche Qualität* to its earlier place beside workmanship and precision.

'Rhineland is wine land.'

Now

In this country of early frosts and harsh winters, the least variation in temperature can just as easily render the ripe grapes sublime or spoilt. The grapevines take refuge on the steep river banks of the Rhine and its tributaries, where they find plenty of sunshine and protection from icy winds. As well as being the world's biggest producer of riesling, the German wine industry is certainly the best adapted to this endemic variety. First brought in by Burgundian Cistercian monks, pinot noir has become the emblematic red. It makes lighter wines with less tannin than in its region of origin and, as in Alsace, is profiting from global warming by becoming more aromatic.

Main varieties

- ● Pinot Noir,* Blauer Portugieser, <u>Dornfelder</u>
- ● <u>Riesling</u>, Müller-Thurgau, Sylvaner

* locally called Spätburgunder

<u>Endemic variety</u>

BERLIN

The Rhine

European river

Long the border between the Roman world and the Germanic tribes, the Rhine has become the symbol of a peaceful continent, crossing all the main founders of the European Union apart from Italy and Belgium: France, Germany and The Netherlands.

During the Middle Ages, the abbeys along the river, not wanting to choose between wine and beer, became the guardians of wine- and beer-making traditions thousands of years old. The Rhine crosses three wine-growing countries, but it's Germany that owes it the most; the river tempers the climate of an area that would otherwise be too cold to support the growth of good grapes. This helps us better understand why virtually all German wines are produced on the banks of the Rhine and the Moselle, and their tributaries.

It's after Lake Constance that the river descends the Swiss mountains, and there becomes navigable and welcomes riesling. While it's difficult to prove the nationality of this almost mythical variety, specialists agree that it was born in the Rhine Valley. It reigns supreme beside pinot noir, an adopted burgundy that thrives in this climate.

In France, the banks of the Rhine aren't planted with vines. The people of Alsace prefer the hillsides of the Vosges, which is home to fabulous terroirs; the plains, too flat and requiring irrigation, are reserved for growing cereal crops. If you make an effort, however, you can see the valley of Münster (which lends its name to the famous cheese) and, if you have a very good view, the geraniums that decorate the balconies of the Alsace villages. Before leaving France, the river regains it romanticism, breaking from its path to meander through the canals of old Strasbourg and admire the half-timbered houses.

Grapevines return to the banks of the river in Germany, and don't leave it again until Cologne. Than, after crossing the northernmost wine-growing region in Germany, the Rhine of wine becomes the Rhine of beer.

Characteristics

Length	1233 km
Main source	Lake Toma (Switzerland)
Mouth	North Sea
Countries crossed	Switzerland, Liechtenstein, Austria, Germany, France, The Netherlands
Main tributaries	Aare, Moselle, Main, Neckar

Legend

- ● Main red variety/ies
- ● Main white variety/ies

NORTH SEA

The Netherlands

ESSEN

Rhine

DÜSSELDORF

COLOGNE

Belgium

Meuse

BONN

Germany

KOBLENZ

FRANKFURT

Main

TRIER

Moselle

MANNHEIM

Rhineland–Palatinate
● Dornfelder
● Müller-Thurgau, Riesling

Neckar

HEILBRONN

KARLSRUHE

BADEN-BADEN

STUTTGART

STRASBOURG

Danube

France

Alsace
● Pinot Noir
● Riesling

COLMAR

Baden

Baden
● Pinot Noir
● Müller-Thurgau

FREIBURG IM BREISGAU

KONSTANZ

Lake Constance

BASEL

ZURICH

Lake Lucerne

Switzerland

Rhine

Lake Geneva

Lake Toma

East Switzerland
● Pinot Noir, Gamay
● Chasselas

NORTH

0   50   100 km

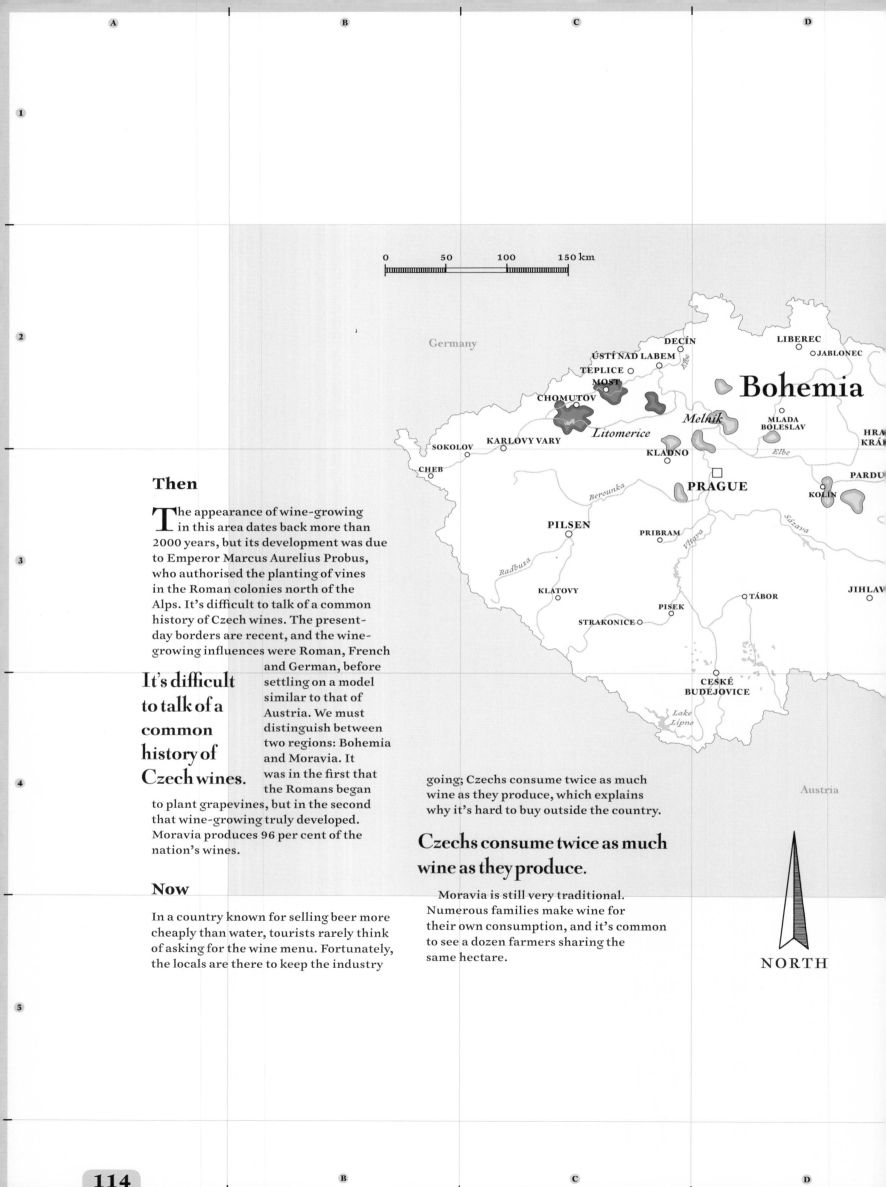

0   50   100   150 km

Germany

DECÍN

LIBEREC

ÚSTÍ NAD LABEM   JABLONEC

TEPLICE

MOST

CHOMUTOV   *Litomerice*   *Melník*   MLADA
BOLESLAV   HRA
KRÁ

SOKOLOV   KARLOVY VARY

CHEB   KLADNO   *Elbe*   PARDU

Berounka   PRAGUE   KOLÍN

PILSEN   PRIBRAM   *Sázava*

Radbuza   *Vltava*

KLATOVY   TÁBOR   JIHLAV

PISEK

STRAKONICE

CESKÉ
BUDEJOVICE

*Lake
Lipno*   Austria

Bohemia

Then

The appearance of wine-growing in this area dates back more than 2000 years, but its development was due to Emperor Marcus Aurelius Probus, who authorised the planting of vines in the Roman colonies north of the Alps. It's difficult to talk of a common history of Czech wines. The present-day borders are recent, and the wine-growing influences were Roman, French and German, before settling on a model similar to that of Austria. We must distinguish between two regions: Bohemia and Moravia. It was in the first that the Romans began to plant grapevines, but in the second that wine-growing truly developed. Moravia produces 96 per cent of the nation's wines.

It's difficult to talk of a common history of Czech wines.

Now

In a country known for selling beer more cheaply than water, tourists rarely think of asking for the wine menu. Fortunately, the locals are there to keep the industry going; Czechs consume twice as much wine as they produce, which explains why it's hard to buy outside the country.

Czechs consume twice as much wine as they produce.

Moravia is still very traditional. Numerous families make wine for their own consumption, and it's common to see a dozen farmers sharing the same hectare.

NORTH

Czech Republic

Born of the fragmentation of the Austro-Hungarian Empire, the Czech Republique has strong similarities with Austria in terms of wine-growing.

Poland

KRNOV
ŠUMPERK
OPAVA
OSTRAVA
HAVÍROV

Moravice

Morava

OLOMOUC
FRÝDEK-MÍSTEK

PREROV
NOVY JICIN

Moravia

KROMĚŘÍŽ
BRNO
ZLÍN

Velké Pavlovice   Uherské Hradiště

jmo

Mikulov   HODONÍN

MO

Slovakia

Main varieties

- ● Saint-Laurent, Zweigelt, Pinot Noir, Blaufränkisch
- ● Müller-Thurgau, Grüner Veltliner, Welschriesling

Global ranking
(by production)

34

Hectares planted

16,000

Annual production
(in millions of litres)

45

Proportion
of red/white grapes

30%   70%

Harvest period

September October

Period when wine-growing appeared

200

AD

Influences

Romans

Hungary

Tokaj
The Danube
Louis XV
The drink of the Tsars
Bor

With its world-famous tokaj (or tokay), Hungary was the first country to devise a meticulously detailed classification of its wine areas.

Global ranking (by production)
18

Hectares planted
68,000

Annual production (in millions of litres)
190

Proportion of red/white grapes
30%
70%

Harvest period
September October

Period when wine-growing appeared
400
AD

Influences
Celts

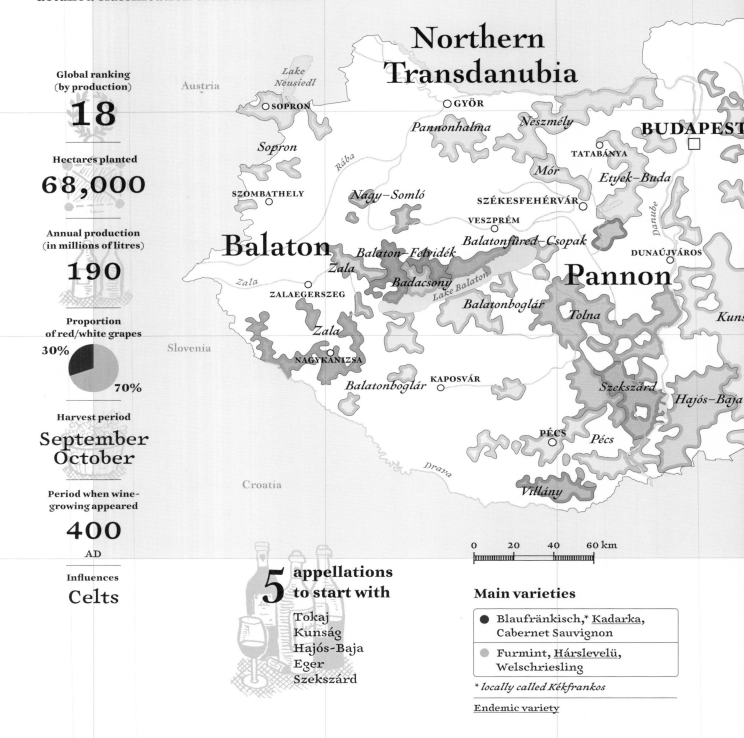

Slovakia

Northern Transdanubia

Austria

Lake Neusiedl

○ SOPRON

○ GYÖR

Pannonhalma

Neszmély

BUDAPEST □

Sopron

Rába

TATABÁNYA ○

Mór

Etyek–Buda

SZOMBATHELY ○

Nagy–Somló

SZÉKESFEHÉRVÁR ○

Danube

Balaton

Zala

VESZPRÉM ○

Balatonfüred–Csopak

DUNAÚJVÁROS

Balaton–Felvidék

Zala

Badacsony

Lake Balaton

Pannon

Zala

ZALAEGERSZEG ○

Balatonboglár

Tolna

Kunsá

Zala

NAGYKANIZSA ○

Balatonboglár

KAPOSVÁR ○

Szekszárd

Hajós–Baja

Slovenia

PÉCS ○

Pécs

Croatia

Drava

Villány

0   20   40   60 km

5 appellations to start with

Tokaj
Kunság
Hajós-Baja
Eger
Szekszárd

Main varieties

● Blaufränkisch,* <u>Kadarka</u>, Cabernet Sauvignon

● Furmint, <u>Hárslevelü</u>, Welschriesling

* *locally called Kékfrankos*

<u>Endemic variety</u>

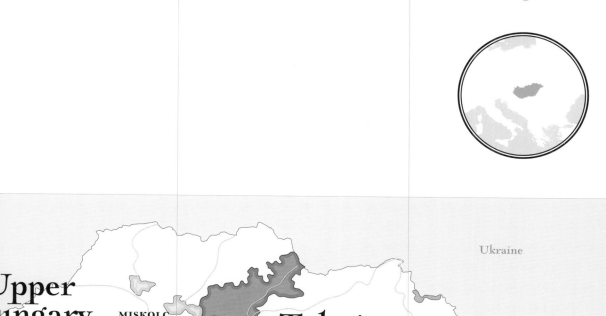

Ukraine

Upper Hungary

MISKOLC ○

Bükk

EGER ○
Eger
EGER ○

Mátra

Tokaj

NYÍREGYHÁZA ○

Szamos

Tisza

Lake Tisza

DEBRECEN ○

Romania

NORTH

SZOLNOK ○

Körös

Danube

CSKEMÉT ○

BÉKÉSCSABA ○

Csongrád

HÓDMEZŐVÁSÁRHELY ○

SZEGED ○

Serbia

Then

The best publicity ever given to to tokaj was by the French King Louis XV. 'Here, Madame, is the wine of kings and the king of wines,' he said to his mistress Madame de Pompadour.

Tokaj (pronounced *tockay*) is a legendary syrupy wine. History tells that soldiers who returned home later than expected discovered a strange

'Here, Madame, is the wine of kings and the king of wines.'

type of rot on their grapes. There was significant surprise when they tasted the wine made with this 'noble rot'; harvesting the grapes when they are overripe gives the wine a remarkable aromatic palate that continues to evolve over time. Rumour of the wine quickly crossed Europe. On the journey from the monarchs of the west to the Tsars of the east, Hungarian wines only improved in taste. Tokaj became the emblem of the country, so much so that it is mentioned in the national anthem: 'For us on the plains of the Kuns, you ripened the wheat; in the grape fields of tokaj, you dripped sweet nectar.'

Apart from Greek, Hungarian is the only language where the word for wine (*bor*) doesn't come from the Latin *vinum*.

Now

No one knows which region was the first to discover the magic of the late harvest: Sauternes, Alsace or Hungary?

Whichever it was, tokaj is the oldest appellation in the world, given it dates back to 1730, making it 125 years earlier than the first classification of the Bordeaux Grands Crus. As is the case with several Eastern European nations, the fall of Soviet Communism renewed investment, and today Hungary exports a quarter of its wine throughout the world.

Kunság (in the Danube region) is the largest wine-growing area in the country, accounting for 30 per cent of national production. When you choose a Hungarian wine, look for the words *minoségi bor* or *különleges minoségu bor*. These measures of quality indicate that the wine belongs to one of the country's 22 appellations. Another point of national pride: while the whole world snaps up American or French oak for making its barrels, the Hungarians make the most of their own oaks, which lend themselves perfectly to the maturation of wine.

Who made wine in 1500?

After the fall of the Roman Empire, the church takes it upon itself to maintain wine-growing traditions. The Ottoman occupation destroys numerous wine-growing industries in the Middle East and Eastern Europe, but production survives thanks to the monks, who make wine for religious purposes. Cross-breeding leads to new types of grapevines, and the notion of varieties is refined.

300   500   700   900

• Belgium

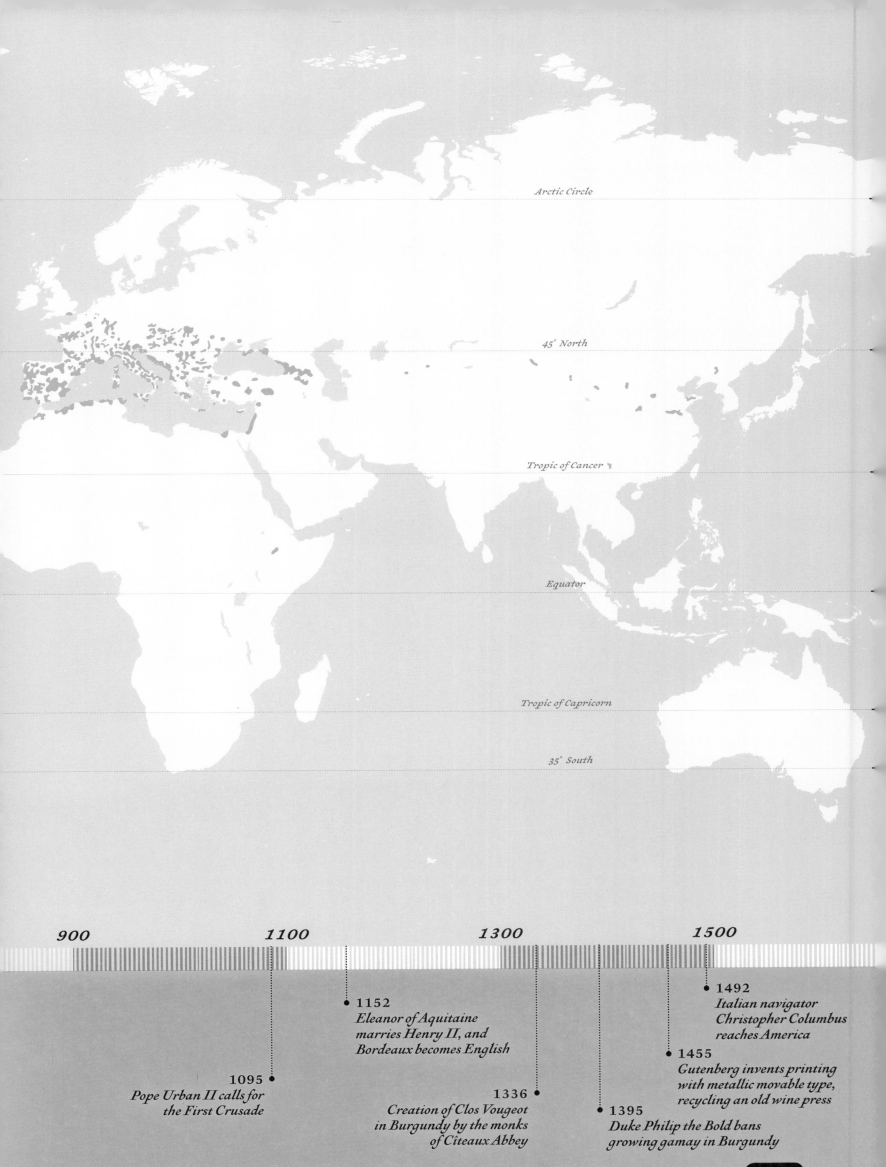

Arctic Circle

45° North

Tropic of Cancer

Equator

Tropic of Capricorn

35° South

900 **1100** **1300** **1500**

1492
*Italian navigator
Christopher Columbus
reaches America*

1152
*Eleanor of Aquitaine
marries Henry II, and
Bordeaux becomes English*

1455
*Gutenberg invents printing
with metallic movable type,
recycling an old wine press*

1095
*Pope Urban II calls for
the First Crusade*

1336
*Creation of Clos Vougeot
in Burgundy by the monks
of Cîteaux Abbey*

1395
*Duke Philip the Bold bans
growing gamay in Burgundy*

Belgium

In the country of beer, a small wine-growing revolution is underway. What do they want? Wine!

5 appellations to start with

Hageland
Haspengouw
Heuvelland
Côtes de Sambre et Meuse
Crémant de Wallonie

OSTEND
BRUGES
GHENT
Scheld
ROESELARE
Lys
Vlaamse Landwijn
KORTRIJK
Heuvelland
Scheldt
MOUSCRON
TOURNAI
M

Then

Belgium shares a similar wine history to England. In the Middle Ages, these two countries saw their vineyards ravaged by the 'Little Ice Age', and they became beer-drinking nations. Beer production only increased in Belgium since the ease of cultivating hops encouraged the abbeys to focus on foam rather than wine, and an improvement in the road system facilitated the arrival of French and German wines the locals couldn't compete with. Due in part to its geographical location, Belgium became an undoubted hub of the global wine trade.

Now

In 1977, the first AOC was created in Flanders, a sign that the national terroir was being recognised. Like their neighbours in Germany and Luxembourg, the Belgians gave white varieties the starring role, better adapted as they are to a northern climate. Production

Belgians consume 284 times more wine than they make.

continues to rise, but is still not large enough to meet the strong local demand: Belgians consume 284 times more wine than they make. Again like England, this low-lying country has announced itself as a serious producer of beautiful sparkling wines.

France

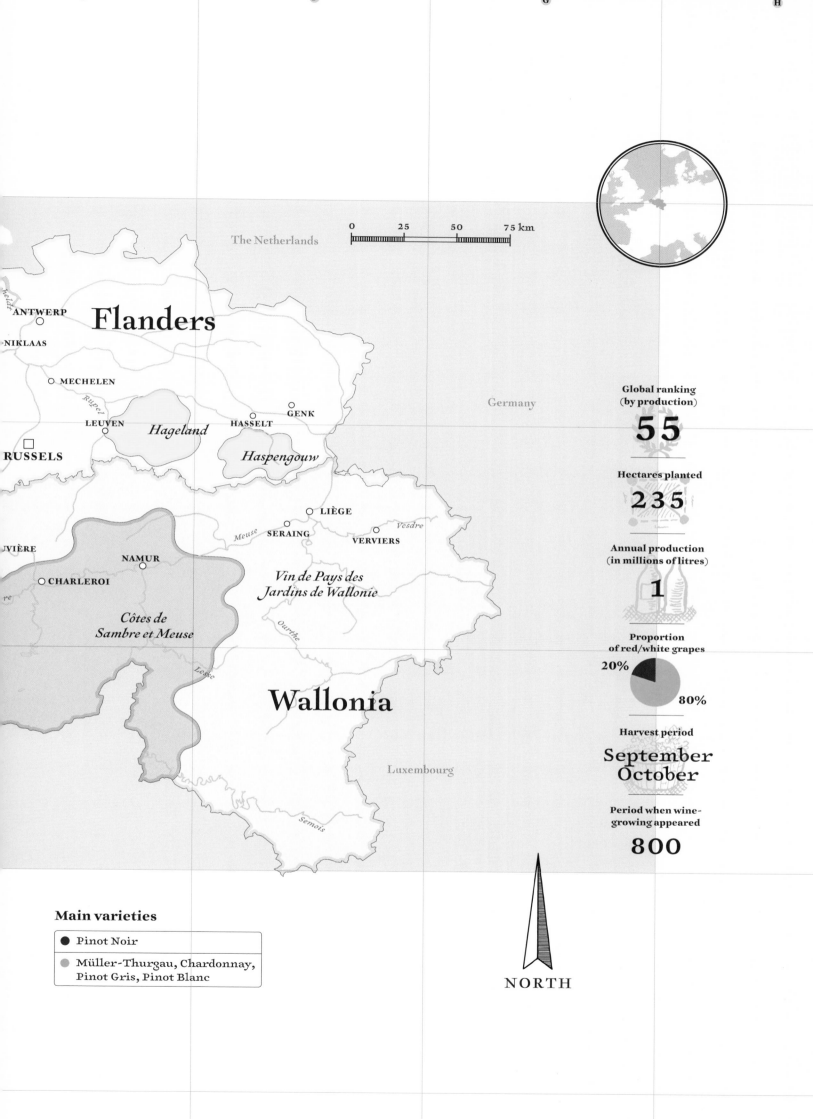

E   F   G   H

1

The Netherlands

0   25   50   75 km

ANTWERP
Flanders
·NIKLAAS

2

○ MECHELEN

Rupel

○ GENK

LEUVEN   HASSELT
Hageland

□
RUSSELS   Haspengouw

Germany

Global ranking
(by production)

55

Hectares planted

235

Annual production
(in millions of litres)

1

○ LIÈGE
Meuse   SERAING
Vesdre
VERVIERS

UVIÈRE   NAMUR

3

○ CHARLEROI
re

Côtes de
Sambre et Meuse

Vin de Pays des
Jardins de Wallonie

Ourthe

Lesse

Proportion
of red/white grapes

20%

80%

Harvest period

September
October

Wallonia

Luxembourg

Semois

Period when wine-
growing appeared

800

4

Main varieties

●   Pinot Noir

●   Müller-Thurgau, Chardonnay,
    Pinot Gris, Pinot Blanc

NORTH

5

E   F   G

Who made wine in 1800?

The Age of Exploration redraws the world's maps as well as those of its vineyards. Spanish, Portuguese, French and Italians take their techniques to the New World. For the first time, wine is produced on five continents.

European colonists

European colonists

Spanish conquistadors

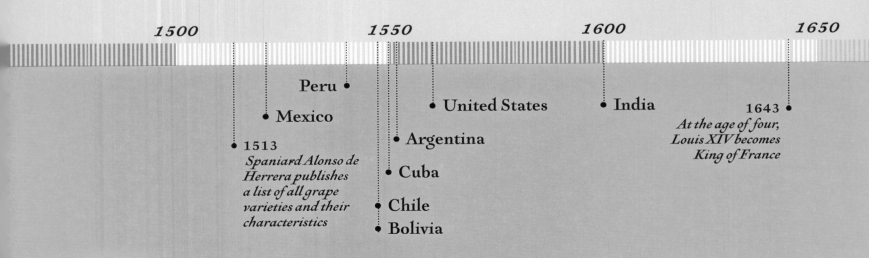

1500   1550   1600   1650

Peru •

• Mexico

• United States

• India

• 1513
Spaniard Alonso de Herrera publishes a list of all grape varieties and their characteristics

• Argentina

• Cuba

1643 •
At the age of four, Louis XIV becomes King of France

• Chile

• Bolivia

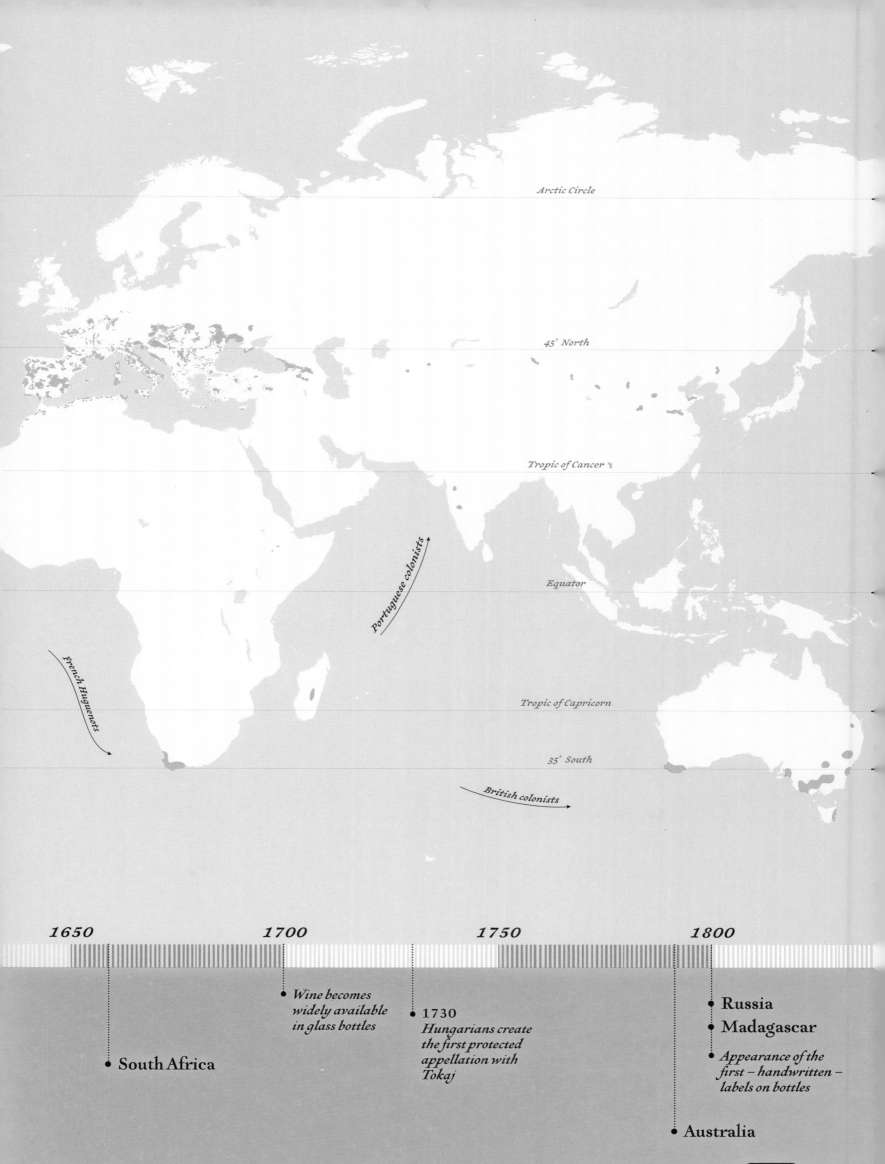

Arctic Circle

45° North

Tropic of Cancer

Portuguese colonists

Equator

French Huguenots

Tropic of Capricorn

35° South

British colonists

1650   1700   1750   1800

• *Wine becomes
widely available
in glass bottles*

• 1730
*Hungarians create
the first protected
appellation with
Tokaj*

• **Russia**

• **Madagascar**

• *Appearance of the
first – handwritten –
labels on bottles*

• **South Africa**

• **Australia**

NORTH

United States of America

EL PASO

HERMOSILLO

CHIHUAHUA

Mexico

Gulf of California

MONTERREY

DURANGO

Cabo San Lucas

Gulf of Mexico

AGUASCALIENTES

TAMPICO

Cabo Corrientes

QUERÉTARO

Bay of Campeche

MÉRID

GUADALAJARA

MEXICO CITY

VERACRUZ

Revillagigedo Islands (Mex.)

TOLUCA

PUEBLA

ACAPULCO

TUXTLA GUTIÉRREZ

Guater

Central America

MEXICO & CUBA

Between the Tropic of Cancer and the Equator, sugar cane grows better than grapes. It was in this region, however, that grapevines first set foot in America. It was via the Caribbean archipelago that Christopher Columbus 'discovered' the New World. Convinced he had reached the Spice Islands in Asia, he was instead on the brink of the most significant encounter between peoples in the history of humanity. Having firmly decided to settle in the region, the Spanish Conquistadors wasted no time bringing in and planting European grapevines. The first wines made in the area were for religious purposes.

0   200   400   600 km

NORTH

ATLANTIC

OCEAN

Bahamas

Straits of Florida

Cuba

Turks & Caicos Islands (GB)

St Kitts & Nevis

HAVANA

Anguilla (GB)

Antigua & Barbuda

Virgin Islands (GB-USA)

○ **CAMAGUEY**

Haiti

Dominican
Republic

Porto Rico (USA)

Montserrat (GB)

Guadeloupe (Fr.)

Dominica

Martinique (Fr.)

Yucatán Channel

St Lucia

○ **CANCÚN**

Cayman Islands (GB)

Barbados

Jamaica

St Vincent & the Grenadines

Grenada

*Gulf of
Honduras*

Trinidad & Tobago

lize

*Cabo Gracias
a Dios*

Aruba (Nl.)

ABC Islands (Nl.)

Honduras

Carribean Sea

El
ador

Nicaragua

*Isthmus
of Panama*

*Gulf of
Darién*

Venezuela

Panama

Costa Rica

Colombia

Brazil

Mexico

Despite a difficult climate, demoralising taxes and compatriots who prefer beer or tequila, Mexican winemakers are making progress. And rather well!

Global ranking (by production)
40

Hectares planted
27,000

Annual production (in millions of litres)
20

Proportion of red/white grapes

20%

80%

Harvest period
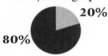
August September

Period when wine-growing appeared
1521

Influences
Spanish Conquistadors

Then

Hernán Cortés decreed in 1524 that each Conquistador must plant, over the following five years, a thousand grapevines or lose his labourer privileges. It's to this measure that Mexico owes the development of wine-growing. But the vineyards grew too quickly in the eyes of the Spanish crown, which saw in this expansion potential competition with its own wines. To check this phenomenon, King Charles II forbade wine-growing for anything other than religious needs. It wasn't until Mexico won independence in 1824 that wine-growers regained their liberty and winemaking autonomy.

The first wine in America was Mexican.

Now

Making a place for oneself isn't easy with dynamos like the United States, Chile and Argentina as neighbours. And with Mexicans only consuming, on average, two glasses of wine a year, the challenge is sizeable! But wine-growers can count on the country's great metropolises, such as Mexico City, Monterrey or even Guadalajara, where the leisured classes are becoming increasingly excited by oenology.

In the meantime, it's the Japanese who are supporting the small number of Mexican wines, given close to 48 per cent of exports are imbibed in the land of the rising sun. Nestled on a quasi-island that gives it a Mediterranean climate, Baja California is the region producing the best-quality wines. It accounts for 85 per cent of national production.

0   200   400   600 km

NORTH

Main varieties

- Barbera, Carignan, Merlot, Cabernet Sauvignon
- Chardonnay, Chenin Blanc, Sauvignon Blanc, Semillon

Cuba

Between its fields of sugar cane and its cigar factories, the largest island of the Caribbean has made space for a few hectares of grapevines.

Global ranking
(by production)

54

Annual production
(in millions of litres)

1

Harvest period

February

Period when wine-growing appeared

16th
century

Influences

Spanish Conquistadors

Then

In the 16th century, grapevines were planted for making communion wine, but the strong heat destroyed the hopes of the Spanish colonists. It took until the 20th century for Italian and Spanish families to reintroduce international varieties and invest in the tools necessary for modern wine-growing.

Now

Production is modest but increasing. Just as in Vietnam or northern Brazil, winemakers meet the challenges of growing grapes in the tropics, and can count on the support of the 4 million tourists who visit the island each year – even if they're thinking more of a mojito than a merlot …

Main varieties

- Carignan, Merlot, Cabernet Sauvignon
- Chardonnay, Sultaniye, Chenin Blanc

Gulf of Mexico

Bahamas

Old Bahama Channel

NORTH

Havana

HAVANA

MATANZAS

Pinar del Río

PINAR DEL RÍO

Yucatán Channel

SANTA CLARA

CIENFUEGOS

SANCTI SPIRITUS

Las Villas

Camaguey

CAMAGUEY

LAS TUNAS

HOLGUIN

Oriente

BAYAMO

Sierra Maestra

MANZANILLO

PALMA SORIANO

GUANTANAMO

Caribbean Sea

SANTIAGO
DE CUBA

Cayman
Islands

Haiti

Jamaica

0   100   200 km

Costa
Rica

Panama

Colombia

Venezuela

PACIFIC

OCEAN

Ecuador

Orinoqu

Río

Japurá

Putumayo

*Gulf of
Guayaquil*

Marañón

Purus

Madeir

PIURA

CHICLAYO

TRUJILLO

Peru

CUSCO

LIMA

Bo

*Lake
Titicaca*

LA PAZ

SANT
DE LA

AREQUIPA

COCHABAMBA

SALTA

Chile

TUCUMÁ

South
America

CÓR

VALPARAÍSO

SANTIAGO

PERU, BOLIVIA, CHILE & ARGENTINA

CONCEPCIÓN

Argenti

*Running from the Peruvian deserts to the snows of Patagonia, the Andes is
the spinal column of the South American wine industry. The various waves of
European immigration shaped the cultural, religious and wine-growing traditions
of each South American country with Italian, Portuguese, Spanish and French
accents. Numerous varieties now forgotten in their original country won their
spurs on this continent, such as tannat in Uruguay and malbec in Argentina.*

*Chiloé
Island (Chile)*

*Chonos
Archipelago
(Chile)*

*San Jo
Gul*

*Golfe
de Peñas*

Map Labels

TALARA
SULLANA
PAITA
CHULUCANAS
PIURA
CHICLAYO
CAJAMARCA
TRUJILLO
CHIMBOTE
HUARAZ
HUÁNUCO
PUCALLPA
BARRANCA
CERRO DE PASCO
HUACHO
Lima
HUANCAYO
LIMA
AYACUCHO
CHINCHA ALTA
ABANCAY
CUSCO
PISCO
ICA
Ica
Arequipa
JULIACA
PUNO
Lake Titicaca
AREQUIPA
Moquegua
MOQUEGUA
ILO
TACNA
Tacna

Brazil
Bolivia
Chili

Javary
Ucayali
Marañón
Huallaga
Urubamba
Alto Purús
Madre de Dios
Apurímac

SOUTH PACIFIC OCEAN

0   200   400 km

Peru

Peru was the first South American country in which the Spanish Conquistadors planted grapevines. Its wine production is modest but of good quality.

Global ranking
(by production)

28

Hectares planted

32,000

Annual production
(in millions of litres)

70

Proportion
of red/white grapes

55%   45%

Harvest period

February March

Period when wine-growing appeared

1540

Influences

Spanish Conquistadors

Then

The first industrialised cities on the continent were born here in Peru, renowned for their mining wealth. Some miners also received part of their wages as wine. The demand for wine never stopped growing, but two important events triggered a decline in Peruvian winemaking. The first was the earthquake that struck the south of the country in 1687, destroying numerous cellars and winemaking set-ups. Then came the 'cotton famine', which redrew the farming landscape. In 1861, the American Civil War provoked a huge drop in cotton exports from the United States to Europe. Many Peruvian wine-growers saw an opportunity and decided to replace their grapevines with cotton fields, which at the time were more lucrative.

Now

Squeezed between the Andes and the Pacific, Peru shares similarities with Chile in terms of climatic conditions. Peru has one of the lowest rainfalls in the world. Ica is undoubtedly the wine capital of Peru. A large part of its harvest is used to produce the grape *eau de vie* that has become the pride of the nation: pisco. Peru is still arguing with Chile over the origin of this drink.

> Peru has one of the lowest rainfalls in the world.

During the past ten years, an increase in buying power among the middle classes has revived interest in the consumption of wine.

Main varieties

- ● Negramoll, Cabernet Sauvignon, Malbec
- ● Italia, Muscat

NORTH

Bolivia

The smallest producer among the South American wine-growing countries is also the most surprising. And it's home to the world's highest vineyard.

Then

Two centuries before the Californian gold rush, the Spanish discovered that their new colonies harboured unimaginable seams of silver. The city of Potosí was founded specifically to mine the deposits found in this region. The business grew rapidly, and the area became, by 1630, more highly populated than London. And to slake the thirst of the main New World city, they made *singani*, a grape spirit destined to warm the hearts and bodies of the miners.

Although the spirit *singani* is still the symbol of the country, the importation of new production equipment and the arrival of French varieties has allowed a new generation to offer a range of wines centred on quality. The slopes make mechanisation impossible, so 100 per cent of the grapes are harvested by hand.

Now

The altitude of the silver deposits explains that of the nearby vineyards, planted between 1600 and 3000 metres. To give you an idea, the highest vines in Europe, in the Valais region of Switzerland, are found at 1300 metres above sea level.

The entire Bolivian wine-growing area is planted between 1600 and 3000 metres altitude.

Main varieties

- ● Cabernet Sauvignon, Malbec, Tannat
- ● Muscat d'Alexandrie, Sauvignon Blanc, Chardonnay

Global ranking (by production)

48

Hectares planted

3000

Annual production (in millions of litres)

5.7

Proportion of red/white grapes

20%
80%

Harvest period

February March

Period when wine-growing appeared

1548

Influences

Spanish Conquistadors

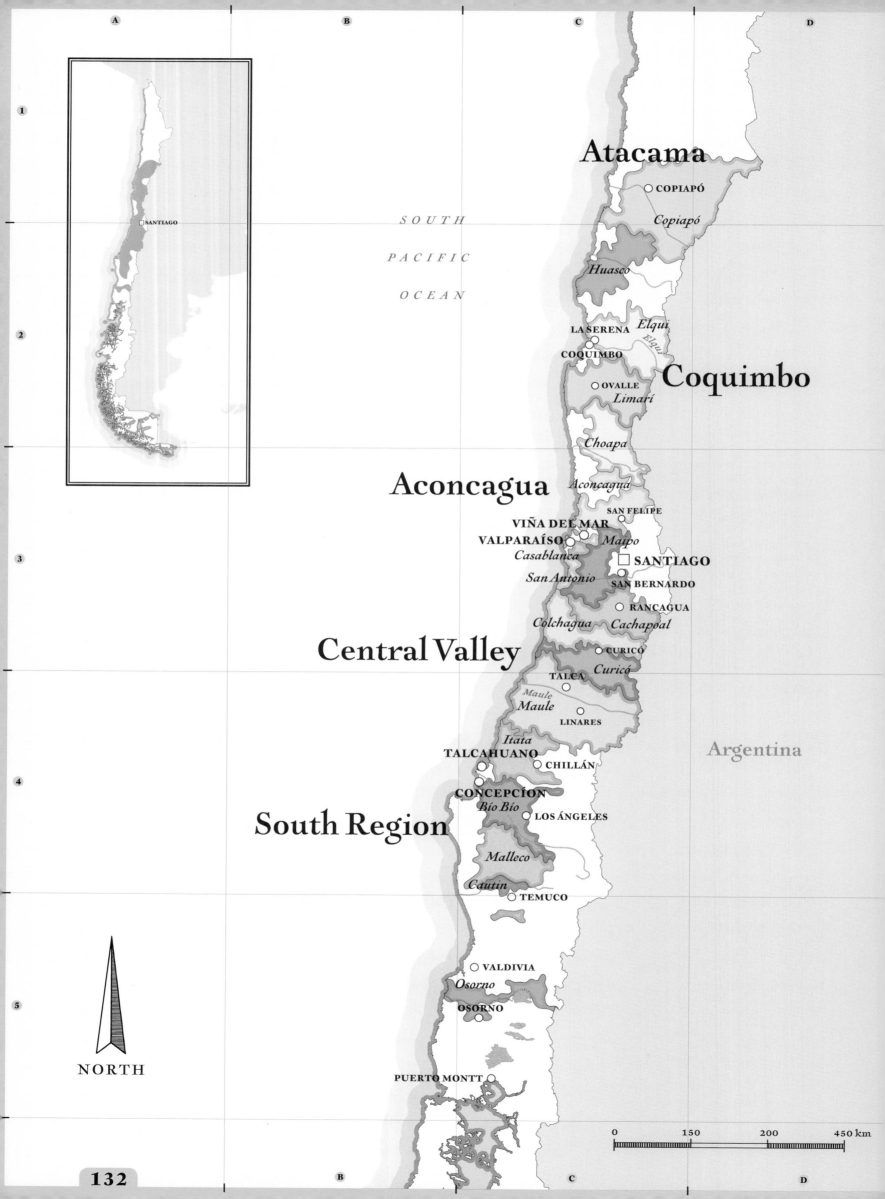

Atacama

COPIAPÓ
Copiapó

Huasco

SOUTH

PACIFIC

OCEAN

LA SERENA
COQUIMBO
Elqui
Elqui

OVALLE
Limarí

Coquimbo

Choapa

Aconcagua

Aconcagua

SAN FELIPE

VIÑA DEL MAR
VALPARAÍSO
Maipo
Casablanca

SANTIAGO

San Antonio
SAN BERNARDO

RANCAGUA
Colchagua
Cachapoal

Central Valley
CURICÓ
Curicó

TALCA
Maule
Maule
LINARES

Itata
TALCAHUANO
CHILLÁN

CONCEPCÍON
Bío Bío
LOS ÁNGELES

South Region

Malleco

Argentina

Cautín
TEMUCO

VALDIVIA
Osorno
OSORNO

NORTH

PUERTO MONTT

0   150   200   450 km

Chile

Enjoying excellent microclimates, in-depth knowledge and determined wine-growers, Chile has made a name for itself, in less than 20 years, as a vital part of the international wine scene.

Global ranking (by production)

8

Hectares planted

215,000

Annual production (in millions of litres)

1010

Proportion of red/white grapes

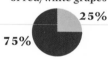

25%

75%

Harvest period

February March

Period when wine-growing appeared

1548

Influences

Spanish Conquistadors

Main varieties

- Cabernet Sauvignon, Carménère, Merlot, Syrah, Pinot Noir
- Sauvignon Blanc, Chardonnay

Then

The first vines were planted by the priest Francisco de Carabantes in 1548 to make the wine needed for his religious rites. Like Mexico, Chile was included in the edict from King Charles II of Spain outlawing wine-growing for anything other than religious practices, but it didn't last long.

Trans-Atlantic voyages encouraged the arrival of French wine experts and varieties.

From the 16th to 20th centuries, the vines were maintained by farmers who made wine for their personal consumption, using a red variety of little interest but high yield: pais, meaning 'peace'. In 1818, Chile won its independence, and trans-Atlantic voyages encouraged the arrival of French wine experts and varieties. Carménère became the jewel in the Chilean wine-growing crown. Long mistaken for merlot, it gained its true identity in 1994, thanks to DNA studies.

Now

Along with Argentina, Chile is the most promising wine-growing country on the continent. Only slightly bigger than the Bordeaux wine-growing area, it has grown by more than 40 per cent in ten years to become the largest wine exporter in the world after the European countries. Its exceptional geographic location is ideal for growing grapevines and for producing terroir wines. The country profits from generous sunshine tempered by fresh breezes blowing off the Pacific and the mild weather that glides down from the Andes during the night. Unlike Argentina, irrigation isn't always necessary, and the vineyards are particularly suited to organic agriculture. Chile also boasts the largest biodynamic estate in the world, which covers close to 1000 hectares in the Colchagua Valley.

5 appellations to start with

Maipo Valley
Colchagua Valley
Cachapoal Valley
Casablanca Valley
Maule Valley

Argentina

The Pampas
MENDOZA
Wine tourism
MALBEC
Bodega

It's without doubt the South American country where the wine-growing tradition is the most established. Long centred on quantity, its wines are becoming more refined, starting to compete with those of Chile and Europe.

Then

Argentina has the largest Spanish population in South America. After the Age of Discovery, the creation of a new civilisation on areas that were almost desert led to less racial diversity than in Brazil or Chile, and winemaking has always retained, in the church and at the table, an important position. In the 19th century, the government consulted specialists, and French agronomist Michel Pougeot introduced a French variety grown in the Cahors region: malbec. This strong red variety rapidly became the signature of Argentinian wines. The wine market enjoyed huge growth after the opening in 1885 of the railway linking Mendoza to the capital, Buenos Aires.

> **Malbec rapidly became the signature of Argentinian wines.**

Now

The arrival of significant foreign investment allowed the development of the Mendoza region, which now accounts for three-quarters of national production and welcomes more than 1 million wine tourists each year. It's one of the Great Wine Capitals, a network of nine global regions established in 1999. In Mendoza, which has the look of the US Far West, rain is rare and the vineyards are irrigated with waters collected from the Andes. It's surely the longest wine trail in the world: you can travel for 2000 kilometres and (almost) always see vines. The bodegas are the equivalent of European cooperatives: large organisations that make wine under the same label using harvests from smaller farms.

> **Mendoza welcomes more than 1 million wine tourists each year.**

Global ranking (by production)

9

Hectares planted

225,000

Annual production (in millions of litres)

940

Proportion of red/white grapes

30%
70%

Harvest period

March
April

Period when wine-growing appeared

1551

Influences

Spanish
Conquistadors

Main varieties

- ● Malbec, Douce Noir, Cabernet Sauvignon
- ● <u>Torrontès</u>, Chardonnay, Pedro Ximénez

<u>Endemic variety</u>

5 appellations to start with

Lujan de Cuyo
San Rafael
Santa Rosa
Cafayate
Valles Calchaquíes

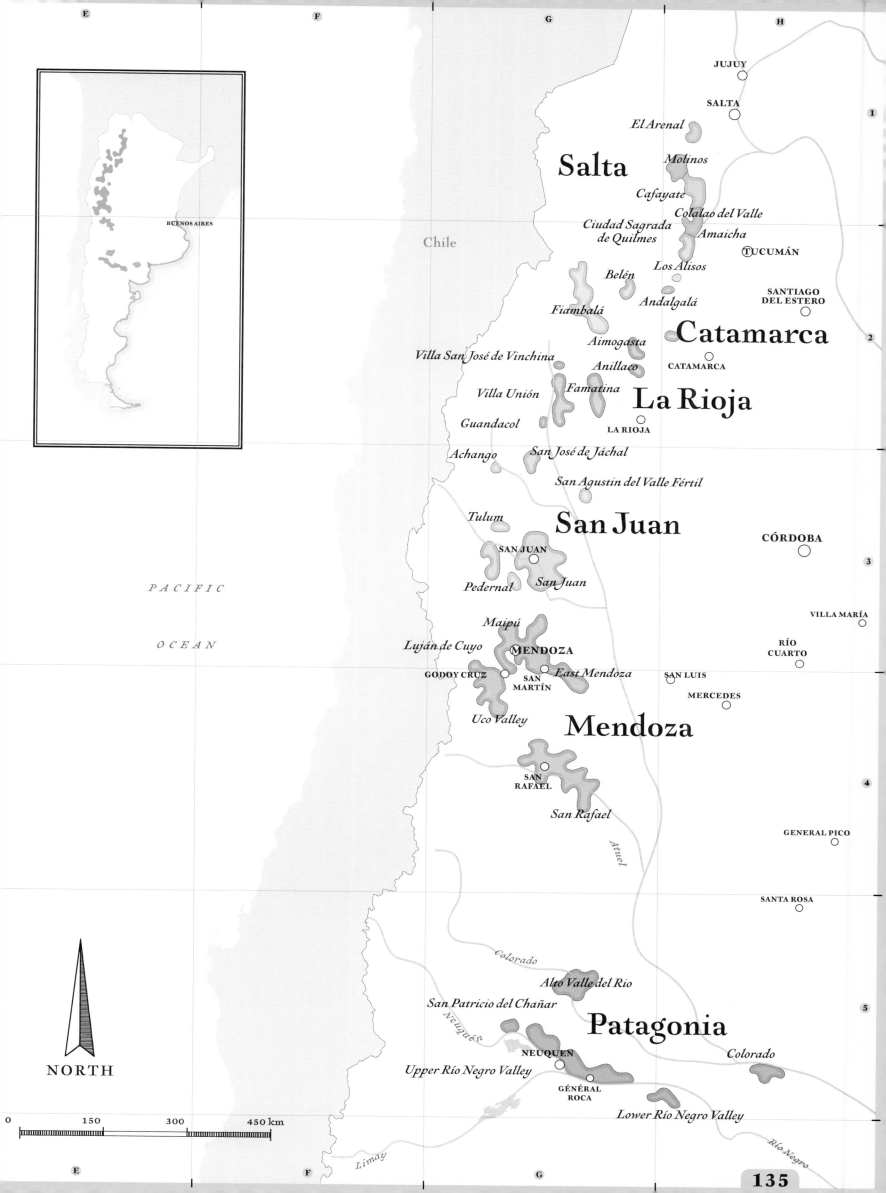

United States

From the Grand Canyon to Niagara Falls, the grapevine has invited itself into all the mind-boggling landscapes of this vast country–continent. All 50 states produce wine, but the majority buy their grapes from regions that are better adapted to wine-growing. Although it's still at the bottom of the list of main producers, the land of Uncle Sam recently became the world's biggest consumer of wine.

Lake Superior

nesota

MINNEAPOLIS

Wisconsin

GREEN BAY

Lake Michigan

Michigan

MILWAUKEE

Lake Huron

New York

Vermont

Maine

Massachusetts

BOSTON

Illinois

DETROIT

Lake Erie

BUFFALO

Rhode Island

Iowa

CHICAGO

CLEVELAND

NEW YORK

Connecticut

Indiana

Ohio

PHILADELPHIA

New Jersey

SPRINGFIELD

INDIANAPOLIS

COLUMBUS

BALTIMORE

Pennsylvania

AS CITY

ST LOUIS

CINCINNATI

Ohio

WASHINGTON

Maryland

Missouri

RICHMOND

Tennessee

Virginia

NASHVILLE

RALEIGH

Arkansas

MEMPHIS

CHARLOTTE

North
Carolina

ATLANTIC

OCEAN

Mississippi

BIRMINGHAM

COLUMBIA

ATLANTA

SHREVEPORT

JACKSON

South
Carolina

EAUMONT

BATON ROUGE

COLUMBUS

Georgia

OUSTON

NEW ORLEANS

JACKSONVILLE

Louisiana

ORLANDO

NORTH

Gulf of Mexico

TAMPA

Florida

MIAMI

The Bahamas

Cuba

0   200   400   600   800   1000 km

Jamaica

Haiti

Global ranking
(by production)

4

Hectares planted

443,000

Annual production
(in millions of litres)

2250

Proportion
of red/white grapes

53% / 47%

Harvest period

September
October

Period when wine-
growing appeared

1560

Influences

European
colonists

Then

Unlike South America, wild grapes were already growing in abundance in North America before the arrival of the colonists. The first wine-growers therefore decided to cultivate endemic varieties, but without success.

It was the well-named Jean-Louis Vignes, a wine-grower freshly arrived from Bordeaux, who planted the first European vines, on the West Coast, in Los Angeles in 1831, a time when the city's population was only 700 souls. Good timing, Jean-Louis! Seventeen years later, the Californian gold rush drew 300,000 adventurers into the region. Few of them made their fortune, but the majority decided to settle in the area, leading to the creation of San Francisco. Wine became a sought-after commodity, and the wine industry took off.

The Californian gold rush saw demand for wine take off.

The history of the United States is intimately linked with that of the railways. In the 19th century, the development of the rail network allowed states without grapevines to obtain stock from the most established vineyards and produce their own wines using their neighbours' grapes.

On 16 January 1919, the 18th Amendment to the Constitution outlawed the making and selling of intoxicating beverages. Prohibition lasted for 14 years and hit the wine industry hard.

Main varieties

●	Cabernet Sauvignon, Zinfandel, Merlot, Pinot Noir, Syrah*
●	Chardonnay, Colombard, Sauvignon Blanc, Riesling

* locally called Shiraz

Now

Long considered too standardised, American wines have increased in complexity, and the diversity of varieties has grown. Each region understands its potential, and the country can rely on the richness of its climates and the curiosity of its countrypeople to allow it to make a name as the most diverse of the New World wine industries.

Since 1980, the United States has defined 224 American Viticultural Areas (AVAs). These are the equivalent of the French AOCs and specify the provenance of the grapes used by the winemaker. As proof of evolving practices, the notion of terroir is winning people over, and details of the production area are taking more and more space on the label, which for many years was the sole preserve of the name of the varieties and the producer.

The notion of terroir is winning people over.

No market in the world is as subject to fashion as that of American wine. All it takes is for a film character or TV series to fall in love with a region or variety, and the winemakers immediately experience an increase in sales.

5 appellations to start with

Sonoma Valley
Napa Valley
Willamette Valley
Finger Lakes
Yakima Valley

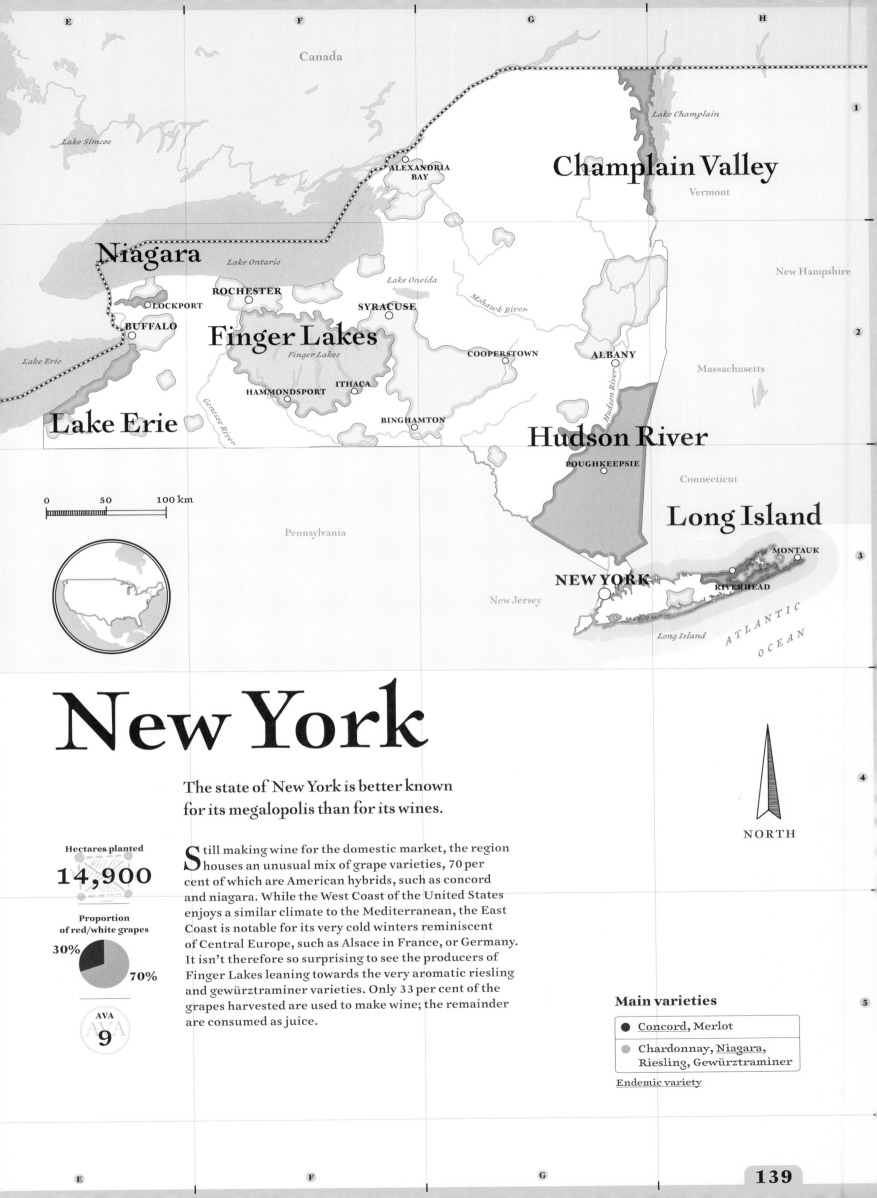

New York

The state of New York is better known
for its megalopolis than for its wines.

Still making wine for the domestic market, the region
houses an unusual mix of grape varieties, 70 per
cent of which are American hybrids, such as concord
and niagara. While the West Coast of the United States
enjoys a similar climate to the Mediterranean, the East
Coast is notable for its very cold winters reminiscent
of Central Europe, such as Alsace in France, or Germany.
It isn't therefore so surprising to see the producers of
Finger Lakes leaning towards the very aromatic riesling
and gewürztraminer varieties. Only 33 per cent of the
grapes harvested are used to make wine; the remainder
are consumed as juice.

Hectares planted

14,900

**Proportion
of red/white grapes**

30%

70%

**AVA
9**

Main varieties

● Concord, Merlot

● Chardonnay, Niagara,
Riesling, Gewürztraminer

Endemic variety

NORTH

Washington

A　B　C　D

1

PACIFIC

OCEAN

NORTH

Columbia Gorge

Chehalem Mountains

Yamhill–Carlton

McMinnville

○ PORTLAND

Ribbon Ridge

Dundee Hills

Eola–Amity Hills

Idah

Snake River
Valley

Willamette Valley

2

Elkton

Red Hill Douglas County

Umpqua Valley

Rogue Valley

Applegate Valley

California

Nevada

3

Oregon

0　50　100　150 km

It's the Burgundy of the New World: with cooler summers than
California and warmer winters than Washington State, Oregon
unites the ideal conditions for growing perfect pinot noir.

Hectares planted

11,300

**Proportion
of red/white grapes**

32%

68%

AVA
18

Winemaking has only been significant in Oregon
since 1960, but it's the most productive state
in the country. Unlike its neighbours, the region
produces variable vintages since the grapes aren't
of the same quality each year. The diversity of soils
and microclimates provides an extraordinary playing
field for the capricious pinot noir, whose price and
elegance draw ever closer to the great burgundies.
The producers resemble farmers more than
businesspeople: the estates are often family owned
and run, and farmed organically.

Main varieties

● Cabernet Sauvignon,
　Pinot Noir

● Pinot Gris, Chardonnay,
　Riesling

B　C　D

Canada

Puget Sound

Lake Chelan

SPOKANE

SEATTLE

Columbia Valley

TACOMA

OLYMPIA

Ancient Lakes

Idaho

PACIFIC

Naches Heights

Wahluke Slope

Rattlesnake Hills

Yakima Valley

Red Mountain

Snipes Mountain

OCEAN

Columbia Gorge

Horse Heaven Hills

Walla Walla Valley

Oregon

NORTH

0   50   100   150 km

Washington

In the past few years, the state has capitalised on a clear craze for its wines to become the second-biggest producer in the country. Between 2000 and 2009, the number of wineries increased by a factor of six.

Hectares planted

20,200

Proportion of red/white grapes

46%   54%

AVA

12

The Washington wine industry is split in two by the natural barrier of the Cascades Range, which stretches from Vancouver to northern California. This range captures the clouds blown in from the ocean and brings regular rain to the east.

The wine-growing area is increasing, but, unlike in Oregon, the majority of the state's winemakers continue to buy their grapes from other producers. This phenomenon is one particular reason why the region displays a strong tendency towards wines made using a blend of varieties. In contrast to Europe, a great winemaker can make wine without owning a single vine, and vice versa. Renowned wine-growers can sell their precious harvest to as many as 30 different winemakers. This might make lovers of terroir gnash their teeth, but Americans find nothing shocking about buying grapes from tens and even hundreds of kilometres away. The main thing is that the wine is good!

Main varieties

● Cabernet Sauvignon, Merlot, Syrah

● Chardonnay, Riesling

California

In a region larger than Italy and with more grapevines than the whole of Argentina, wine has become an institution. In this hot spot for technology, modernity often prevails over tradition.

Hectares planted

246,000

Proportion of red/white grapes

34%

66%

AVA

135

California is a land for fantasy, a factory of dreams. What's striking is the proximity of polar opposites. Just like the sea and the national parks, vineyards are often at the outskirts of the cities, spreading for close to 1000 kilometres, enjoying generous sunshine tempered by the freshness of Pacfic breezes.

It was the first region in the New World to be recognised in Europe for the quality of its wines. During a blind tasting organised in Paris in 1976, two Californian wines created a stir by winning against the great bordeaux and burgundies.

Today, the region accounts for more than 90 per cent of national production, and is home to half the country's appellations. To meet a demand that often surpasses production capacity, wineries have invested in the vast deserts of the Central Valley, irrigating

soils scorched by the sun with water from the rivers of the Sierra Nevada.

Despite its small size, the Russian River has created a gap in the mountains that allows the entry of sea breezes, without which it would be impossible to grow grapes. With little variation in

The region accounts for more than 90 per cent of national production, and is home to half the country's appellations.

temperature, the vineyards yield grapes of a similar quality year after year.

For reds, cabernet sauvignon is king. For whites, it's chardonnay that reigns unchallenged over the state. Although unfamiliar with the coast, it can still rely on the freshness of the Pacific to not overheat. Its routine maturation in barrels confers the toasted and vanilla aromas that have made it such a success.

Main varieties

- ● Cabernet Sauvignon, Merlot
- ● Chardonnay

Sonoma & Napa

These West Coast twins are together the showcase for Californian wines. Spoilt for choice with a mosaic of terroirs, they are home to an unequalled number of appellations. While Napa enjoys greater fame, Sonoma fascinates with its perfectionism.

Sonoma

Hectares planted

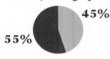

24,200

Proportion of red/white grapes

45%

55%

AVA **16**

This new star of American wine stretches out 30 minutes from San Francisco. Its size and its proximity to the ocean bring great variety in its soils. The heat of the north is suitable for wines based on zinfandel, while the gentler south has become the land of choice for chardonnay.

Main varieties

- ● Pinot Noir, Zinfandel
- ● Chardonnay

Napa

Hectares planted

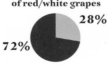

18,200

Proportion of red/white grapes

28%

72%

AVA **17**

Nestled between two mountain ranges – the Vacas to the east and the Mayacamas to the west – this wine region owes its name to the river that crosses it: the Napa. At the end of the 1970s, this 'Promised Land' inspired the whole wine-growing community in its quest for modernisation and adaptation to terroir. The region has become an obligatory visit for any wine buff. The wineries have developed a superb wine tour experience, with tasting rooms and winemaker meet and greets – a sort of Disneyland of wine!

Main varieties

- ● Cabernet Sauvignon, Merlot
- ● Chardonnay

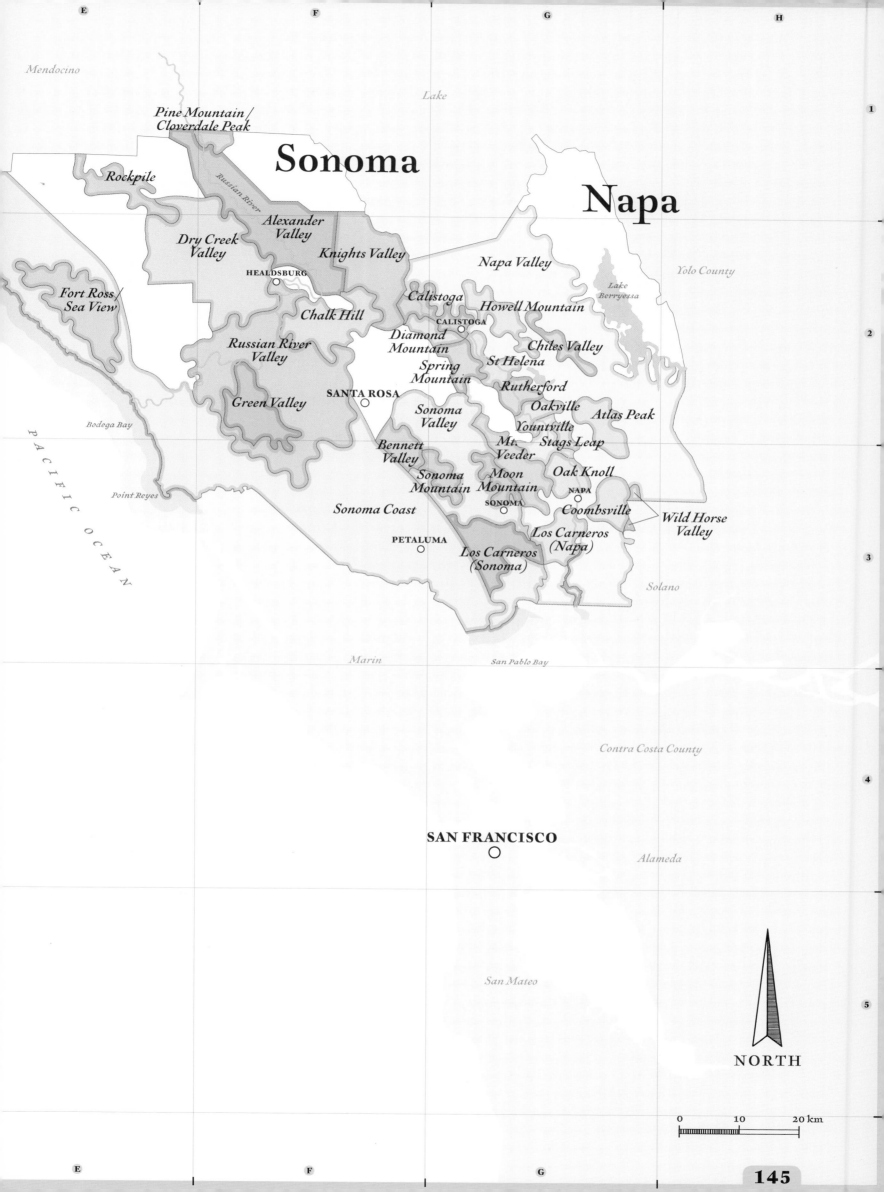

India

In a country that disapproves of drinking alcohol and endures the strong monsoons of its tropical climate, it would seem unthinkable to develop wine-growing regions. And yet India plans on taking its place among the wine producers of the New World.

Global ranking
(by production)

42

Hectares planted

114,000

Annual production
(in millions of litres)

17

Proportion
of red/white grapes

40%   60%

Harvest period

February

Period when wine-growing appeared

16th
century

Influences

English
Portuguese

Then

Although growing grapes for the table dates back thousands of years, the true birth of grape-growing in India was encouraged by two European colonising nations who followed each other into the region: the Portuguese and the English. In 1498, Vasco de Gama (Portugal's Christopher Columbus) was the first European to sail to India via the Cape of Good Hope in South Africa. This has had been Christopher Columbus's intention, but he instead found himself in the land of Uncle Sam. The Portuguese wasted no time in reproducing the thing they knew how to do well: fortified port-style wine. By the 17th century, the English influence dominated, but the importation of wine from Europe was costing them a fortune. The English decided to therefore expand the local wine-growing industry to meet their needs. At the end of the 19th century, the phylloxera plague brought an abrupt end to this surge in production.

Now

India is the country with the lowest per capita wine consumption in the world: 9 ml per year, equal to about 2 teaspoons. By comparison, the French consume 44 litres of wine per person each year. As in many New World countries, the growth in production is striking (up 30 per cent in 2016). This promising rise is dominated by five producers who supply 90 per cent of the volume. The regions in the south of the country experience

> **This promising rise is dominated by five producers who supply 90 per cent of the volume.**

such high temperatures that they can harvest twice a year, a surprising phenomenon that also occurs in the north of Brazil.

Main varieties

- Cabernet Sauvignon, Merlot, Syrah
- Ugni Blanc, Chardonnay, Chenin

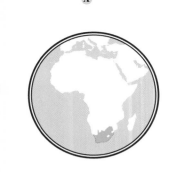

South Africa

Within the confines of the African continent, a wine industry has emerged in response to Mediterranean climates and to inspiration. It was the first region in the New World to put flagons on the tables of European monarchs during the Enlightenment. We mainly know its emblematic national variety: pinotage.

5 appellations to start with

Constantia
Darling
Cape Peninsula
Stellenbosch
Paarl

Lutzville Valley

○ VREDENDAL

Olifants River

St Helena Bay

Citrusdal Valley

Cape Columbine

Coastal Region

SALDANHA ○

Swartland

Breede River Valley

Tulbagh

Worcester

Darling

Wellington   *Breedekloof*

Tygerberg

PAARL ○ **WORCESTER**

□ *Paarl*

Klein Karoo

Calitzdorp

OUDTSHOORN ○

STELLENBOSCH

○

Robertson

Langeberg–Garcia

CAPE TOWN ○

Constantia

□ *Stellenbosch*

Elgin

SOMERSET WEST

○

Overberg

Swellendam

GEORG

Cape Peninsula

Cape South Coast

Cape of Good Hope

Walker Bay

Danger Point   *Cape Agulhas*

SOUTH
ATLANTIC OCEAN

Cape Agulhas

0   50   100   150 km

Then

In the middle of the 17th century, Jan van Riebeeck, the first governor of South Africa, ordered that Dutch grapevines be planted. South Africa is certainly the only wine-growing area in the world whose first grape harvest is possible to date: 1659. Although the colonists didn't know terribly much about winemaking, production was given a lift by the arrival of a handful of Huguenot families (French Protestants who left the country after the revocation in 1688 of the Edict of Nantes that had allowed them freedom of religion) – an early French touch!

Between the phylloxera plague and the Apartheid crisis that led to an international boycott of South African products, the wine industry lost its lustre before being reborn at the beginning of the 1990s after the liberation of Nelson Mandela.

Main varieties

- Cabernet Sauvignon, Syrah, Merlot, <u>Pinotage</u>
- Chenin Blanc, Colombard, Chardonnay

<u>Endemic variety</u>

Now

Among the winemakers of the New World, the first producer from the African continent has certainly been the fastest to make its mark in Europe. The coolness of the South African coasts is favourable for white wines, while the interior offers good conditions for reds. Pinotage is the national variety. This cross between pinot noir and cinsault was obtained in 1952 by Abraham Perold, a researcher at the University of Stellenbosch, making it one of the youngest varieties in the world. It relies on sunshine and is suited to the dry heat of the country, producing classy wines with aromas of dark fruit, coconut and coffee. Used alone or with other varieties, it makes a cellaring wine that deserves time to express itself fully.

Pinotage is the national variety.

Among the appellations, we distinguish 'Regions' (Coastal Region, Breede River Valley Region, Olifants River Region), 'Districts' (Stellenbosch, Paarl, Overberg, Worcester, etc.), 'Wards' (Constantia, Durbanville, Elgin, etc.) and 'Estates', which complete the circle of exceptional wines.

Global ranking (by production)

7

Hectares planted

101,000

Annual production (in millions of litres)

1050

Proportion of red/white grapes

45% 55%

Harvest period

February

Period when wine-growing appeared

1659

Influences

French

Plettenberg Bay

KNYSNA

NORTH

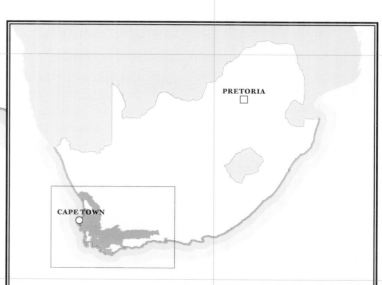

PRETORIA

CAPE TOWN

A   B   C   D

Gascoyne

Murchison

WARBURTON

1

MEEKATHARRA

Lake Austin

Lake Carnegie

GERALDTON

SHIRAZ
Tasmania
Barossa Valley
Island continent

*Mongers
Lake*

*Lake
Barlee*

KALGOORLIE

Swan District

Lake Moore

PERTH

EYRE

2

MANDURAH   *Peel*

Western Australia

Geographe

ESPERANCE

*Great Australian
Bight*

Margaret River
Manjimup   *Great Southern*
Pemberton

ALBANY

Cape Leeuwin

Australia

NORTH

3

Drawing on high-performance production equipment, great
climatic variations and an appropriate choice of varieties,
the largest island on the planet has become an important
figure among the countries of the New World.

Then

Vine cuttings were brought to
Australia with the First Fleet in
1788, but it was 30 years before the first
bottle of Australian wine was exported.
Lacking the necessary ideal conditions
in their own country, the British saw
an opportunity to create their own wine
industry here.
It is widely
believed that the
first shiraz (as
syrah is locally
known) plants
were introduced
from Europe in
1832 by James Busby, who brought over
300 varieties into the country, planting
them in the Botanic Gardens in Sydney
and at his Hunter Valley property.
At the end of the 19th century, a great
construction project began to bring
water to the arid plains and increase
the area available for agriculture.

The British saw
an opportunity to
create their own
wine industry.

Now

To profit from their Mediterranean-
type climate, Australian vineyards are
concentrated around the southern coastal
areas. Australia is the only New World
producer to have
adopted shiraz,
originally from the
Rhône Valley, as
the flagship variety
for its reds. In the
South Australian
and New South Wales wine regions,
it yields strong wines with aromas of
mature fruit and spicy notes. Benefiting
from a gentler climate, Victoria and
Tasmania are renowned for their pinot
noir and chardonnay. The strength of the
Australian dollar has stimulated imports
to a critical point: the bestselling wine
in the country is from New Zealand ...

Shiraz is the
country's
flagship variety.

Already at the limit of aridity, the
Australian wine industry is threatened
by global warming, which risks rendering
wine-growing impossible.

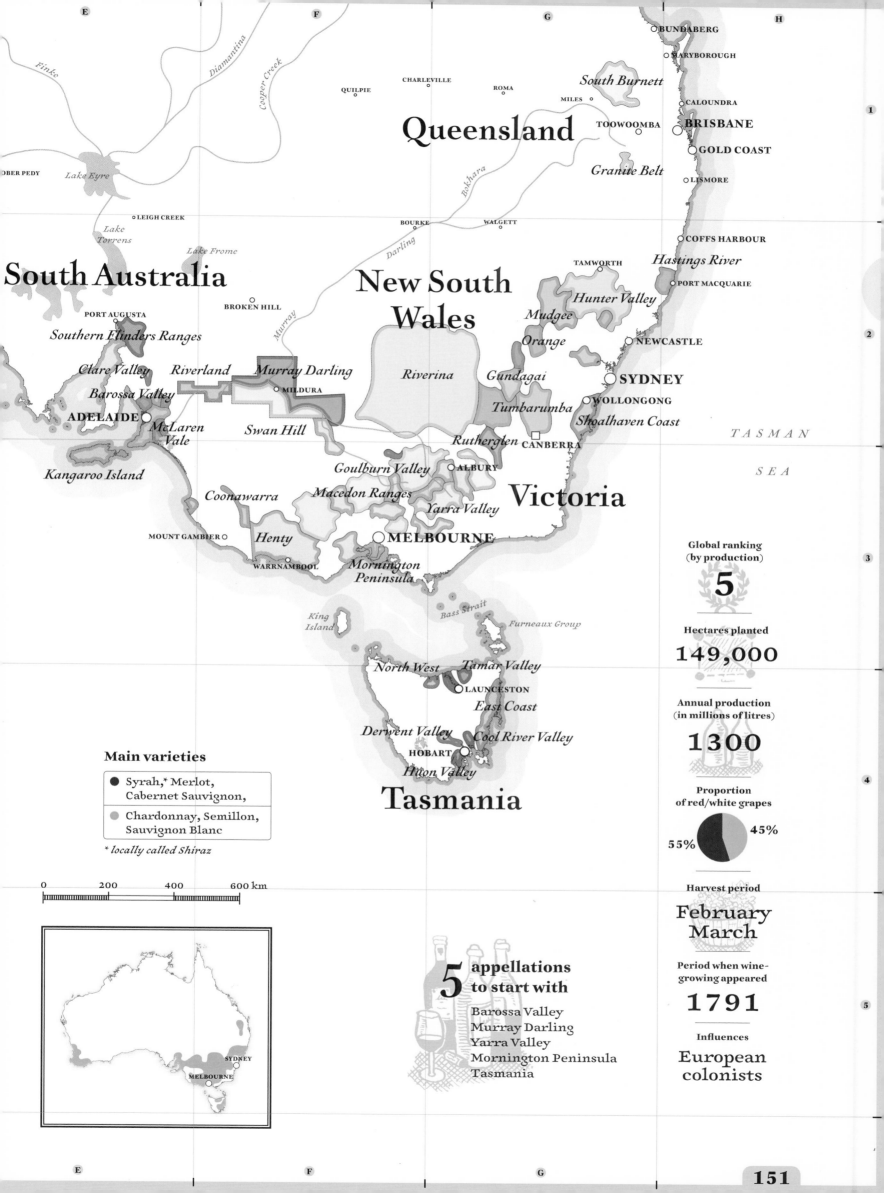

E   F   G   H

Finke

Diamantina

Cooper Creek

QUILPIE   CHARLEVILLE   ROMA

South Burnett

◉ BUNDABERG

◉ MARYBOROUGH

CALOUNDRA

MILES

Queensland

TOOWOOMBA

◉ BRISBANE

◉ GOLD COAST

Granite Belt

LISMORE

OBER PEDY

Lake Eyre

LEIGH CREEK

Lake Torrens

Lake Frome

PORT AUGUSTA

South Australia

BOURKE   WALGETT

Darling

COFFS HARBOUR

Hastings River

TAMWORTH

PORT MACQUARIE

New South Wales

BROKEN HILL

Southern Flinders Ranges

Hunter Valley

Clare Valley

Riverland

Murray Darling

Murray

Riverina

Mudgee

Orange

◉ NEWCASTLE

Barossa Valley

MILDURA

Gundagai

SYDNEY

ADELAIDE

McLaren Vale

Swan Hill

Tumbarumba

◉ WOLLONGONG

Shoalhaven Coast

T A S M A N

Kangaroo Island

Rutherglen

CANBERRA

S E A

Coonawarra

Goulburn Valley

ALBURY

Macedon Ranges

Victoria

MOUNT GAMBIER

Yarra Valley

Henty

MELBOURNE

WARRNAMBOOL

Mornington Peninsula

Bass Strait

Furneaux Group

King Island

North West   *Tamar Valley*

LAUNCESTON

East Coast

Derwent Valley   *Cool River Valley*

HOBART

Huon Valley

Tasmania

Global ranking (by production)
5

Hectares planted
149,000

Annual production (in millions of litres)
1300

Proportion of red/white grapes

55% — 45%

Harvest period
February March

Period when wine-growing appeared
1791

Influences
European colonists

Main varieties

- ● Syrah,* Merlot, Cabernet Sauvignon,
- ● Chardonnay, Semillon, Sauvignon Blanc

* locally called Shiraz

0   200   400   600 km

5 **appellations to start with**

Barossa Valley
Murray Darling
Yarra Valley
Mornington Peninsula
Tasmania

SYDNEY

MELBOURNE

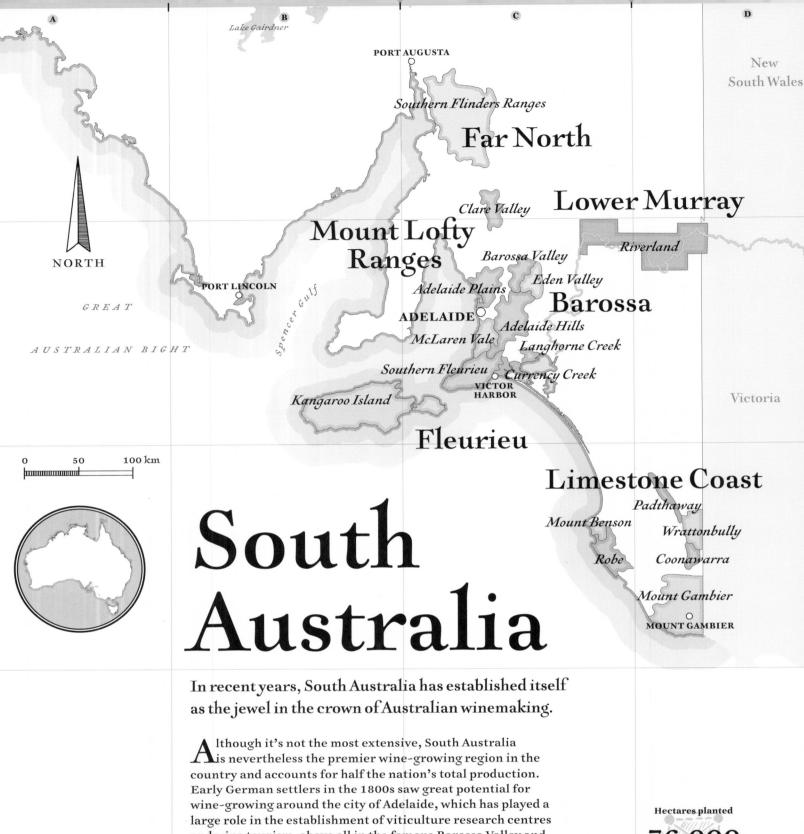

A
B
Lake Gairdner
C
D

New
South Wales

1

PORT AUGUSTA

Southern Flinders Ranges

Far North

Clare Valley

Lower Murray

NORTH

**Mount Lofty
Ranges**

Barossa Valley

Riverland

Eden Valley

PORT LINCOLN

Adelaide Plains

Barossa

GREAT

ADELAIDE

Adelaide Hills

2

AUSTRALIAN BIGHT

McLaren Vale

Langhorne Creek

Victoria

Southern Fleurieu

Currency Creek

VICTOR
HARBOR

Kangaroo Island

Fleurieu

Limestone Coast

Padthaway

Mount Benson

Wrattonbully

0   50   100 km

Robe

Coonawarra

3

South
Australia

Mount Gambier

MOUNT GAMBIER

In recent years, South Australia has established itself
as the jewel in the crown of Australian winemaking.

A lthough it's not the most extensive, South Australia
is nevertheless the premier wine-growing region in the
country and accounts for half the nation's total production.
Early German settlers in the 1800s saw great potential for
wine-growing around the city of Adelaide, which has played a
large role in the establishment of viticulture research centres
and wine tourism, above all in the famous Barossa Valley and
Clare Valley, nicknamed the 'riesling trail'.

Hectares planted

76,000

4

Spared the phylloxera plague, this region is haven to
some of the world's oldest varieties. It is rare for a region to
equally support red and white varieties that were originally
considered opposites, such as syrah (shiraz) and riesling.
In Europe, the former grows best in the warmth of the Rhône
Valley, while the latter prefers the freshness of the banks of
the Rhine. Here, thanks to scorching days and chilly nights,
everyone is happy!

**Proportion
of red/white grapes**

42%

58%

5

Main varieties

●	Syrah,* Cabernet Sauvignon
●	Chardonnay, Riesling, Semillon

* locally called Shiraz

**Barossa Valley
Clare Valley
Coonawarra
Eden Valley**

B
C
D

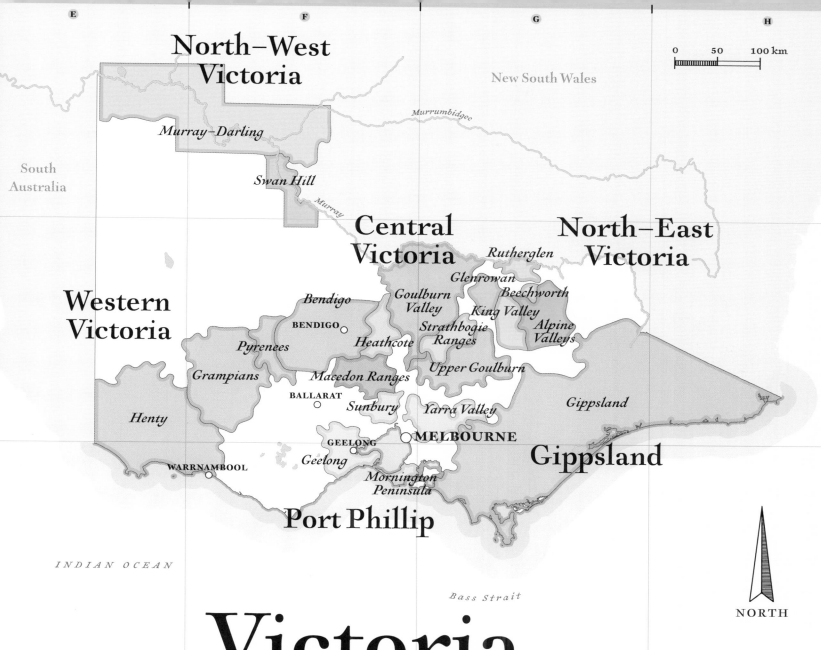

Victoria

This is one of the most surprising regions in the world in terms of the diversity of its production, which ranges from pinot noir to syrah (shiraz), and sparkling to dessert wines.

Historically the showcase of Australian wines, this region lost ground from 1875 due to the phylloxera plague, which led to the removal of vines under government order. The region has the same number of producers as South Australia but produces three times less wine, which indicates that the vineyards here are smaller, family-run concerns.

Hectares planted

23,000

Proportion of red/white grapes

52% 48%

5 appellations to start with

Heathcote
Rutherglen
Geelong
Pyrenees
Yarra Valley

Main varieties

- Syrah,* Cabernet Sauvignon, Pinot noir
- Chardonnay, Riesling

* locally called Shiraz

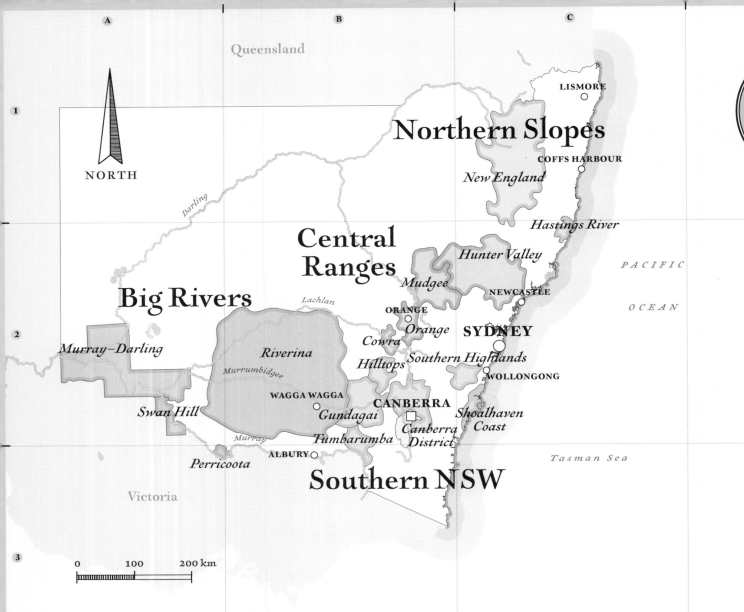

Queensland

NORTH

Northern Slopes

Darling

LISMORE

COFFS HARBOUR

New England

Hastings River

Central Ranges

Lachlan

Hunter Valley

Big Rivers

Mudgee

NEWCASTLE

PACIFIC

OCEAN

ORANGE

Murray–Darling

Riverina

Orange

SYDNEY

Murrumbidgee

Cowra

Hilltops

Southern Highlands

WAGGA WAGGA

CANBERRA

WOLLONGONG

Swan Hill

Murray

Gundagai

Canberra District

Shoalhaven Coast

Tumbarumba

Tasman Sea

ALBURY

Perricoota

Southern NSW

Victoria

0   100   200 km

New South Wales

Larger than France, this region is home to a great diversity of soils
and climates, and accounts for 30 per cent of national production.

Hectares planted

39,000

Proportion of red/white grapes

45%   55%

Long restricted to mainly just
producing syrah (shiraz) and chardonnay,
this region now welcomes new wine-growers
who are willing to take on the challenges of the
soil and gamble on interesting varieties such as
verdelho and tempranillo. North of Sydney, the
Hunter Valley produces some of the best semillons
in the world. Winemakers here can rely on the
international drawcard that is Sydney to develop
their wine tourism.

Main varieties

⬤ Syrah,* Cabernet Sauvignon

⬤ Chardonnay, Semillon

* locally called Shiraz

Western Australia

The isolation of Perth has hampered the exportation of wines from this region, meaning they are largely destined for local consumption.

Whue this is the land of syrah (shiraz), Margaret River has built its reputation on another king: cabernet sauvignon. This variety is planted the world over, but seems to have found a new terroir of choice. In the westernmost part of the country, the gravelly soils are reminiscent of the left bank of France's Bordeaux region. The gluttony of the region's birds has forced wine-growers to protect their vines with huge nets at fruiting time, to avoid seeing their precious harvest fly away.

- ● Cabernet Sauvignon, Syrah*
- ● Chardonnay, Sauvignon Blanc

* locally called Shiraz

Hectares planted
9000

Proportion of red/white grapes

44% **56%**

Greater Perth

Swan District

PERTH
Perth Hills
ROCKINGHAM
MANDURAH
Peel
BUNBURY
Geographe
Margaret River   Blackwood Valley

South–West Australia

Manjimup
Pemberton   Great Southern
Cape Leeuwin
ALBANY

OCÉAN INDIEN

NORTH

0   50   100 km

Tasmania

The island's island enjoys a cooler climate than the rest of the country.

Originally notable for its production of sparkling wines, Tasmania has shown great promise with non-sparkling types. The young wine-growers who come to this far corner of the globe express the uniqueness of the island state through surprising pinot noirs, chardonnays and pinot gris.

- ● Pinot noir, Cabernet Sauvignon
- ● Chardonnay, Sauvignon Blanc, Pinot Gris

Hectares planted
1538

Proportion of red/white grapes

48% **52%**

Bass Strait
Furneaux Group

North

Pipers River
DEVONPORT   North East
North West   **LAUNCESTON**
Tamar Valley

East Coast

East Coast

Coal River Valley
Derwent Valley   **HOBART**
South   **PORT ARTHUR**
Huon Valley   Tasman

INDIAN OCEAN

Sea

NORTH

0   50   100 km

Who makes wine today?

The 20th century is one of wine appellations. Producers understand that quality comes from an identifiable terroir. Regions are meticulously defined and mapped. Some unexpected producers, such as Sweden and Vietnam, are knocking on the door of the great wine family, but at the moment it's still difficult to speak of true wine-growing traditions in those countries where production remains small.

Basque and Italian immigrants

1760　　　　　1800　　　　　1840　　　　　1880

New Zealand

Canada

Brazil

Japan

Uruguay

Russia

Madagascar

1855
Official classification of wines from the Bordeaux region

1863
First appearance of phylloxera in the French department of Gard

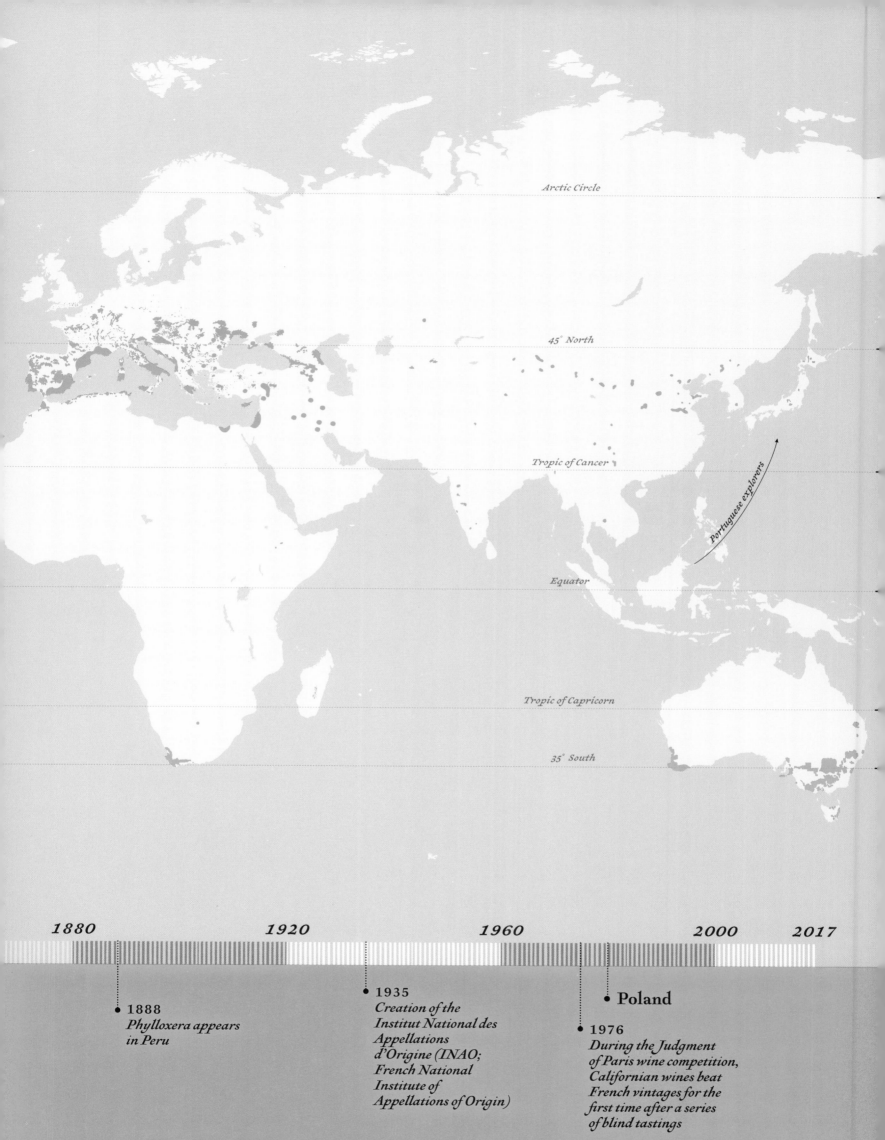

Arctic Circle

45° North

Tropic of Cancer

Equator

Portuguese explorers

Tropic of Capricorn

35° South

1880   *1920*   *1960*   *2000*   *2017*

1935
*Creation of the
Institut National des
Appellations
d'Origine (INAO;
French National
Institute of
Appellations of Origin)*

Poland

1888
*Phylloxera appears
in Peru*

1976
*During the Judgment
of Paris wine competition,
Californian wines beat
French vintages for the
first time after a series
of blind tastings*

Ethiopia

The winemakers of Ethiopia must dig deep pits around their grapevines to protect the grapes from pythons and hippopotamuses. Who could claim to do more than that?

Then

Vines discovered near convents seem to indicate that the introduction of grapevines in Ethiopia is linked to the arrival of Christianity as the official religion in the fourth century. Mussolini invaded the country in 1935 and the occupation lasted for six years. The Italians planted vines without really giving any structure to the wine industry. The local wine, called Tej, is fermented with the leaves of the gesho, a plant similar to hops.

Now

Near the Equator, the vines adopt an extremely short vegetative cycle and allow two harvests per year. This phenomenon swells the volumes of wine, but prevents the vines from entering dormancy and thus from gaining in quality. Since the arrival of a French merchant in 2007, Ethiopia plans on closing the gap to the continent's leading wine producer: South Africa. With only two companies sharing one vineyard, the road ahead is still a long one.

Global ranking
(by production)

46

Annual production
(in millions of litres)

7

Harvest period

**November
December
June
July**

Period when wine-growing appeared

4th
century

Influences

Christianity

Main varieties

- ● Sangiovese, Merlot, Syrah
- ● Chenin Blanc, Chardonnay, Sauvignon Blanc

NORTH

0   150   300 km

Madagascar

In a country with a tropical climate, subjected to monsoons from December to April, wine-growing is as surprising as it is interesting.

Global ranking
(by production)

45

Hectares planted

2700

Annual production
(in millions of litres)

8

Harvest period

January to March

Priod when wine-growing appeared

19th century

Influences

French

Then

Views differ as to when the first grapevines arrived on the island. Some writings attribute them to the Arabs who were among the first to explore the coasts, others to Protestant missionaries already installed in Cape Town in South Africa. Whoever it was, we have French botanists and explorers to thank for the first attempts at wine-growing in the 19th century. In 1971, the Malagasy Republic and the Swiss Agency for Development and Cooperation signed an agreement supporting the development of wine-growing on the island. A nationalised company called Lazan'i Betsileo (Pride of Betsileo) encouraged farmers to plant grapevines, with the undertaking to buy their harvests for making wine.

Now

On this island more than twice the size of the United Kingdom, the vines are grown on terraces, using the same methods as for the widespread rice paddies. The altitude of the wine-growing area, located between 500 and 1500 metres above sea level, lifts it from the tropical climate of the plains,

> **On this island, more than twice the size of the United Kingdom, the vines are grown on terraces.**

which is too heavy to support grapes. These unfavourable climatic conditions restrict the possibility of expansion. The country produces no glass, which necessitates the importation of bottles, complicates the winemakers' job and raises the price of production. Despite all these obstacles, production has risen constantly for the past 50 years.

Main varieties

- ● Villard Noir, Chambourcin, Varousset, Petit Bouchet
- ● Couderc 13, Villard Blanc

Hautes Terres du Sud

Cap d'Ambre

ANTSIRANANA

AMBANJA

Mahavary

SAMBAVA

ANDAPA

ANTSOHIHY

Mozambique Channel

MAHAJANGA

Sofia

MAROANTSETRA

MAROVOAY

Mahajamba

MANANARA

Lake Kinkony

SOANIERANA-IVONGO

Lake Alaotra

VOHIBINANY

AMPARAFARAVOLA

TOAMASINA

TSIROANOMANDIDY

ANTANANARIVO □

MIANDRIVAZO

ANTANIFOTSY

MAHANORO

Tsiribihina

ANTSIRABE

MORONDAVA

NOSY VARIKA

AMBATOFINANDRAHANA

MANANJARY

FIANARANTSOA

Mangoki

AMBALAVAO

IKONGO

Lake Ihotry

NORTH

TOLIARA

Onilahy

VANGAINDRANO

INDIAN

BETIOKY

OCEAN

Mandrare

AMPANIHY

TÔLANARO

AMBOVOMBE

Cape Sainte-Marie

0   100   200   300 km

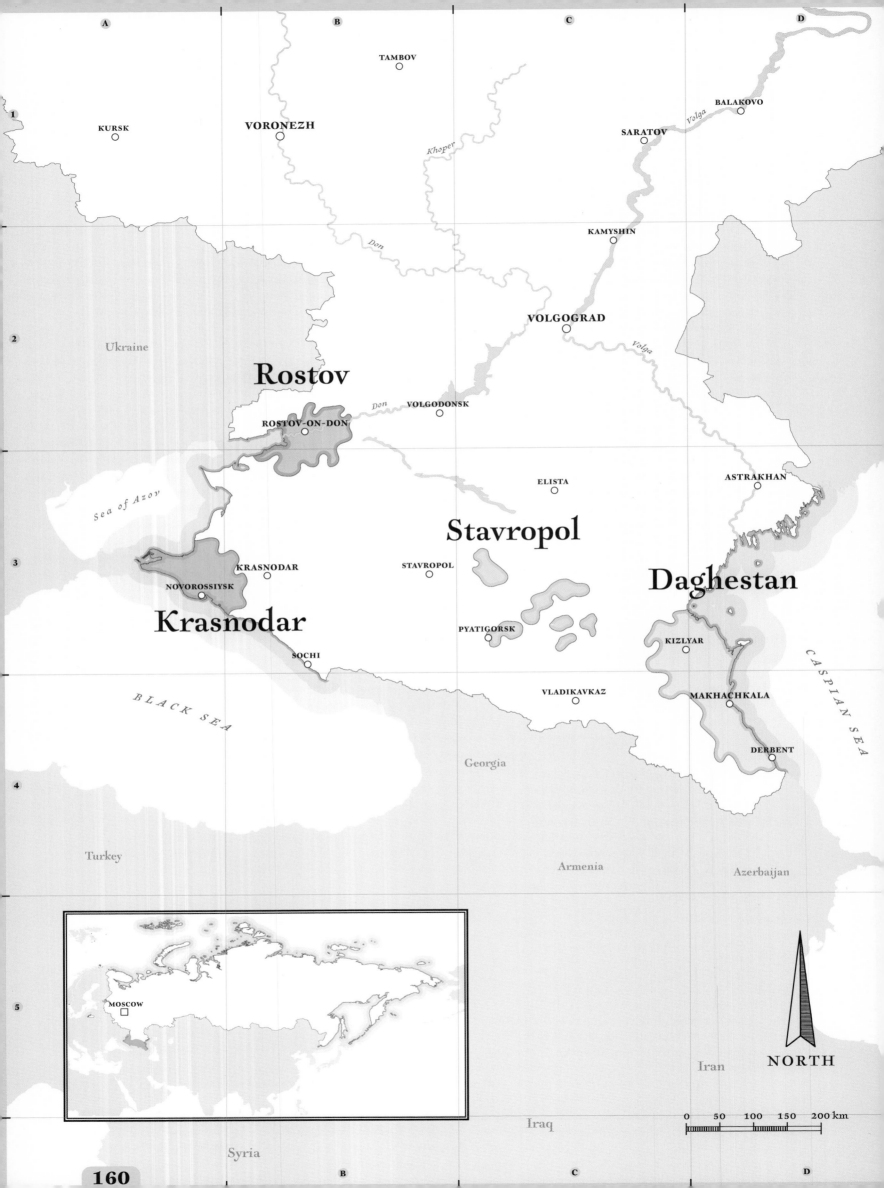

A   B   C   D

1

KURSK ○

TAMBOV ○

VORONEZH ○

Khoper

SARATOV ○   *Volga*   BALAKOVO ○

KAMYSHIN ○

Don

VOLGOGRAD ○   *Volga*

2   Ukraine

Rostov

Don   VOLGODONSK ○

ROSTOV-ON-DON ○

ELISTA ○

ASTRAKHAN ○

Sea of Azov

Stavropol

3

KRASNODAR ○

STAVROPOL ○

Daghestan

NOVOROSSIYSK ○

Krasnodar

PYATIGORSK ○

KIZLYAR ○

SOCHI ○

CASPIAN SEA

VLADIKAVKAZ ○

MAKHACHKALA ○

BLACK SEA

Georgia

DERBENT ○

4

Turkey

Armenia   Azerbaijan

MOSCOW □

5

Iran

NORTH

Iraq

0   50   100   150   200 km

Syria

Kazakhstan

Russia

Celebrated by the tsars before being snubbed by the Soviet regime, the Russian wine industry clings on in a country where they consume twice as much vodka as wine.

Then

Grapevines have been cultivated in the Caucasus region for millennia, but the true birth of the wine industry dates back to the 19th century and to Prince Lev Golitsyn, creator of 'Russian champagne'. To combat alcoholism, the USSR encouraged wine production and consumption – after all, it's better to drink a glass of red than of vodka, isn't it? In 1956, the authorities again tried to reduce alcohol consumption by increasing the national price of all alcohol. Good news: the consumption of wine has tripled in ten years. The bad news is that vodka intake hasn't changed … Good old Russians!

> **To combat alcoholism, the USSR encouraged wine production and consumption.**

Now

Apart from in the 2000s, the great wine estates have used the services of winemaking experts from Bordeaux or Champagne to move forward. How does a country with three times fewer vines than Portugal get to be the 13th biggest wine producer in the world? By importing grapes! A large proportion of their wine, made using grapes from South America, is still of mediocre quality.

Turkmenistan

Main varieties

- ● Cabernet Sauvignon, Merlot
- ● Rkatsiteli, Aligoté, Muscat, Riesling

Global ranking (by production)

12

Hectares planted

63,000

Annual production (in millions of litres)

480

Proportion of red/white grapes

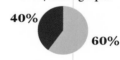

40% **60%**

Harvest period

September October

Period when wine-growing appeared

19th century

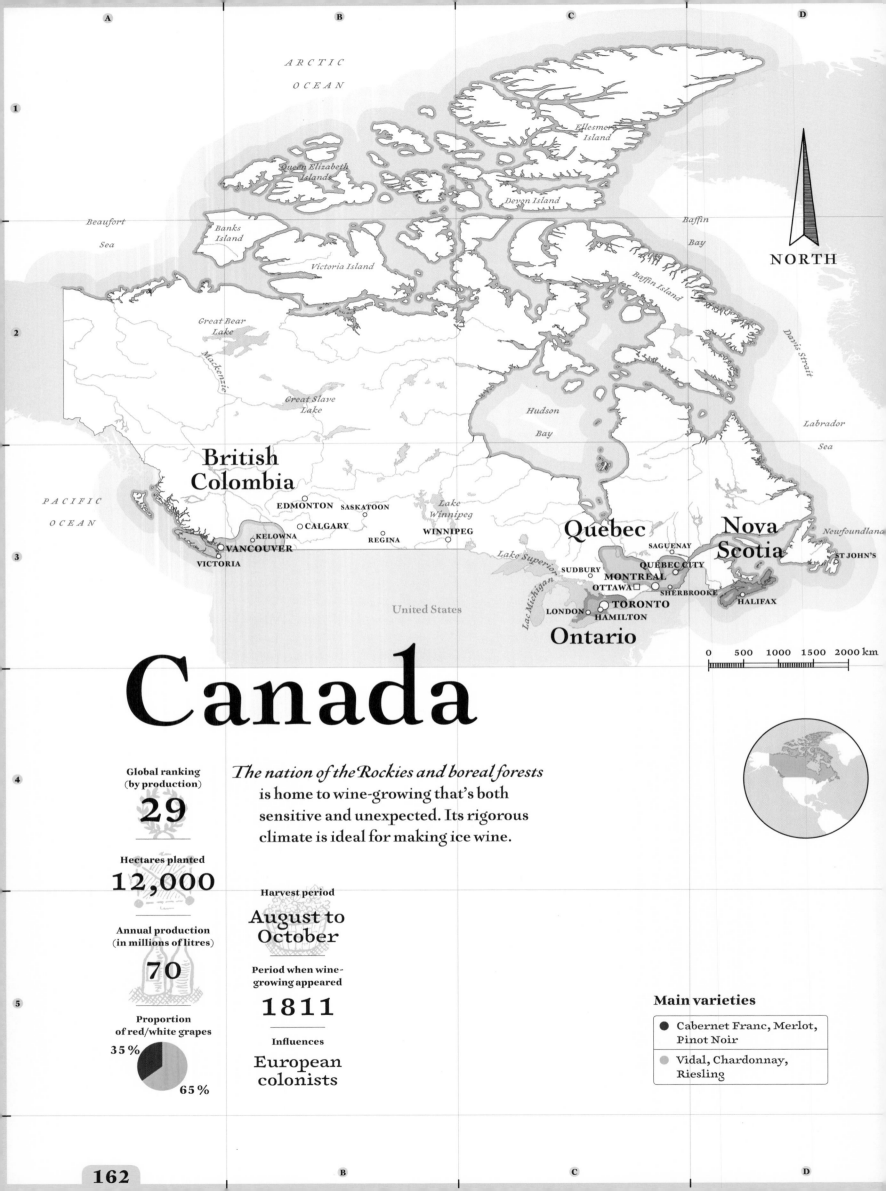

Canada

The nation of the Rockies and boreal forests is home to wine-growing that's both sensitive and unexpected. Its rigorous climate is ideal for making ice wine.

Global ranking
(by production)
29

Hectares planted
12,000

Annual production
(in millions of litres)
70

Proportion
of red/white grapes
35%
65%

Harvest period
August to October

Period when wine-growing appeared
1811

Influences
European colonists

Main varieties

- Cabernet Franc, Merlot, Pinot Noir
- Vidal, Chardonnay, Riesling

Then

Before Christopher Columbus sailed to America, Icelandic Vikings, in the year 1000, reached the lands of modern-day Canada via the icy waters of Greenland. History tells us that they called the area 'Vinland' due to the abundance of wild grapevines. Johann Schiller is considered the father of Canadian wine-growing. This former soldier and cobbler, originally from Germany, succeeded in taming the wild vines in the suburbs of Toronto in 1881. His wine was intended only for sale to his neighbours. The Canadian climate, notable for winters as long as they are cold and its hot summers, forced winemakers to the Great Lakes, which temper the strong heat and postpone frosts. In 1987, the free trade agreement signed with the United States encouraged winemakers to grow European varieties and propelled Canadian wines onto the world stage.

Now

Canadians have always preferred beer to wine, which could explain the relative late appearance of the local wine industry. The provinces of Ontario and British Colombia account for 80 per cent of national production. Canada is one of the rare countries where you can still produce 'ice wine'. This practice consists of leaving the grapes to freeze on the vine to prolong their maturation and thus increase their sugar concentration in order to produce a sweet wine. The technique comes from Austria and Germany, but Canada has recently become the world's main producer of ice wine.

> **Canada has recently become the world's main producer of ice wine.**

Ontario

Nova Scotia

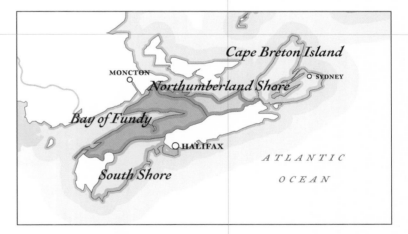

Quebec

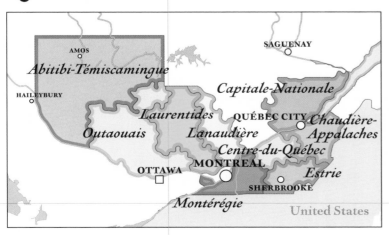

British Colombia

New Zealand

In 20 years, the nation of the All Blacks has announced itself as the jewel of the New World and an expert in sauvignon blanc, which takes up more than 60 per cent of its wine area.

Global ranking (by production)

14

Hectares planted

36,000

Annual production (in millions of litres)

313

Proportion of red/white grapes

20%

80%

Harvest period

February March

Period when wine-growing appeared

1820

Influences

British

Then

Lying at the edge of the world, New Zealand was one of the last territories on the planet to be discovered by humans when it was first occupied by the Maoris in 1050. The island was colonised by Europeans in the early 19th century. The history of wine on the islands is as short as that of colonisation. The Frenchman François Jean-Baptiste Pompallier and the Englishman James Busby (yes, the same one who developed wine-growing in Australia) were the pioneers of wine-growing and quickly passed on their expertise to the country's farmers during the 19th century. It took until after the Second World War to see a major planting campaign. After China, it's the fastest growing wine industry in history. Very quickly, New Zealand wines have carried home accolades from all corners of the globe and wine has become, after rugby, the pride of the nation.

The island's wine industry is young but growing quickly.

Now

To understand the wine industry, we must distinguish between the country's two main islands. The North Island, closer to the Equator, offers beautifully ripe cabernet sauvignon, merlot and

New Zealand wines are distinctive for their freshness and precision.

chardonnay. The South Island is the promised land for the great sauvignon blanc and pinot noir. In fact, thanks to the Southern Alps, a mountain chain running the length of the island (not to be confused with the European range), the east coast is sheltered from humid westerly winds. This explains why the vineyards are the clustered in the east. Filtered by these peaks, the cool oceanic breezes make New Zealand wines distinctive for their freshness and precision. The variations in soil and climate, in combination with the diverse inspirations of winemakers, makes possible a large palette of varieties. Marlborough perfects sauvignon blanc, Hawke's Bay syrah (shiraz), Central Otago pinot noir, Waipara Valley riesling and Gisborne chardonnay. Although the country owes its wine reputation to the great wineries that pushed open the doors to international markets, the industry is still composed of myriad small family producers who are always perfecting their knowledge of vines.

Main varieties

●	Pinot Noir, Merlot, Syrah
●	Sauvignon Blanc, Pinot Gris, Chardonnay, Riesling

SOUTH

PACIFIC

OCEAN

Northland

WHANGAREI

Auckland

Matakana   *Waiheke Island*

AUCKLAND

MANUKAU

Bay of Plenty

NORTH ISLAND

HAMILTON   TAURANGA

ROTORUA

Waikato

TAUPO

Gisborne

Lake Taupo   *Hillsides*   *Manutuke*

NEW PLYMOUTH   *Coastal Areas*

Tasman Sea

HAWERA   *Alluvial Plains*   NAPIER   *Hawke's*

WANGANUI   HASTINGS   *Bay*

Hawke's Bay

PALMERSTON NORTH

Nelson

Gladstone

Martinborough

NELSON   LOWER HUTT

Marlborough

Wairau Valley   WELLINGTON

Awatere Valley   # Wairarapa

Clarence   *Cook Strait*

Canterbury

Waipara Valley

Canterbury Plains

SOUTH ISLAND

Rakaia

CHRISTCHURCH

ASHBURTON

Waitaki Valley

Lake Wanaka   TIMARU

Waitaki

QUEENSTOWN   *Wanaka*   OAMARU

Lake Te Anau   *Gibbston*   *Bendigo*

Bannockburn

Alexandra   # Central Otago

GORE   DUNEDIN

INVERCARGILL

Foveaux Strait

Stewart Island

5 appellations to start with

Marlborough
Central Otago
Hawke's Bay
Gisborne
Waipara Valley

NORTH

0   100   200   300 km

Uruguay

Lying at the same latitudes as Argentina, Chile, South Africa and Australia, Uruguay has positioned itself as the formidable outsider of the New World.

Then

The first grapevines arrived with the Spanish Conquistadors in the 16th century, but the true birth of the wine industry was marked by

From the Pyrenees to Uruguay, tannat discovered its second childhood.

the arrival of Basque immigrants in 1870. And in their luggage, the future visiting card of Uruguayan wines: tannat. Who would have believed that this red variety, originally from the Pyrenees and grown solely for making blended wines, would earn its spurs on the other side of the Atlantic? Since the 1990s, the wine industry has taken giant leaps forward while concentrating on quality.

Now

Between very limited production and compatriots who love the finer things of life, few bottles manage to cross the border. The proof: the country exports only 5 per cent of the wine it produces. Of the 18 departments in the country, 15 produce wine, but that of Canelones accounts for 60 per cent of national production. Like most New World producers, Uruguay found the 'signature variety' for its reds: tannat. This allows it to make unique wines without entering into competition with the standards of the great winemaking countries. It only remains to find a white wine

The country exports only 5 per cent of the wine it produces.

to seduce every taste. Chardonnay? Too classic, and cultivated the world over. Torrontés? Already taken by the Argentinians. Why not albariño? Recent studies have shown that this white variety, originally from north-western Spain, does very well in the south of the country. Watch this space ...

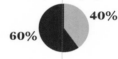

5 appellations to start with

Canelones
Montevideo
Colonia
Maldonado
San José

Main varieties

●	Tannat, Cabernet Sauvignon, Merlot
●	Ugni Blanc, Chardonnay, Sauvignon Blanc

Global ranking (by production)
26

Hectares planted
9000

Annual production (in millions of litres)
100

Proportion of red/white grapes
40%
60%

Harvest period
February March

Period when wine-growing appeared
1870

Influences
Spanish

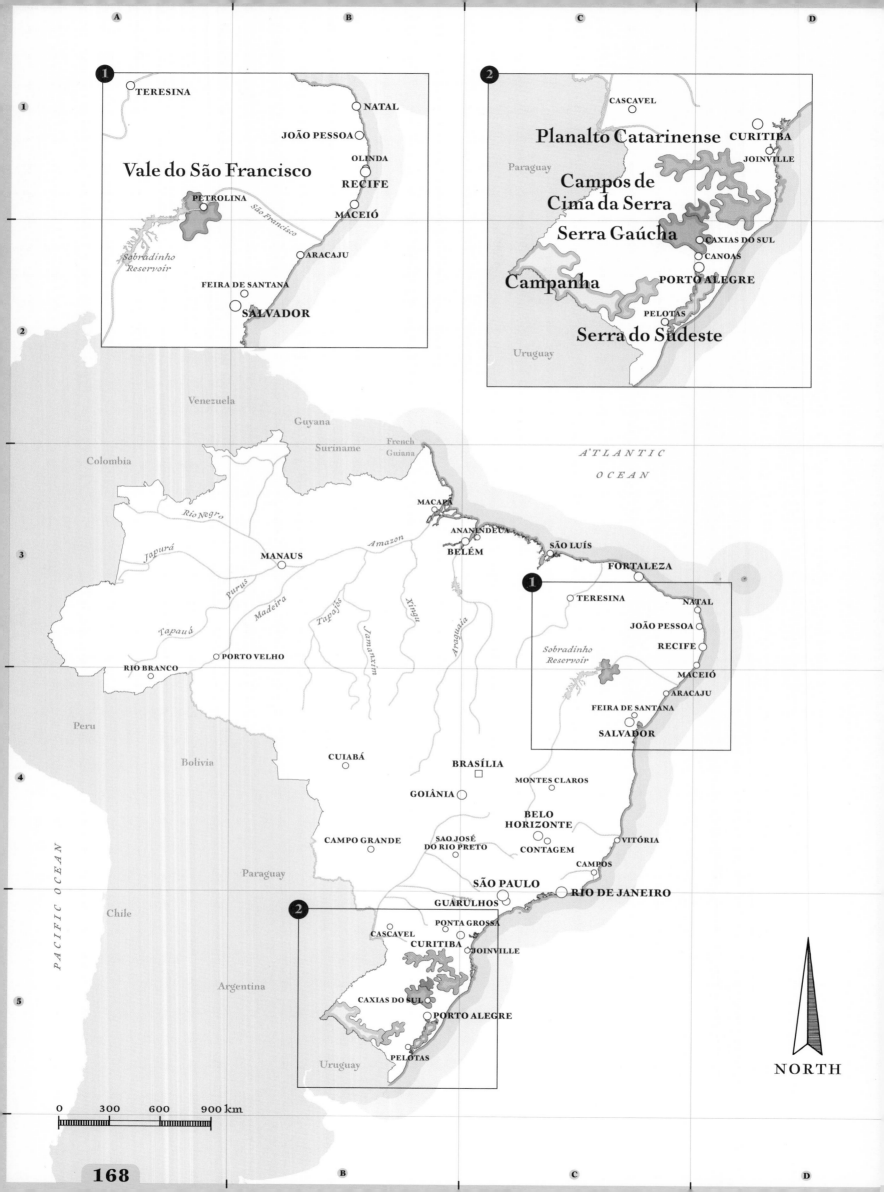

Inset 1 — Vale do São Francisco

TERESINA
NATAL
JOÃO PESSOA
OLINDA
RECIFE
PETROLINA
São Francisco
MACEIÓ
Sobradinho Reservoir
ARACAJU
FEIRA DE SANTANA
SALVADOR

Inset 2

CASCAVEL
Planalto Catarinense
CURITIBA
JOINVILLE
Paraguay
Campos de Cima da Serra
Serra Gaúcha
CAXIAS DO SUL
CANOAS
PORTO ALEGRE
Campanha
PELOTAS
Uruguay
Serra do Sudeste

Main map

Venezuela
Guyana
Suriname
French Guiana
Colombia
ATLANTIC OCEAN
MACAPÁ
ANANINDEUA
BELÉM
SÃO LUÍS
Rio Negro
Japurá
FORTALEZA
Amazon
MANAUS
Purus
Madeira
Tapauá
Tapajós
Jamanxim
Xingu
Araguaia
TERESINA
NATAL
JOÃO PESSOA
RECIFE
Sobradinho Reservoir
MACEIÓ
ARACAJU
FEIRA DE SANTANA
SALVADOR
PORTO VELHO
RIO BRANCO
Peru
Bolivia
CUIABÁ
BRASÍLIA
MONTES CLAROS
GOIÂNIA
BELO HORIZONTE
CONTAGEM
VITÓRIA
CAMPO GRANDE
SAO JOSÉ DO RIO PRETO
CAMPOS
Paraguay
SÃO PAULO
RIO DE JANEIRO
GUARULHOS
PONTA GROSSA
CASCAVEL
CURITIBA
JOINVILLE
Chile
Argentina
CAXIAS DO SUL
PORTO ALEGRE
Uruguay
PELOTAS
PACIFIC OCEAN

0   300   600   900 km

NORTH

Indicação de Procedência
Espumante
Vale dos Vinhedos
Saúde!

Brazil

South America's third-largest wine producer is also its most recent. It's the only country in the world where vineyards are grown in two radically different climates: tropical in the north and continental in the south.

Global ranking (by production)

22

Hectares planted

85,000

Annual production (in millions of litres)

140

Proportion of red/white grapes

40%

60%

Harvest period

February March

Period when wine-growing appeared

1875

Influences

Italian immigrants

Then

It's with the American variety isabella that the Brazilian wine industry developed at the end of the 19th century. This variety, better known for its yield than its refinement, ceded its place to European varieties with the arrival of Italian immigrants in the 19th century. These families settled in the Vale dos Vinhedos around Porto Alegre, which they covered with grapevines and buildings that brought to mind their beloved Italy. At the beginning of the 20th century,

Brazil is the best producer of sparkling wines in the southern hemisphere.

the region suffered through months of drought. A chapel absolutely had to be built but there wasn't enough water to make the cement. Without a moment's hesitation, the inhabitants decided to replace the water with wine. We know that religion is intimately linked with wine, and the Brazilians built the solid proof of this.

Now

If you order a Brazilian wine in Rio de Janeiro, you risk being greeted with surprise: very few Brazilians are aware of the existence of their own wine industry. The size of the country and the absurdity of each state taxing the others prevents national distribution of wine. It's more economical, for example, to obtain a Brazilian wine in Miami than in Brasilia. The Serra Gaúcha region accounts for 60 per cent of national production, and lays claim to virtually all the quality wines.

Brazil exports less than 1 per cent of the wines it produces, but it's always remarkable for its bubbles, which make it the best producer of sparkling wines in the southern hemisphere. The potential for evolution is significant, given only 10 per cent of the possible wine-growing area is planted with *Vitis vinifera*. In the north of the country, the very recently established wine area of Vale do São Francisco is located in a desert region with a tropical climate. There are no seasons, but the 300 days of sunshine and a customised irrigation system allow two harvests per year.

Main varieties

●	Isabella, Cabernet Sauvignon, Merlot
●	Chardonnay, Niagara, Muscat

Japan

Although wine is now a growing trend among the wealthiest classes, it's still low-profile in the land of sake.

Global ranking (by production)

27

Hectares planted

18,000

Annual production (in millions of litres)

86

Proportion of red/white grapes

35%

65%

Harvest period

September

Period when wine-growing appeared

1875

Influences

Portuguese

Then

Arriving via the Silk Road, grapevines were grown by Buddhists without making wine. Great navigators, the Portuguese missionnaries reached the islands at the end of the 16th century and offered their wines to Emperor Go-Nara. Kawakami Zenbei (1868–1944) was the father of modern Japanese wine-growing and of cross-breeding, giving rise to the main local red variety: muscat bailey A.

Koshu, a grape that seems to have Chinese origins, has become the emblem of Japanese white wines. In the 1970s, liberalisation of alcohol importation allowed the Japanese to discover the wines of the world, before they even tasted their nation's own wines.

> **The Buddhists grew grapevines without making wine.**

Main varieties

- ● Merlot, <u>Muscat Bailey A</u>, Cabernet Sauvignon
- ● <u>Koshu</u>, Müller-Thurgau, Chardonnay

<u>Endemic variety</u>

Now

The wine-growing area is concentrated on the two main islands of the archipelago, and the best terroirs are found on the oceanic soils in the foothills of Mt Fuji, south-west of Tokyo. The market is monopolised by five companies that account for 80 per cent of national production, and the majority of the wine is made using grape must imported from South America. It's therefore important to distinguish between true 'Japanese wines' and 'wines fermented in Japan'. This is a difficult exercise, as the law allows 'Japanese wine' to appear on the label as long as 10 per cent of the grapes were grown locally. The country hasn't succumbed to the fashion for European varieties, which make up less than 5 per cent of the grapes grown, but it does produce interesting bottles. Japan has no laws limiting alcohol advertising, so it's common to see advertisements for wine on television.

Oki Islands

Korea Strait

Tsushima Island

OKAYA

HIROSHIMA

Shikoku

FUKUOKA

MATSUYAMA

KUMAMOTO

NAGASAKI

Russia

Soya Strait

Sea of Okhotsk

Rishiri Island

ASAHIKAWA

Sorachi

Furano

Hokkaido

Yoichi

SAPPORO

Tokachi

Okushiri
Island

Hokkaido

HAKODATE

Tsugaru Strait

PACIFIC

AOMORI

Sea of Japan

OCEAN

AKITA

MORIOKA

Yamagata

Mogami Gawa

Sado
Island

YAMAGATA

SENDAI

NIIGATA

FUKUSHIMA

Nagano

IWAKI

TOYAMA

KANAZAWA

NAGANO

Gawa Valley

Alps Valley

UTSUNOMIYA

Gahara Valley

Yamanashi

TOKYO

KAWASAKI

NAGOYA

YOKOHAMA

KYOTO

TOYOTA

KOBE

YOKKAICHI

OKAZAKI

SHIZUOKA

OSAKA

SAKAI

HAMAMATSU

WAKAYAMA

PACIFIC

OCEAN

NORTH

0   100   200   300 km

Poland

Better known for making vodka, this country is witnessing the birth of a wine industry as modest as it is determined.

Then

Writings and archaeological digs attest to modest wine-growing activity at the time Christianity arrived in the tenth century. The Cistercian and Benedictine monks controlled the entire chain, from production to consumption. The true birth of the Polish wine industry is, however, much more contemporary. Since the fall of the Berlin Wall, becoming open to the world and Poland's entry into the bosom of the European Union in 2004, wine-growing has been reborn. In 2008, the Polish parliament passed a law recognising the winemaking profession and allowing each grape producer to make and sell their own wine.

> **Wine-growing has been reborn since the country entered the European Union in 2004.**

Now

The majority of the Polish wine-growing area is located in the foothills of the Carpathians, a mountain range in Central Europe. Roman Mysliwiec is the father of modern Polish wine-growing. To endure the rigorous winters and best capture the sunlight, the vines are trained on high trellises held up to 1.5 metres from the ground by concrete posts. In a country where people prefer beer and vodka, annual wine consumption remains the lowest in Europe, with 5.5 litres of wine consumed by each adult per year.

Global warming favouring the maturation of reds, along with improvements in buying power among the Polish population, are the two main factors that will influence the future of this young wine-growing country. It remains to be seen if wine production will be confined to supplying the local market, or if it will become a true quality product made specifically for export.

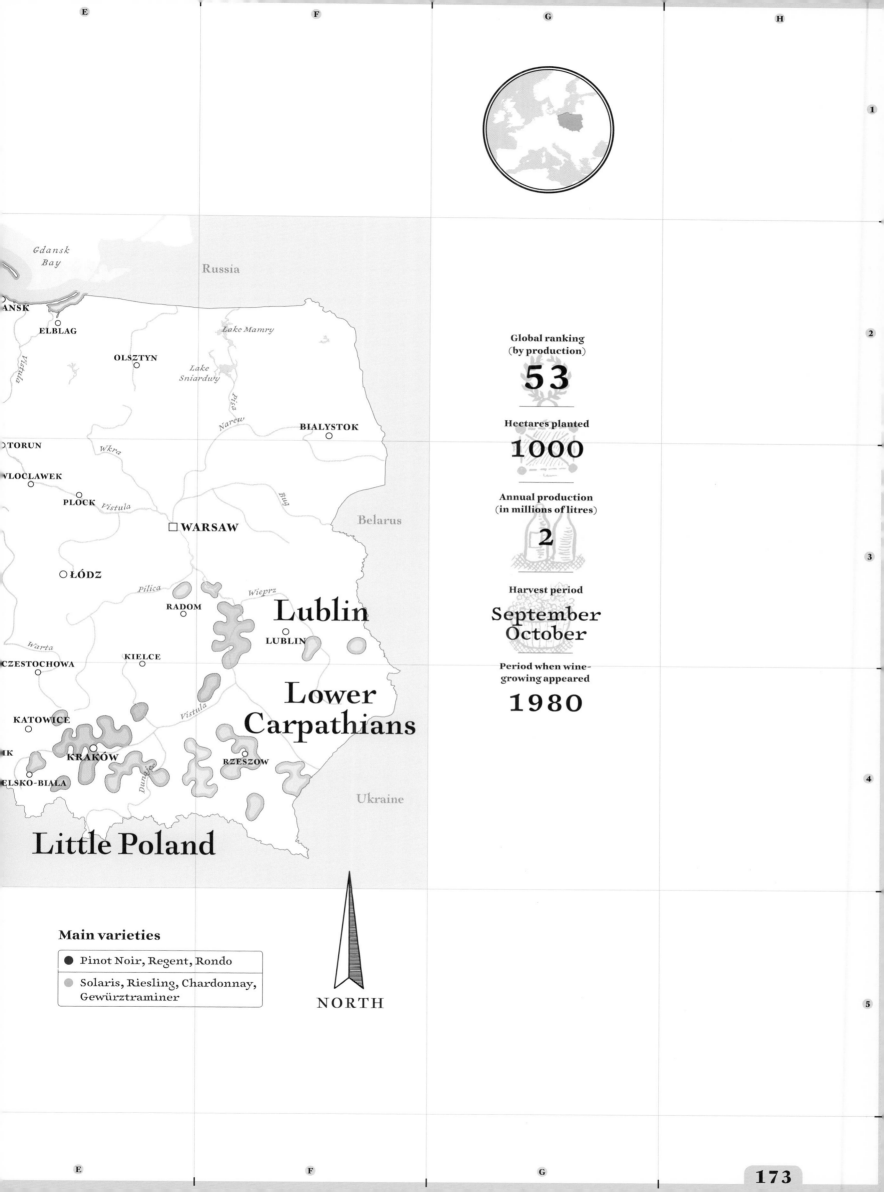

Russia

Gdansk
Bay

ANSK

ELBLAG

OLSZTYN

Lake Mamry

Lake
Sniardwy

Pisa

Narew

BIALYSTOK

TORUN

Wkra

WLOCLAWEK

PLOCK   Vistula

Bug

Belarus

☐ WARSAW

ŁÓDZ

Pilica

Wieprz

RADOM

Lublin

LUBLIN

Warta

KIELCE

CZESTOCHOWA

**Lower
Carpathians**

KATOWICE

Vistula

IK

KRAKÓW

Dunajec

RZESZOW

ELSKO-BIALA

Ukraine

Little Poland

Global ranking
(by production)

53

Hectares planted

1000

Annual production
(in millions of litres)

2

Harvest period

September
October

Period when wine-
growing appeared

1980

Main varieties

● Pinot Noir, Regent, Rondo
● Solaris, Riesling, Chardonnay,
  Gewürztraminer

The outsiders

They are young, beautiful, full of energy and ready to face the challenges of Mother Nature to produce wine. It's difficult to map these countries where there are no real wine-growing regions and where production is still small, but you can't make a wine atlas without saluting their perseverance.

Sweden

How do you produce wine in such a cold country? Thanks to the sun! Located close to the North Pole, Sweden has longer days than most European countries. During the summer, the grapes ripen by making the most of two hours more daily sunlight than in France. Wine production remains as small as it is fragile: each year, the extreme cold snaps of November threaten the country's dozen or so hectares of grapevines.

Paraguay

Paraguay tends to be forgotten when talking about South American wine-making. While its Argentine and Chilean neighbours are becoming the stars of the New World, Paraguay is barely managing to keep its head above water. It's the only wine producer on the continent without a coastline and that's removed from the famous Andes mountain range, the source of the greatest South American terroirs.

Zimbabwe

Like the majority of African countries, Zimbabwe owes the renaissance of its wine-growing industry to its independence, won in 1980. Confronted with a Sub-Saharan climate, the grapevines have climbed to altitudes of 1500 metres to enjoy more favourable conditions than those of the arid plains. Given the costs of production, some winemakers have no other choice than to package their wines in 1 litre cardboard cartons.

Thailand

Grapevines were introduced by the French in the 17th century, but it wasn't until after the Second World War that entrepreneurs invested in the region. Since 1995, a dozen or so winemakers have shared the 300 wine-growing hectares of this most dynamic South-East Asian country. Growing interest in wine among the middle classes offers a real opportunity for local producers.

Tahiti

Lost in the Pacific Ocean, this island belongs to French Polynesia, but shares only its nationality with Paris. Today, we could count only one active wine producer. This makes its product the wine produced the furthest from a continent. Imagine the adventure just to obtain the corks …

Kazakhstan

Little known but not small, the Kazakh wine area covers 13,000 hectares and is thus larger than that of Canada. The scorching summers force the producers to concentrate on dessert wines of varying sweetness.

South Korea

Koreans are still modest producers, but they're not small consumers – the country imports more than 31 million litres of foreign wine each year. The wine-growing area is in the neighbourhood of 20 hectares, about the size of a single Burgundian estate.

Share of worldwide production

Humans produce 800 litres of wine per second in more than 60 countries, but the trio at the top accounts for half this volume.

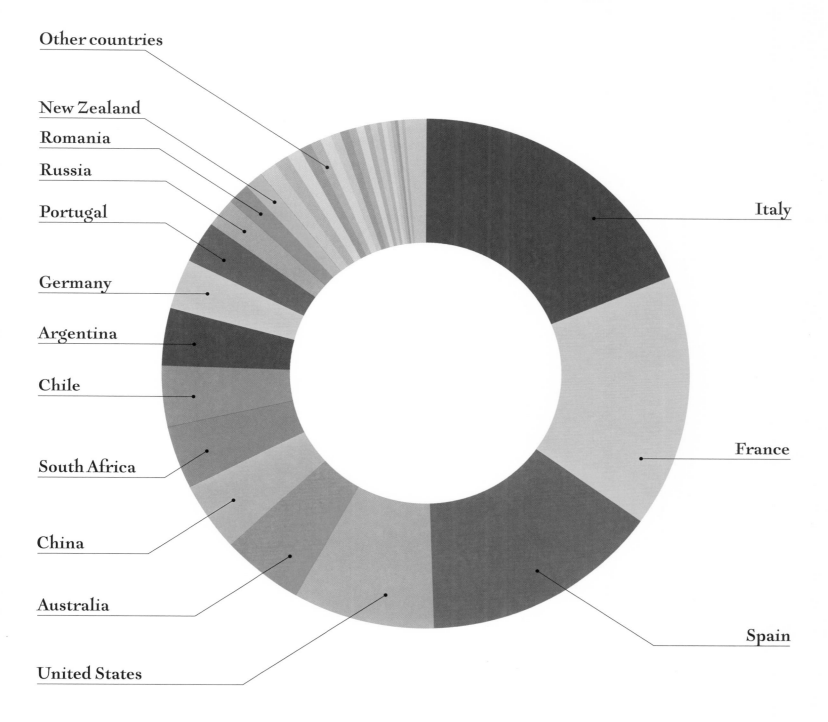

Other countries

New Zealand

Romania

Russia

Portugal

Germany

Argentina

Chile

South Africa

China

Australia

United States

Italy

France

Spain

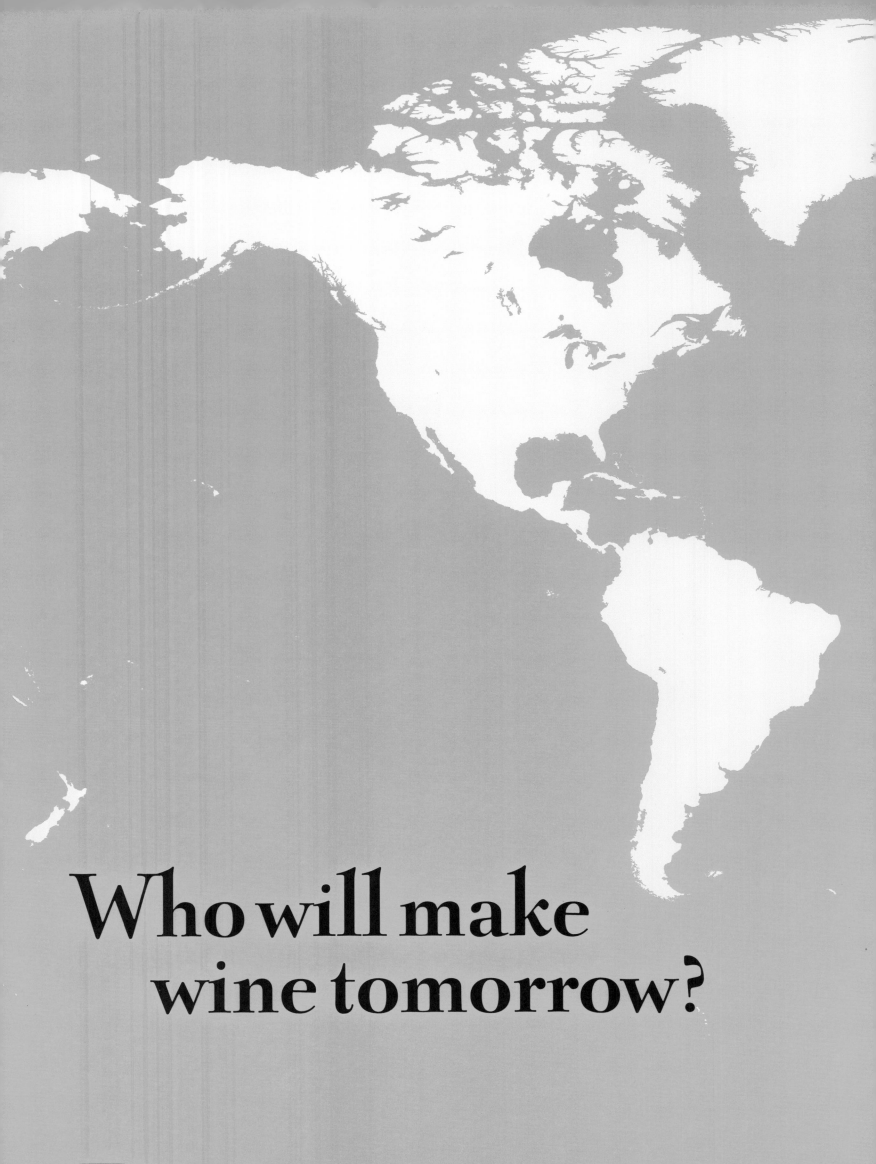

Who will make wine tomorrow?

The wine map never stops evolving, and global warming has become the worst nightmare of certain wine-growing regions. A recent study led by American climatologist Professor Gregory Jones shows that in 50 years, the geographic zone favourable for wine-growing will move 180 kilometres towards the poles. Will Icelanders be making rosé? Will Burgundians have to give up pinot noir for syrah (shiraz)? Watch this space ...

The world's grape varieties

As for all plants, each grape variety deserves a particular terroir to express itself fully. The same variety won't give the same wine in Tuscany as in Chile. The list of grapevine varieties numbers 6000, but about 20 account for virtually all wine production worldwide.

Merlot

267,000 hectares planted globally

More supple than cabernet sauvignon, with which it's often blended, merlot yields fruity reds and surprising rosés. Because it ripens early, it's one of the varieties that's most threatened by global warming.

1 France
2 Italy
3 United States
4 Spain
5 Romania

Pinot Noir

**86,000 hectares
planted globally**

*The freshest of the red varieties.
Despite its capricious and
delicate side, this king of
Burgundy has conquered
the New World's wine industry.*

1 France
2 United States
3 Moldova
4 Italy
5 New Zealand

Sauvignon Blanc

**110,000 hectares
planted globally**

*Not too hot, not too cold, this variety
prefers a temperate climate. Long
the showcase for Sancerre and Pessac-
Léognan, it has become the most
planted variety in New Zealand.
Has the student become the master?*

1 France
2 New Zealand
3 Chile
4 South Africa
5 Moldova

Chardonnay

**198,000 hectares
planted globally**

*When your CV says 'Dominant
white variety in Champagne and
Burgundy', the job is yours, of course!
Chardonnay's structure allows it to
stand up to time in barrels and offer
a remarkable cellaring potential.*

1 France
2 United States
3 Australia
4 Italy
5 Chile

Grenache

**184,000 hectares
planted globally**

*Simply saying its name makes
you want to taste it. It blossoms
under the Mediterranean sun
and gives gourmet wines.*

1 France
2 Spain
3 Italy
4 Algeria
5 United States

Cabernet Sauvignon

**290,000 hectares
planted globally**

*This is the most planted variety in
the world. From Bordeaux to Chile,
its tannins make it the quintessential
cellaring wine, and it often needs
a few years to express itself fully.*

1 France
2 Chile
3 United States
4 Australia
5 Spain

Riesling

**50,000 hectares
planted globally**

*A true mirror of the soil, it
expresses its terroir brilliantly.
In Alsace and in Germany, there
are surely as many Rieslings
as villages! It's notable for its
uprightness and minerality.*

1 Germany
2 United States
3 Australia
4 France
5 Ukraine

Syrah (Shiraz)

**185,000 hectares
planted globally**

Having acquired its patents of nobility in the Rhône Valley, where it gives fruity and powerful wines, syrah has become idolised by the Australians, who call it shiraz.

1 France
2 Australia
3 Spain
4 Argentina
5 South Africa

Chenin Blanc

**35,000 hectares
planted globally**

It's worth getting to know this smallest of the big varieties! Originally from the Loire, it has become a star in South Africa. Its natural acidity allows it to yield sparkling wines.

1 South Africa
2 France
3 United States
4 Argentina
5 Australia

Global ranking of varieties

BY HECTARES PLANTED

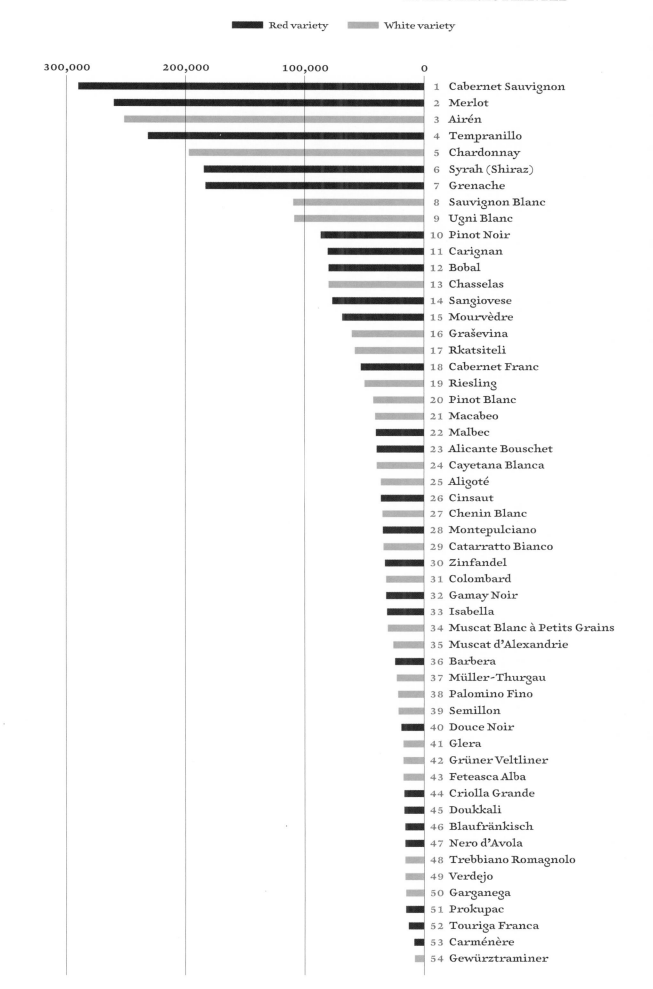

Red variety White variety

300,000 200,000 100,000 0

1 Cabernet Sauvignon
2 Merlot
3 Airén
4 Tempranillo
5 Chardonnay
6 Syrah (Shiraz)
7 Grenache
8 Sauvignon Blanc
9 Ugni Blanc
10 Pinot Noir
11 Carignan
12 Bobal
13 Chasselas
14 Sangiovese
15 Mourvèdre
16 Graševina
17 Rkatsiteli
18 Cabernet Franc
19 Riesling
20 Pinot Blanc
21 Macabeo
22 Malbec
23 Alicante Bouschet
24 Cayetana Blanca
25 Aligoté
26 Cinsaut
27 Chenin Blanc
28 Montepulciano
29 Catarratto Bianco
30 Zinfandel
31 Colombard
32 Gamay Noir
33 Isabella
34 Muscat Blanc à Petits Grains
35 Muscat d'Alexandrie
36 Barbera
37 Müller-Thurgau
38 Palomino Fino
39 Semillon
40 Douce Noir
41 Glera
42 Grüner Veltliner
43 Feteasca Alba
44 Criolla Grande
45 Doukkali
46 Blaufränkisch
47 Nero d'Avola
48 Trebbiano Romagnolo
49 Verdejo
50 Garganega
51 Prokupac
52 Touriga Franca
53 Carménère
54 Gewürztraminer

Flavours of the varieties

A variety – the very soul of a wine – takes its inspiration from the soil, the climate and the winemaker to offer a unique bouquet. Each variety does, however, provide distinctive flavours that allow it to be identified.

Legend

Variety adapted to a:

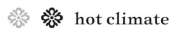 hot climate

cold climate

temperate climate

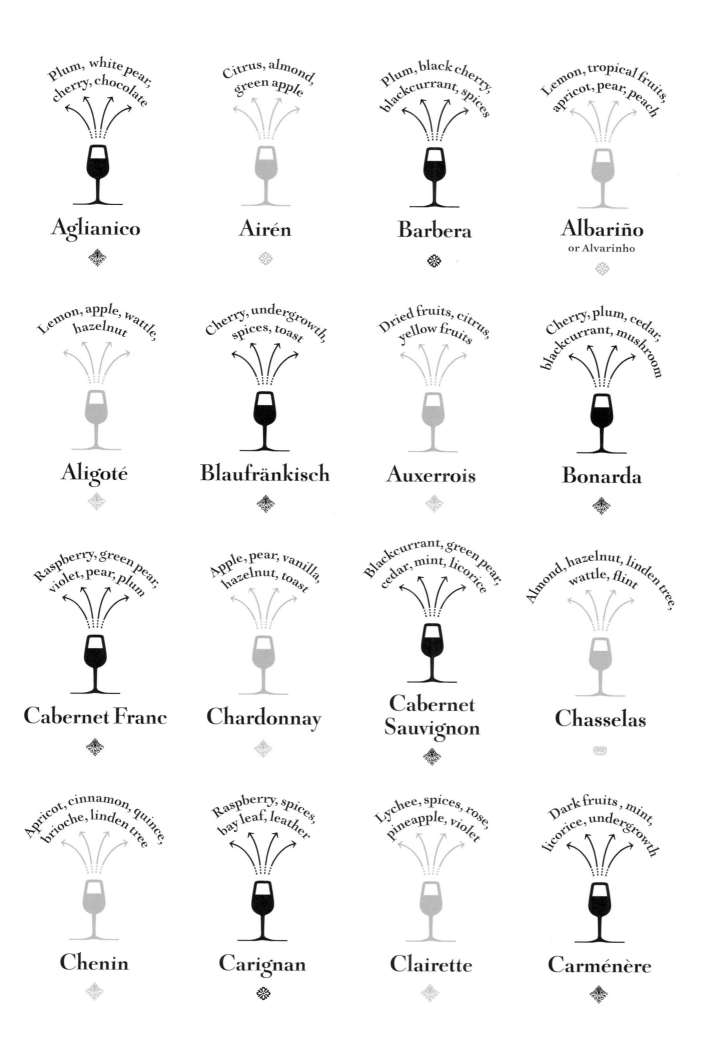

Plum, white pear,
cherry, chocolate

Aglianico

Citrus, almond,
green apple

Airén

Plum, black cherry,
blackcurrant, spices

Barbera

Lemon, tropical fruits,
apricot, pear, peach

Albariño
or Alvarinho

Lemon, apple, wattle,
hazelnut,

Aligoté

Cherry, undergrowth,
spices, toast,

Blaufränkisch

Dried fruits, citrus,
yellow fruits

Auxerrois

Cherry, plum, cedar,
blackcurrant, mushroom

Bonarda

Raspberry, green pear,
violet, pear, plum

Cabernet Franc

Apple, pear, vanilla,
hazelnut, toast

Chardonnay

Blackcurrant, green pear,
cedar, mint, licorice

**Cabernet
Sauvignon**

Almond, hazelnut, linden tree,
wattle, flint

Chasselas

Apricot, cinnamon, quince,
brioche, linden tree

Chenin

Raspberry, spices,
bay leaf, leather

Carignan

Lychee, spices, rose,
pineapple, violet

Clairette

Dark fruits, mint,
licorice, undergrowth

Carménère

Pomegranate, raspberry, rose, orange, peach,

Cinsault

Lime, grapefruit, white flowers, box tree

Colombard

Red fruits, spices, game, varnish,

Concord

Lemon, grapefruit, white flowers

Folle Blanche
or Gros Plant

Citrus, cinnamon, pear, spices,

Furmint

Cherry, green pear, cinnamon, almond

Corvina

Lychee, spices, rose, pineapple, violet

Gewürztraminer

Raspberry, violet, coffee, chocolate

Dolcetto

Strawberry, redcurrant, cherry, spices

Gamay

White flowers, apple, pear

Glera

Pear, licorice, herbes de Provence, bay leaf, black cherry,

Grenache

Peach, fennel, aniseed, dill

Grenache Blanc

Apple, pear, white pear, tropical fruits, flint

Grüner Veltliner

Cherry, cocoa, blackcurrant, leather, spices,

Malbec

Ripe fruits, aniseed, fennel

Macabeo

Cherry, cocoa, pomegranate, licorice, vanilla

Mencía

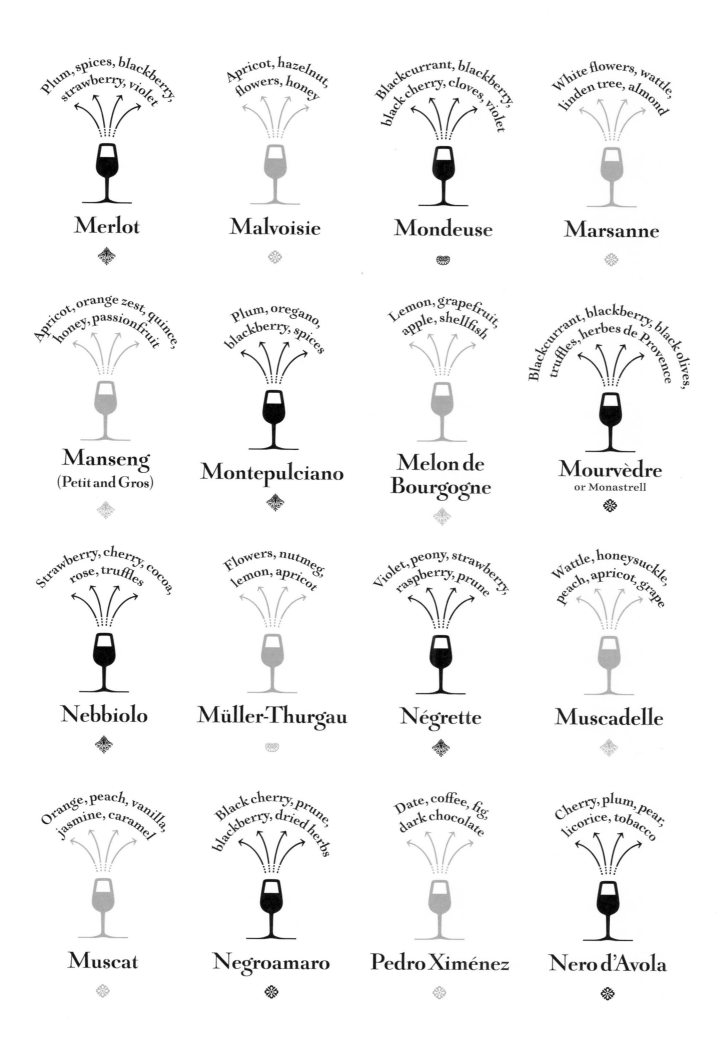

Plum, spices, blackberry, strawberry, violet,

Merlot

Apricot, hazelnut, flowers, honey,

Malvoisie

Blackcurrant, blackberry, black cherry, cloves, violet,

Mondeuse

White flowers, wattle, linden tree, almond

Marsanne

Apricot, orange zest, quince, honey, passionfruit,

Manseng
(Petit and Gros)

Plum, oregano, blackberry, spices

Montepulciano

Lemon, grapefruit, apple, shellfish

Melon de Bourgogne

Blackcurrant, blackberry, black olives, truffles, herbes de Provence,

Mourvèdre
or Monastrell

Strawberry, cherry, cocoa, rose, truffles,

Nebbiolo

Flowers, nutmeg, lemon, apricot

Müller-Thurgau

Violet, peony, strawberry, raspberry, prune,

Négrette

Wattle, honeysuckle, peach, apricot, grape

Muscadelle

Orange, peach, vanilla, jasmine, caramel,

Muscat

Black cherry, prune, blackberry, dried herbs,

Negroamaro

Date, coffee, fig, dark chocolate

Pedro Ximénez

Cherry, plum, pear, licorice, tobacco

Nero d'Avola

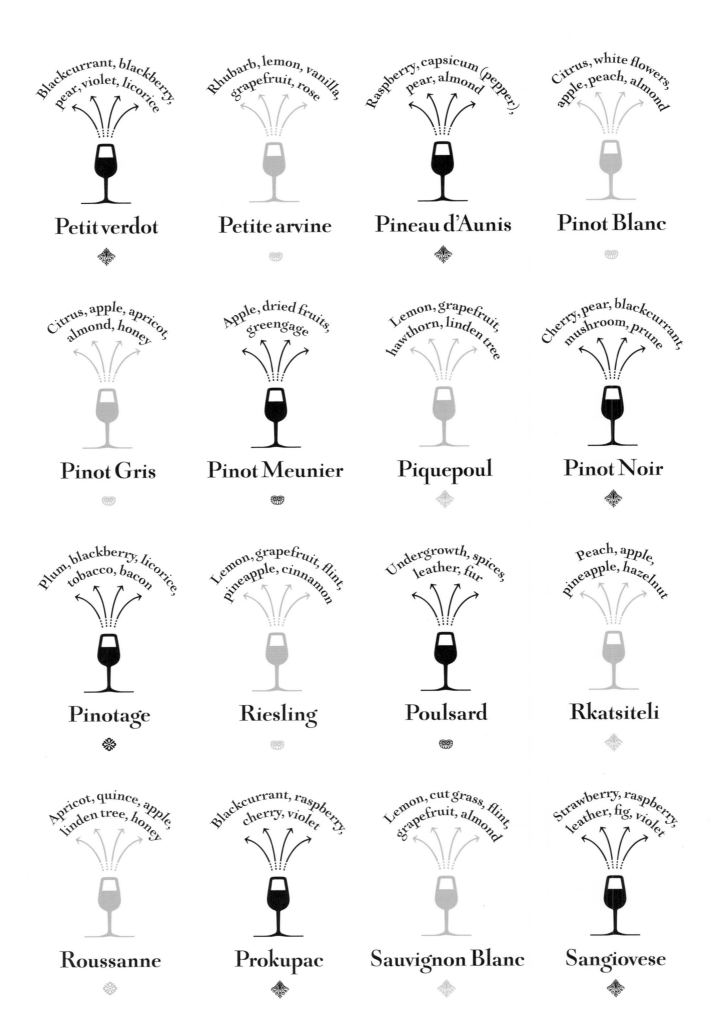

Blackcurrant, blackberry, pear, violet, licorice,

Petit verdot

Rhubarb, lemon, vanilla, grapefruit, rose

Petite arvine

Raspberry, capsicum (pepper), pear, almond

Pineau d'Aunis

Citrus, white flowers, apple, peach, almond

Pinot Blanc

Citrus, apple, apricot, almond, honey

Pinot Gris

Apple, dried fruits, greengage

Pinot Meunier

Lemon, grapefruit, hawthorn, linden tree

Piquepoul

Cherry, pear, blackcurrant, mushroom, prune

Pinot Noir

Plum, blackberry, licorice, tobacco, bacon

Pinotage

Lemon, grapefruit, flint, pineapple, cinnamon

Riesling

Undergrowth, spices, leather, fur

Poulsard

Peach, apple, pineapple, hazelnut

Rkatsiteli

Apricot, quince, apple, linden tree, honey

Roussanne

Blackcurrant, raspberry, cherry, violet

Prokupac

Lemon, cut grass, flint, grapefruit, almond

Sauvignon Blanc

Strawberry, raspberry, leather, fig, violet

Sangiovese

Blackcurrant, pear, blackberry, violet, cocoa

Syrah
or Shiraz

Walnut, green apple, coffee, curry, cinnamon

Savagnin Blanc

Blackberry, licorice, undergrowth, blackcurrant, blueberry

Tannat

Lemon, honey, fig, walnut, apricot

Semillon

Lemon, melon, iodine, almond

Soave

Cherry, plum, tomato, licorice, tobacco

Tempranillo

Citrus, white flowers, honey, almond, cut grass

Sylvaner

Raspberry, plum, blackcurrant, violet, mint

Touriga Nacional

Strawberry, cherry, undergrowth, pepper, smoky note

Trousseau

Lemon, peach, rose, white flowers

Torrontés

Raspberry, blackcurrant, black cherry, cinnamon, pepper

Zinfandel
or Primitivo

Citrus, quince, pine resin

Ugni Blanc
or Trebbiano Toscano

Citrus, peach, honeysuckle, tropical fruits, apricot

Verdejo

Cherry, cinnamon, violet, spices

Zweigelt

Lemon, peach, aniseed, hawthorn, linden tree

Vermentino
or Rolle

White peach, apricot, honey, orange zest, wattle

Viognier

Index

WINE-GROWING COUNTRIES

Bibliography

REFERENCE WORKS

ANDERSON, Kym, *Which Winegrape Varieties Are Grown Where?*, University of Adelaide Press, Adelaide, 2013

BELL, Bibiane & DOROZYNSKI, Alexandre, *Le Livre du Vin*, Éditions des Deux Coqs d'Or, Paris, 1968

JOHNSON, Hugh, *Une Histoire Mondiale du Vin*, Hachette, Paris, 2012

NOCHEZ, Henri & BLANCHARD, Guy, *La Loire: Un Fleuve de Vins*, Thoba's Editions, Roanne, 2006

ORHON, Jacques, *Les Vins du Nouveau Monde*, vol. I & II, Éditions de l'Homme, Montreal, 2009

PHILPOT, Don, *The World of Wine and Food*, Rowman & Littlefield, Lanham, Maryland, 2017

ROBINSON, Jancis, *The Oxford Companion to Wine*, vol. IV, Oxford University Press, Oxford, 2015

WEBSITES

www.suddefrance-developpement.com/fr/fiches-pays.html

www.oiv.int/fr

www.wine-searcher.com

www.winesofbalkans.com

www.italianwinecentral.com

About the authors

When Adrien Grant Smith Bianchi and Jules Gaubert-Turpin first became interested in oenology, they noticed a lack of up-to-date and beautiful guides. With Jules writing the words and Adrien drawing the maps, the duo embarked on creating a new way of approaching wine and its terroirs through a collection of guides and posters about wine-growing regions.

Since their first *Carte des Vins de Bordeaux* (*Map/Menu of the Wines of Bordeaux*) in 2014, they have published four guides in four languages and mapped 92 wine regions. Discover the whole French-language collection at lacartedesvins-svp.com.

Jules Gaubert-Turpin

Adrien Grant Smith Bianchi

This edition published in 2018 by Hardie Grant Books,
an imprint of Hardie Grant Publishing
First published in 2017 by Hachette Livre (Marabout)

Hardie Grant Books (Melbourne)
Building 1, 658 Church Street
Richmond, Victoria 3121

Hardie Grant Books (London)
5th & 6th Floors
52–54 Southwark Street
London SE1 1UN

hardiegrantbooks.com

A catalogue record for this
book is available from the
National Library of Australia

Journey Through Wine
ISBN 978 1 74379 474 6

10 9 8 7 6 5 4 3 2

French editor: Véronique Dussidour
Translator: Nicola Young

Colour reproduction by Splitting Image Colour Studio
Printed in China by 1010 Printing International Limited